The
rsonal
world

DATE DUE			
Dec 4 '72			
NOV 1 1 1985			

Originally published under the title of
*FIRO: A Three-Dimensional Theory
of Interpersonal Behavior*
by Holt, Rinehart and Winston, 1960

The
Interpersonal
Underworld

BY WILLIAM C. SCHUTZ

Department of Psychiatry
Albert Einstein College of Medicine
Yeshiva University

SCIENCE & BEHAVIOR BOOKS, INC.

577 College Avenue, Palo Alto, California

To Ruth and Carl

and the elephant

with the upturned trunk

Fourth Printing, 1970

Reprint edition:
© **1966 by Science & Behavior Books, Inc.**
Printed in the United States of America
Library of Congress Catalog Card Number: 66-28683
ISBN: 0-8314-0011-0

Preface to This Edition

The general reaction to the appearance of *FIRO* in 1958 was one of skeptical optimism. Most reviewers remarked on the ambitiousness of undertaking to evolve a theory of interpersonal behavior. The potential value of such a system was acknowledged, along with the need for more research to establish the soundness of the theory.

The past years have seen a slow, steady increase in the publication of articles and dissertations testing the FIRO concepts and using the questionnaires presented in the book. Because the field of interpersonal behavior is so ubiquitous, research on FIRO has taken place in a wide variety of fields, including:

1) The use of FIRO–B in marriage counseling and in selection of marital partners.

2) Study of the effect of compatibility on the outcome of several real-life dyads such as doctor-patient, experimenter-subject, teacher-student, salesman-customer. The studies have indicated that there is generally a positive effect as a result of compatibility—that is, patients seem to improve more, subjects do better, etc.

3) Evaluation of human relations workshops, such as the T-groups or sensitivity training groups of the National Training Laboratories. The FIRO–B questionnaire has been used often to measure changes in interpersonal relations during and following such workshops.

4) In clinical work, exploration of inclusion, control, and affection as possible dimensions for psychiatric classification. The relation between FIRO categories and standard psychiatric classifications —schizophrenic, neurotic, psychopathic, etc.—has also been investigated with some success.

5) Exploration of the relation of the FIRO dimensions of inter-

personal needs—inclusion, control, and affection—to other dimensions such as birth order, need affiliation, social-class variables, scientific creativity, and differences among occupational groups.

6) Use of the FIRO techniques of compatibility as a method of group composition for teaching teams, therapy and training groups, task groups, and even string quartets!

In addition to these investigations the author has been engaged for the past several years in a large study of the applicability of the FIRO theory to the educational context, particularly the relation of the school administrator to the school board members, teachers, and parents. This study, soon to be published, attempts to use the hypotheses of the theory to understand and predict the success of an administrator under particular social conditions. It also extends the theory to incorporate cognitive and sociological factors more adequately than before.

Another important development in the theory is the construction of several tests previewed in the book. Since the original presentation of FIRO–B in 1958, the following tests have been developed[1]:

FIRO–F (for Feelings), a measure of an individual orientation toward expressed and wanted feelings in the areas of inclusion, control, and affection. These feelings are respectively, importance, competence, and lovability.

COPE (Coping operations preference enquiry), when involved with an interpersonal anxiety the respondent's preference for using the defense mechanisms of denial, isolation, projection, regression, or turning-against-self.

LIPHE (Life interpersonal history enquiry), a measure of the respondent's interpersonal behavior and feelings toward his parents when he was a child.

VAL–ED (Educational values), the values a person holds about the relations among teacher, student, school administrator, and community, in the school situation.

All of these tests are derived from the FIRO theory. Under development at the present time are MATE (Marital attitudes evaluation), an evaluation of interpersonal satisfaction in marriage, and VAL–DOC (Doctor-patient values), an assessment of values governing the relations between doctor and patient.

Development of these questionnaires is a key effort in advancing the theory since they represent precise definitions of the theoretical concepts, and they allow for extensive testing of the theory. Further, to have a series of tests covering a wide variety of phenomena at different levels and in different areas of interaction, but generated from the same theoretical structure, provides the basis for a wide variety of studies interrelating

---

[1] They are available through Consulting Psychologists Press, 577 College Avenue, Palo Alto, California.

distant areas of investigation. Data relevant to one questionnaire have implications for all the others since they are connected by the same theory.

Looking back on the theory after seven years, I find that one area in particular is unresolved, that of the relation of task-oriented behavior (also called "work," "competence," "creativity," or the "conflict-free ego sphere") to the three interpersonal needs. I vacillate between a need-reduction notion that asserts that work is simply one way of trying to gratify interpersonal needs, and an ego psychology approach stating a separate autonomous energy source (as in Maslow's deficiency motivation and being motivation). I have tried to deal with this problem, leaning toward the second conception, but I still feel dissatisfied with the formulation. The best impression I have at the moment is that some of the current work on creativity will fill this void and help clarify the problem.

I also have regrets about including the very flimsy empirical justification (pointed out quite properly by one reviewer) of the dimensions presented at the end of chapter three (pages 54–56). It should be omitted entirely.

In spite of these reservations, the present edition is substantially the same as the original. The only important changes are omission of a detailed history of the development of the FIRO–B questionnaire, and addition of a new title, which I believe is less cryptic and more descriptive of the content.

My feelings about the material in this book range from thinking that it is not only a remarkable system but a way of life, to wondering how anyone could possibly take it seriously. This seems to be a splendid reason for exposing the theory to others less involved for a somewhat more dispassionate view and for the accumulation of more evidence.

W. C. S.

New York
May, 1966

Preface

This book has three objectives: (1) theoretical—to present the current status of a theory of interpersonal behavior which is consistent with psychodynamic personality theory, and from which experimental hypotheses are readily derivable; (2) empirical—to report data from about fifteen previously unpublished experiments which provide an empirical basis for the theory of interpersonal behavior; (3) methodological—to discuss and demonstrate an approach to the problem of applying the techniques of the logicians and philosophers of science to the problems of behavioral science.

"FIRO" stands for "Fundamental Interpersonal Relations Orientation." It is chosen as the title of this book because it signifies the basic idea that every person orients himself in characteristic ways toward other people, and the basic belief that knowledge of these orientations allows for considerable understanding of individual behavior and the interaction of people. The word is pronounced to rhyme with "Cairo."

Work leading toward the theory began in 1952 at the Naval Research Laboratory in Washington, D.C. At that time I was on active duty in the Navy with the Systems Coordination Division, assigned the task of understanding and improving the performance of a CIC—Combat Information Center—a room aboard ship where several men must receive, collate, evaluate, and disseminate various items of intelligence, primarily radar data. From this beginning the work continued briefly at Tufts College in 1953 in the Systems Analysis Department. This department was short-lived and the project moved to Harvard and the Social Relations Department, where it is at the present time.

There are several sources of inspiration for this book. When I was a graduate student at the University of California, Los Angeles, I became fascinated by the clarity and penetration of the scientific philosophers, particularly Hans Reichenbach and Abraham Kaplan. The thought processes they taught and exhibited were to me the objects of deep admiration. After leaving U.C.L.A. I underwent another experience that held the same intellectual thrill. I discovered that Freud's psychoanalytic theory was a great deal richer and more sophisticated than its critics had led me to believe. Strangely enough, it seemed to me that the writings of Freud had a great deal in common with the writings of logicians and scientific philosophers. Both were remarkable for their penetration, for seeing through a maze of complication and confusion and selecting out those elements and their configurations that made the whole problem simple—even obvious in the more successful cases. It was certainly true that Freud's theory could be criticized on the basis of its lack of experimental support, but this always impressed me as an uneasy criticism, one in which the critic knew somehow that Freud would probably turn out to be largely correct.

One other event strongly influenced the methodological course I have since taken. At the University of Chicago I met Rudolf Carnap. From just a few brief talks I became infused with the notion that here was a man, who, with Reichenbach, Kaplan, and others, had explored far and wide the problems of science and scientific method. These men had evolved techniques, or at least habits, of thinking, that were remarkable and that should—even must —be applied to problems of empirical science. The challenge was how profitably to join the techniques of the scientific philosopher with the insights of the psychoanalysts.

In addition to these inspirational influences I owe much to three persons who were invaluable in the development of the substantive aspects of the theory. I am indebted to Elvin Semrad, a psychoanalyst, for his naively brilliant insights into individual and group processes, which I found so profound and so useful. His wisdom pervades many pages of this book. In Warren Bennis, I found the kind of friend almost necessary for this type of project, one who provides stimulating ideas, discussion, and support. And I owe much to my wife Edith, whose original insights and impatience with my inability to explain ideas clearly was of great value, and whose understanding and enthusiasm provided the impetus to continue in this pursuit even when the results failed to reach the .05 level. To these three I owe my greatest debt and offer my warmest thanks.

In addition, many others contributed importantly to the progress and results. Wesley Salmon provided expert counsel on the logical aspects, especially Chapters 1 and 10 and Appendix A; several research assistants provided untiring efforts, including Nancy Waxler, Douglas Bunker, Eugene Gross, Bruce Finnie, Cathy Hampton, Saul Sternberg, Warren Bachelis, Norman Berkowitz, and Sylvia Mitchell. Dorothy Stock was important in the original theoretical formulations and introduced me to the work of Bion, Redl, and others when I was a complete neophyte in the field.

Paul Hare contributed much through discussion and through his attempt to adapt and extend these ideas to the experimental literature on behavior of small groups. (His book is to appear soon.) Freed Bales made many disturbingly incisive comments, forcing me to search for more adequate formulations. Theodore Mills has patiently pointed out my slighting of sociological factors. (I hope Chapter 8 is the start toward a satisfactory reply.) Samuel Stouffer has provided support and encouragement. Eugene Cogan's comments on the first draft of the book were very helpful. And the students in the seminar, Small Groups, which I have taught with Bales since 1954, have given the type of stimulation possible only from graduate students.

Finally, the patient, persistent, and remarkably competent work of Miriam Blank in reading and correcting the proofs, creating the index, and generally guiding the text from manuscript to final product was invaluable.

If this preface begins to sound rhapsodic, as if written by someone feeling very grateful and expansive while drinking beer after just finishing the manuscript of the book—it should. But perhaps that's when all prefaces should be written.

W. C. S.

Harvard University
June, 1958

This study was conducted under contract number Nonr–494 (03) between the Systems Analysis Department of Tufts College and the U.S. Navy, Office of Naval Research; and contracts N5ori–07668 and Nonr–1866 (06) between the Laboratory of Social Relations of Harvard University and the U.S. Navy, Office of Naval Research. Since June 1, 1957, the work has been given additional support by Grant No. M–1831, made by the Department of Health, Education and Welfare, Public Health Service, to Harvard University, with the author as the principal investigator.

The opinions expressed in this volume are those of the author and are not to be construed as reflecting the views or endorsement of the United States Navy. Permission is hereby granted to the United States Government for reproduction, translation, publication use, and disposal of this book in whole or in part.

Table of Contents

1

Introduction

People need people.

Laurie was about three when one night she requested my aid in getting undressed. I was downstairs and she was upstairs, and ... well.

"You know how to undress yourself," I reminded.

"Yes," she explained, "but sometimes people need people anyway, even if they do know how to do things by theirselves."

As I slowly lowered the newspaper a strong feeling came over me, a mixture of delight, embarrassment, and pride; delight in the realization that what I had just heard crystallized many stray thoughts on interpersonal behavior; anger because Laurie stated so effortlessly what I had been struggling with for months; and pride because, after all, she is my daughter.

In a sense, this book and the theory it presents may be considered an elaboration of the phrase, "people need people." Starting from this simple statement, the book sets out to elaborate, to test, to speculate about, to systematize, and finally to understand the phrase, "people need people."

The first elaboration of this idea could be stated, "People need people for three kinds of relations." I've called them *Inclusion* ("No, Laurie, you can't come down and join the company"); *Control* ("I said go to bed!"); and *Affection* ("Yes, I still love you; I was just angry at what you did"). The next elaboration is, "People need people to receive from, and to give to." I've called these "wanted behavior" and "expressed behavior." The second chapter of the book discusses these two elaborations and develops the general notion of an "interpersonal need" as having properties closely analogous to those of a biological need.

Chapter 3 briefly reviews some of the literature in an attempt to show that it is not unreasonable to postulate these three needs for everyone. The fourth chapter presents a measuring instrument, FIRO–B, developed to assess how people characteristically behave with respect to these needs. A discussion of the validity and reliability of the test dominates the chapter.

The fifth chapter tries to point out the close relation between the way people act as adults and the way they acted as children—the constancy principle; and also the way people act as adults and the way their parents acted toward them—the identification principle. Some data are presented to support these principles, which together constitute the Postulate of Relational Continuity.

Chapter 5 closes the first section, which deals in general with the orientations of persons toward interpersonal relations and the origins of these orientations. The second part of the book deals with people in interaction. It is based on the premise that if the characteristic ways of approaching interpersonal situations of two individuals are measurable, their interaction pattern is predictable.

Chapter 6 presents a theoretical discussion of the concept of compatibility and the derivation of specific formulas for its measurement. The formulas are all based on scores obtained from FIRO–B. It presents the idea that incompatibility is of two basic types, interchange incompatibility (differences in total amount of interpersonal interchange desired) and originator incompatibility (differences regarding who initiates and who receives behavior). This chapter also reports the stability over time of these measures of compatibility between persons. The concept of compatibility is central to the second section of the book.

The seventh chapter presents data from a study of the predictability of the selection of roommates; two studies that try to predict the productivity of groups composed of members said to be compatible or incompatible solely on the basis of their individual orientations to interpersonal relations ("personalities"); one study that explores the relation between compatibility and cohesion; and several related empirical studies.

Chapter 8 is a respite from the mass of data of the previous chapter. Environmental influences on interpersonal behavior are discussed, and certain standard sociological terms are given precise definitions within the interpersonal theoretical framework. These terms include "role definition," "role expectation," "enacted role," "norm," "sanction," and "task situation." A few data are presented, but the main purpose of the chapter is to demonstrate the relation between these important sociological concepts and those suggested in this book, and how the two may be integrated into a common framework.

The ninth chapter takes up the interesting problem of group development. The Postulate of Group Development asserts that every group handles the same interpersonal problems in the same sequence, and that this sequence is the same as that encountered by the developing child as he learns to relate to people. First come problems of inclusion, then problems of control, and finally problems of affection. Further, it is asserted that the process of group resolution proceeds in the opposite order.

Chapter 10 presents the ideas of the book as a formal theory including primitive and defined terms, postulates, and theorems. More about this enterprise is discussed below.

Appendix A presents details of various technicological points mentioned in the text, especially those related to the theory of Bayes. Appendix B presents experimental material mentioned in the text. Some of these materials were usable for other projects in their original form while others (e.g., POP, ASIA) have since been revised into more satisfactory measuring instruments.

RANGE OF THE THEORY

The book is organized around a formal theory. The range of phenomena to which this theory is applicable may be called interpersonal behavior. The term "interpersonal" is defined and discussed in Chapter 2. With a presently existing interpersonal relation as a starting point, three kinds of interpersonal behavior may be delineated: (a) *prior*—relations between early interpersonal relations and present ones, (b) *present*—relations between elements of the present interpersonal situation, and (c) *consequent*—relations between present interpersonal orientations and other behavior and attitudes.

The *prior* category includes the childhood origins of adult interpersonal orientations, the constancy of these orientations, factors that lead to alteration of interpersonal orientations during childhood and adolescence, relation between parents' and children's orientations to interpersonal relations, and so on.

The *present* category includes the compatibility or cohesion of interpersonal relations, the leadership structure of a group, the sociometric patternings within a group, the developmental stages of an interpersonal relation, interpersonal relations and situational factors such as task, societal norms, and the larger social structure.

The *consequent* category includes relations between interpersonal orientations and attitudes and behavior toward other aspects of life such as social attitudes, political attitudes, occupational choice, and tastes in art, plays, and music.

THE ORGANIZING PRINCIPLES OF THIS BOOK

In writing a book there are at least three questions an author is inevitably asked either by himself or others. Although they are stated in various ways, usually euphemistically, they seem to reduce to these: (1) "What's different?" (2) "Who cares?" and (3) "So what?" Trying to answer these questions generated the framework for organizing the material in this book.

"What's Different?"

Unless a book offers something unavailable in other sources it has little justification. In this book data from many unreported studies are presented, together with central propositions that may explain the results. These propositions help form a theory of interpersonal behavior which has not been hitherto presented. In addition, there is somewhat different discussion of the appropriateness of the application of formal theories to data of the behavioral sciences. Thus, "what is different" is (a) certain new empirical results, (b) a theory of interpersonal behavior, and (c) various views on the relation between scientific method and behavioral science.

"Who Cares?"

This question is often phrased, "For what audience are you writing?" This is an especially difficult question to answer because interpersonal behavior is of virtually universal interest. However, this book was written primarily for my professional colleagues, and also for interested nonpsychologists, including educators, businessmen, administrators, group leaders and members—in short, for virtually everyone who has more than a passing interest in how people get along together. The problem of writing for both a professional and nonprofessional audience is relatively simple when the author has a thorough grasp of his subject matter. Then he can state the most complex ideas in simple, straightforward language. If, however, he hasn't lived with the ideas long enough to call them his own, he must explain them to himself as well as to the reader; the result is usually difficult reading. Examples of both simple and difficult writing can be found in this book. In all instances, however, simplicity and clarity are the goals.

One organizational feature that aids in presenting a simpler picture is the placing of the extended discussions of more technical points in the appendix, where the interested reader may dwell further.

"So What?"

"What use is the whole thing even if you accomplish your goal?" is an omnipresent question. The chief purpose of this book is to add to the knowledge of human behavior. If the theory presented in this book proves reasonable, applications follow directly for child training; treatment of adolescents; gang behavior; selection of effective and satisfied work teams, roommates, committees, and other participants in group activities; leadership of groups; and perhaps ultimately even selection of marital partners. Let me hasten to add that these are mainly *ultimate* applications not immediately available. The general application of the theory presented here is toward increasing our understanding and enjoyment of interpersonal relations as well as making them more productive.

If, indeed, these are the book's objectives, how can they best be met? How can the data and ideas be presented so that they will offer a sound and accurate picture of results obtained, and at the same time generate further exploration and testing in the area of interpersonal behavior? The answer, I believe, is to present these ideas in the form of a formal or axiomatic theory. To demonstrate why this type of formulation is preferable, a short description of the properties of a formal system follows, with a specification of the value of using such a system, and the most efficient manner of utilizing formal theories in the behavioral sciences.

THE FORMAL THEORY

In the literature of the philosophy of science, and increasingly in the empirical sciences, there are references to structures called "formal systems," "axiomatic systems," "postulate systems," or what is now somewhat more in vogue, "mathematical models."

Elements of a Formal Theory

A formal theory consists of the following elements:

1. Basic or primitive terms
2. Defined terms
3. Formation rules
4. Transformation rules (or rules of inference or deduction)
5. Postulates (or axioms, or primitive propositions)
6. Theorems (or derived propositions)

Normally, for application to empirical material, the language of logic and mathematics is utilized without making it a part of the theory. This language includes the formation and transformation rules. In the theory presented in this book, these languages will be assumed without being made a part of the system.

The primitive terms are not defined within the formal system but represent the minimal set of terms needed to develop the theory. Defined terms are introduced into the theory as equivalent to certain combinations of primitive terms. The postulates of the system are a minimal set of propositions from which all true statements in the logical system are derivable. The most familiar example of a formal system is Euclidean geometry. All the elements of a formal system are present: primitive terms, for example, "point"; defined terms, for example, "triangle"; axioms, for example, "If a straight line meets two straight lines, so as to make two interior angles on the same side of it taken together less than two right angles, these straight lines, being continually produced, shall at length meet on that side on which are the angles which are less than two right angles" (the famous "parallel postulate"); and rules for deducing the theorems from the axioms, for example, "If B is true whenever A is true, and A is true, then it follows that B is true (*modus ponens*)."

Presentation of scientific material in the framework of a formal system has many important advantages over more informal or discursive presentations, particularly with regard to the scientific utilization of the material. Some of these advantages are

1. *To achieve conceptual clarity.* The necessity to state ideas explicitly leads to the identification of contradictions, omissions, repetitions, and confusions. Formalization fosters clear statements, explicit definitions, and clear logical sequences. For example, although the ideas of Harry Stack Sullivan (88) are extremely provocative, it is difficult to find explicit statements in his work about several vital areas, for example, dimensions of personality.

2. *To detect hidden assumptions.* Formalization requires that all steps leading to the statement of a theorem be made explicit. If the chain of reasoning is incomplete, a hidden assumption may be revealed. For example, the fact that several social theories apply only to a particular culture is often not made explicit because the range of applicability of the theory is not systematically stated.

3. *To gain from indirect verification.* If the relations between theorems are made explicit, then the verification of one theorem may indirectly verify the other because they are parts of a logically interconnected system. For example, in Newtonian mechanics, evidence for the laws of falling bodies gives indirect evidence for laws of movement of astronomical bodies since these sets of laws are logically connected.

4. *To specify the range of conceptual relevance.* Formalization makes clear which aspects of a theory are affected by particular data. It makes explicit which theorems follow from which postulates and therefore which theorems and postulates are affected by a particular experimental result. For example, because of the weak formal properties of psychoanalytic theory it is virtually impossible to tell how evidence refuting the mechanism of repression affects the theory of psychosexual development. More formalism would make explicit the postulates required to deduce the mechanism of repression and allow for comparison of such postulates with those required to deduce the theory of psychosexual development. The extent of the overlap of postulates would indicate the degree to which evidence for one is relevant to the other.

5. *To identify equivalent theories and theorems.* If theorems are explicitly stated in two theories it is possible to see in what respects they are the same (that is, lead to the same consequences) and in what respects different (that is, lead to different consequences).

6. *To achieve deductive fertility.* By constructing a powerful set of postulates many theorems are derivable, and the derivations may be mechanically checked. Deductive fertility is probably the primary goal of a formal system, although, unfortunately, not one that can be achieved to a significant degree in the theory offered here or in any behavioral theory at the present time.

FORMAL THEORIES AND BEHAVIORAL SCIENCE

It is not accidental that the most familiar example of an axiomatic formal system occurs in mathematics, a nonempirical science. In the empirical sciences there have been fewer attempts at formalization. A look into the most highly developed science, physics, reveals a remarkably small number of rigorously executed formal theories. McKinsey, Sugar, and Suppes have axiomatized particle mechanics (61) for one example. In other sciences this type of rigor has not even been approached.

Attempts at partial formalization have been made with great sophistication by Woodger in biology (96), and with less sophistication by Dodd in sociology (31), and by Hull in psychology (50). Others, such as Freud (38) and Parsons (67), have referred to their systems of thought as theories, but they indicated no special concern about the formalism of their work.

Attempts at formalization have met with varying degrees of success; in fact, the effect of formalization, or lack of it, on the ultimate value of the work of these men is still unknown. Although it has been assumed that a formal theory is a desirable form for organizing knowledge, apparently application of formal theories to the behavioral sciences has been uninspiring. One is therefore inclined to ask to what extent this lack of success is due to the nature of the data of behavioral science, and to what extent it is due to our failure to apply the formal theories most fruitfully to these data.

The conceptual inelegance of behavioral science contrasts with the logical elegance of a formal theory. Serious scientific study of human behavior is of relatively recent origin, and the field is too vast and complex to submit to simple solution. Observed alongside the vagueness and ambiguity of the subject matter of interpersonal relations, the formal system appears overelaborate and perhaps inappropriate. However, the complexity of the subject matter need not mean that no use whatever can be made of formalization in the solution of empirical social science problems.

I believe that a postulate system may be utilized profitably if one considers it the *model toward which systematizing efforts are aimed,* and realizes that present attempts should not be expected to achieve the rigor required in a completely formal model. The formal system is an ideal to be successively approximated. (This is not to say the formal approach supercedes other techniques, merely that it is a useful way of gaining the values of a formal system.)

The conception of the formal system as a model has several important consequences for the formulation and presentation of the present material:

1. Primitive and defined terms are approximated by using terms that refer to observable and, if possible, measurable entities.

2. Postulates are approximated by attempting to formulate observed relations in as few propositions as possible.

3. Basic and defined terms are successively approximated by specifying the meaning of terms in such a way that the meaning is alterable through the introduction of empirical evidence. Relevant to this are the approaches to definition of Kaplan (53) and the techniques of latent structure analysis and factor analysis.

Since formation and transformation rules are assumed, selection of the formal system as a model for presenting the theory in this book calls for the presentation of primitive and defined terms and postulates. Introduction of the terms, as mentioned above, presents no special problem, but the postulate presentation merits further discussion. The most adequate model for introducing and describing the postulates is, in my judgment, the rule of Bayes.

THE RULE OF BAYES

Postulates, though logically prior, are empirically very late in the sequence of theoretical development. In order to identify and develop postulates a field of inquiry has to be so well researched that it is possible to discern the small number of important propositions from which all the others are derivable. In fact, this stage must be arrived at inductively by a process of successive approximations. Various hypotheses are proposed and tested, and some are confirmed. Gradually certain of these become applicable to a larger and larger range of phenomena. They are then on the road to attaining the status of postulates.

The immediate problem, then, is to establish the truth of various propositions from empirical evidence and then to generate propositions that are even more general. This will be the technique whereby postulates are successively approximated. The most satisfactory formulation of the method of relating evidence to hypotheses is given by the rule of Bayes.

Although postulates are by definition not proved *within the system* of which they are postulates, they may be very carefully and convincingly established outside the system. Indeed, for an empirical interpretation of a formal system it is important that the postulates be true, since the formal system may be regarded as a vast and complex (logical) argument. Its premises are the axioms, and its conclusion is the conjunction of all the theorems deduced (28). Hence the premises, that is, the postulates, must be true if the deductions are to be meaningfully true. This fact demonstrates the importance of establishing the truth of the postulates or, more accurately, the truth of the theorems derived from the postulates.

The rule of Bayes asserts that the truth of a hypothesis is a function of

1. The probability that the proposition is true, given all possible propositions and all the relevant knowledge available—this is called the *antecedent probability*—and
2. The probability that a particular sort of evidence would occur if the proposition is true—the *evidential probability*.

For example, prior to the Duke experiments (71) the phenomenon of extrasensory perception (ESP) was highly improbable. That is, the proposition, "ESP is a human property," had very little support from all that was known; in other words, it had low antecedent probability. Since that time many experiments have been performed to test this proposition, and many observers feel that the evidential probability is disturbingly high; that is, there are people who perform as the ESP hypothesis would predict and guess cards consistently better than chance.

The rule of Bayes is more complicated than this presentation, which nevertheless conveys the important point for the organization of this book. (A more detailed discussion of the Bayes theorem is given in Appendix A.) In the presentation of the theory, attention will be given to the antecedent probabilities for the theorems as well as the evidential probability for the theorems.

The antecedent probability shall be called an argument for plausibility. To illustrate how this will be presented, Postulate 1 (Chapter 2) asserts that people have three interpersonal needs. A review of selected literature from the fields of parent-child relations, personality types, group behavior, and miscellaneous studies is presented (Chapter 3) in an attempt to demonstrate that many investigators have independently concluded that these three are important variables. This review obviously does not *prove* or even confirm the theorems derived from the postulate in a strict sense, nor is it so intended. The purpose of the review is to establish the antecedent probability, or plausibility, of the postulate, in other words, to demonstrate that it is reasonable in terms of what is already known in this field of knowledge and does not do violence to existing knowledge or data.

PLAN OF THE BOOK

Hence, the two principles for organizing the book are the formal theory and the rule of Bayes. The chapters are organized around the postulates of the system, except for Chapter 4, which presents a measuring instrument, and Chapter 10, which summarizes the theory. The rule of Bayes is used as the framework for presenting each postulate of the theory. This framework allows for the presentation of the most complete justification for the theory.

A typical chapter begins with the presentation of a postulate, followed by an explanation of the terms introduced (primitives and defined terms) and an informal discussion of the meaning of the postulate. Whenever possible, specific measuring instruments are introduced and described to give specific content and "operationism" to basic terms. The next section of the chapter presents the antecedent probability or plausibility argument for the postulate. In general, there are two types of plausibility arguments; (a) report of available evidence, such as might be revealed by reanalysis of old data, and (b) argument from experience, a kind of "common sense" discussion. Each will be used where appropriate. Theorems derived from the postulate are presented next, followed by a standard presentation of experimental results relevant to the postulate. At this point in the chapter new experiments are reported (perhaps fifteen throughout the book); these provide evidential probability for the theorems derived from the postulate. Finally, a section on future research completes each chapter. This section provides an opportunity to report research in progress, and theoretical and experimental ideas suggested by the previous material, as well as suggestive results obtained on very small samples.

In addition to these chapters there is one devoted to FIRO–B, an instrument for measuring an individual's fundamental interpersonal relations orientations. A special chapter is devoted to this instrument; because it is so central in the development of the theory it seemed to merit a complete presentation as a new psychological questionnaire, including data on reliability (stability), intercorrelations of scales, and reproducibility, as well as a discussion of the theory underlying the questionnaire.

Finally, in Chapter 10 the theory is compiled and discussed *as a theory* in an attempt to present the most parsimonious and succinct statement of the fundamental ideas of this book.

PART I

Individual Orientations
to Interpersonal Relations

2

The Postulate of Interpersonal
Needs: Description

Postulate 1. *The Postulate of Interpersonal Needs.*

    (a). Every individual has three interpersonal needs: inclusion, control, and affection.
    (b). Inclusion, control, and affection constitute a sufficient set of areas of interpersonal behavior for the prediction and explanation of interpersonal phenomena.

Explanation: In studying interpersonal behavior it is important to isolate the relevant variables. "People need people" serves as a good starting point, but, if the frontiers of knowledge are to recede, the next question must be investigated: *"In what ways* do people need people?"

The literature is not lacking in contestants for the mantle of "basic interpersonal variables." French (35) in a recent report summarizes the factors found in the factor analysis of various personality tests; he was able to reduce the number of apparently unrelated factors to forty nine! Clearly this number is unmanageable for use in future investigation.

If the strictly statistical techniques for reducing variables still leaves forty nine, some other exploratory method must be employed or at least added. A developmental approach to isolating variables has several appealing features. It seems promising to attempt to trace the developing individual through his sequence of typical interpersonal dealings, as a method of identifying the most basic interpersonal areas from which others are derivable. A consideration of this developmental process (discussed in more detail below), and some formulations presented by certain investigators, notably Bion, led the author to the conclusion that three interpersonal areas seemed to cover most interpersonal behavior. Later analysis of certain relevant literature (see Chapter 3) lent weight to the proposition that three areas would prove adequate for fruitful investigation.

As the description of these three areas, here called inclusion, control, and affection, progressed, the fable came to mind of the blind men who disagreed over the characteristics of an elephant because each was exploring a different sector. It seems that various investigators are describing different aspects of the elephant—the three need areas—but apparently they are describing the same elephant. Thus clinicians discuss unconscious forces, small-group investigators describe overt behavior, child psychologists report on early interpersonal relations, and sociologists are interested in roles and group structures. But there seems to be heartening convergence toward the same set of variables, even though the approaches differ. The problem, then, is to give a complete description of the "elephant" and point out which aspects are being described by each observer. This chapter attempts to provide a complete description of the three basic interpersonal areas as basic needs, by showing how they appear in personality structure, in overt behavior, and in pathological behavior. In Chapter 3 a brief summary is given of selected studies which seem to fit into various parts of this schema.

INTERPERSONAL NEED

The concept of interpersonal need, often called "social need," has been discussed by many authors (65), but because it forms the central part of this book it is important to describe in what sense the term will be used.

The term "interpersonal" refers to relations that occur between people as opposed to relations in which at least one participant is inanimate. It is assumed that, owing to the psychological presence of other people, interpersonal situations lead to behavior in an individual that differs from the behavior of the individual when he is not in the presence of other persons. An optimally useful definition of "interpersonal" is one such that all situations classified as interpersonal have important properties in common—properties that are in general different from those of noninterpersonal situations. With this criterion for a definition in mind, the following specifies the meaning of "interpersonal situation." (The term "interpersonal" shall be used as equivalent to the term "group.")

An *interpersonal situation* is one involving two or more persons, in which these individuals take account of each other for some purpose, or decision, D. It is described from a particular point of reference, usually either that of one of the participants or of an outside observer. It is also specified as existing during a stated time interval. Thus a complete statement of an interpersonal situation has the form:

"From the standpoint of O (or A, or B), A takes account of B for decision D during time interval t_1 to t_n."

"*A* takes account of *B* for decision *D*" means that when *A* considers what alternative to select for decision *D* one criterion for his choice is his expectation of *B*'s response to his choice. This expectation does not require that *A* make a different decision because of the influence of *B;* it simply means that his criteria for making the decision are supplemented.

For example, if a man who is sitting on a bus trying to decide whether or not to give up his seat to an elderly lady considers the reaction of the attractive young woman across the aisle, he is taking account of the young woman whether or not he gives up his seat. From *his* point of view the relation is interpersonal, since he takes account of her. From the standpoint of the young woman the situation may not be interpersonal at all, since she may not even be aware of his presence. Further, *A* may take account of *B* for one decision, for example, giving up a bus seat, as in the previous example, but not for another, for example, deciding which cobbler to patronize a week later. In addition, the degree to which *A* takes account of *B* varies with time. Our bus rider may be taking account of the lady during the bus ride (i.e., t_1 to t_n) but not at all when watching television that evening (i.e., after t_n).

The type of investigation will determine which point of reference for defining the term "interpersonal" will be most useful. Sometimes it is useful to consider an interpersonal situation from the standpoint of an individual, as when we speak of an interpersonal need. Sometimes it is more advantageous to consider a situation interpersonal only if the "taking account of" relation is reciprocal, that is, perceived by both members of a dyadic (two-person) relation (see Chapter 7). Sometimes the point of view of observers will decide whether a situation is interpersonal, regardless of the reports of the individuals involved in the relation. For conceptual clarity the important requirement in describing an interpersonal relation is that the point of reference be specified.

The phrase "face-to-face" used frequently by other writers when defining "interpersonal" or "group" has been omitted from the present definition. As shall be elaborated below, the property of physical presence is an important variable within the scope of interpersonal behavior, closely related to the area of inclusion. Further, it is often useful to consider situations as interpersonal in which behavior is determined by *expectations* of the behavior of others, even if the others are not physically present. It therefore seems more useful to leave the term "interpersonal" free of the face-to-face condition and consider as a separate problem the effect of that condition on behavior.

The other term in the phrase under discussion is "need." A "need" is defined in terms of a situation or condition of an individual the nonrealization of which leads to undesirable consequences. An interpersonal need is one that may be satisfied only through the attainment of a satisfactory relation with other people. The satisfaction of a need is a necessary condition for the avoidance of the undesirable consequences of illness and death. A discrepancy between the satisfaction of an interpersonal need and the present state of an organism engenders a feeling in the organism that shall be called *anxiety*.

There is a close parallel between biological needs and interpersonal needs, in the following respects:

1. A biological need is a requirement to establish and maintain a satisfactory relation between the organism and its *physical* environment. An interpersonal need is a requirement to establish a satisfactory relation between the individual and his *human* environment. A biological need is not satisfied by providing unlimited gratification. An organism may take in too much water and drown, as well as too little water and die of thirst. The need is satisfied by establishing an equilibrium between the amount of water inside and outside the organism. The same is true for the "commodities" exchanged between people. An individual's needs may be unfulfilled either by having, for example, too much control over his human environment and hence too much responsibility, or too little control, hence not enough security. He must establish a satisfactory relation with his human environment with respect to control.

2. Nonfulfillment of a biological need leads to physical illness and sometimes death. Nonfulfillment of an interpersonal need leads to mental (or interpersonal) illness and sometimes death. Unsatisfactory personal relations lead directly to difficulties associated with emotional illness. Death, either through suicide or resulting from the more general loss of motivation for life, results when interpersonal dissatisfaction is prolonged.

3. The organism has characteristic modes, which are temporarily successful, of adapting to lack of complete satisfaction of biological needs. The organism also has characteristic ways, which are temporarily successful, of adapting to nonsatisfaction of interpersonal needs. For the interpersonal situation the terms "conscious" and "unconscious" needs are sometimes used to describe the phenomena at issue.

The distinction between a conscious and an unconscious need finds a parallel in a biological condition such as drug addiction. In drug addiction the immediate (conscious) need is to satisfy the immediate craving and to adjust the body chemistry so that the pain is reduced. The more basic (unconscious) need is to adjust the body chemistry back to the state where the drug is no longer required. The pain or anxiety felt when the organism is in a situation which does not allow for the satisfaction of these two needs is different in each case. In the first there is the immediate deprivation, analogous to an interpersonal situation in which an individual's characteristic psychological adjustment mechanisms (for example, defenses) cannot operate. To illustrate, if denial were the defense used by an individual in the affection area and he were placed in a situation in which close personal relations were called for, he would feel an *immediate anxiety* caused by the discrepancy between the demands of the situation and his most comfortable behavior pattern. The more *basic anxiety* or interpersonal imbalance stemming from the general inadequacy of the defense to ward off the need for affection is analogous to the physical discomfort caused by the discrepancy between the chemical balance produced by the drug addiction and the normal chemical balance.

This analogy assumes a particular interpersonal relation that optimally satisfies interpersonal needs, parallel to an optimal chemical balance. This assumption is made, although it is difficult to test. Perhaps it parallels the condition in which the psychoanalyst attempts to place his patient. The analyst has a conception of an optimal psychological condition for a given individual toward which the person strives. This condition goes deeper than the reinforcement of the patient's defense mechanisms, which protect him from undesirable impulses. The optimal state is one in which defenses are only minimally required. It is this psychological state that is analogous to the concept of an optimal interpersonal relation.

These parallels between the interpersonal and biological needs will be specified more precisely in the following discussion. Other aspects of this problem could be mentioned at this point, such as the phylogenetic continuity of interpersonal needs, their universality cross-culturally, and possible physiological correlates. However, this would take the discussion too far afield. The main point is that in many important ways interpersonal needs have properties closely parallel to those of biological needs.

INCLUSION, CONTROL, AND AFFECTION

Now comes the problem of describing the elephant, that is, providing a complete description of interpersonal variables sufficient to provide a framework for integration and future investigation in the field.

To construct such a schema it is necessary to determine the most relevant parameters for describing important aspects of the interpersonal variables. These parameters may then be used as the classification variables for generating a matrix to encompass the interpersonal behavior of interest. This process is called "substructing" by Lazarsfeld and Barton (55), and "facet analysis" by Guttman (45). It has the virtue of providing all possible combinations of parameter values so that omissions or duplications are easily recognized.

The parameters chosen should delineate salient differences worthy of preservation in personality description. Differences on these parameters represent important behavioral differences which are helpful, even necessary, when behavioral characteristics are related to external factors, for example, childhood experiences, productivity, compatibility, leadership. The matrix generated by the parameters represents the *types of available data*. The methods of obtaining the data (such as introspection, questionnaire, observation, projective test) are independent of the matrix. Any method of data collection is permissible for any type of data. The parameters:

1. *Observability*—the degree to which an action of an individual is observable by others. This parameter is dichotomized into *action* and *feeling*. An action is usually more observable to outsiders, a feeling usually more observable to the self.

2. *Directionality*—the direction of the interaction with respect to originator and target. This parameter is trichotomized into (a) self toward other, (b) other toward self, and (c) self toward self. The last category is interpersonal in the sense that it represents interaction between the self and others who have been interiorized early in life.

3. *Status of Action*—whether the behavior is in the inclusion, control, or affection area.

4. *State of Relation*—whether the relation is desired, ideal, anxious or pathological.

Table 2–1 summarizes the terms and concepts discussed in this chapter. This table, in a sense, is the "elephant."

The Three Interpersonal Needs

The interpersonal need for inclusion is defined behaviorally as the need to establish and maintain a satisfactory relation with people with respect to interaction and association. "Satisfactory relation" includes (1) a psychologically comfortable relation with people somewhere on a dimension ranging from originating or initiating interaction with all people to not initiating interaction with anyone; (2) a psychologically comfortable relation with people with respect to eliciting behavior from them somewhere on a dimension ranging from always initiating interaction with the self to never initiating interaction with the self.

On the level of feelings the need for inclusion is defined as the need to establish and maintain a feeling of mutual interest with other people. This feeling includes (1) being able to take an interest in other people to a satisfactory degree and (2) having other people interested in the self to a satisfactory degree.

With regard to the self-concept, the need for inclusion is the need to feel that the self is significant and worth while.

The interpersonal need for control is defined behaviorally as the need to establish and maintain a satisfactory relation with people with respect to control and power. "Satisfactory relation" includes (1) a psychologically comfortable relation with people somewhere on a dimension ranging from controlling all the behavior of other people to not controlling any behavior of others and (2) a psychologically comfortable relation with people with respect to eliciting behavior from them somewhere on a dimension ranging from always being controlled by them to never being controlled by them.

With regard to feelings, the need for control is defined as the need to

		INCLUSION			CONTROL			AFFECTION		
		Self to Other (Actions)	**Other to Self (Reactions)**	**Self to Self**	**Self to Other (Actions)**	**Other to Self (Reactions)**	**Self to Self**	**Self to Other (Actions)**	**Other to Self (Reactions)**	**Self to Self**
DESIRED INTERPERSONAL RELATIONS (NEEDS)	Act	Satisfactory interaction behavior	Satisfactory relation re inclusion behavior 1		Satisfactory power and behavior	Satisfactory relation re control behavior 19		Satisfactory love and behavior	Satisfactory relation re affection behavior 37	
	Feel	Satisfactory feelings of mutual interest	Satisfactory relation re mutual interest 2	Feeling that I am significant 15	Satisfactory feelings of mutual respect	Satisfactory relation re mutual respect 20	Feeling that I am responsible 33	Satisfactory feelings of mutual affection	Satisfactory relation re mutual affection 38	Feeling that I am lovable 51
IDEAL INTERPERSONAL RELATIONS	Act	Social 3	People include me 4		Democrat 21	People respect me 22		Personal 39	People are friendly to me 40	
	Feel	I am interested in people 5	People are interested in me 6		I respect people 23	People respect me 24		I like people 41	People like me 42	
ANXIOUS INTERPERSONAL RELATIONS (ANXIETIES) — Too much activity	Act	Over-social 7	Social-compliant 8	I am insignificant (I don't know who I am; I am nobody) 16	Autocrat 25	Rebel 26	I am incompetent (I am stupid, irresponsible) 34	Over-personal 43	Personal-compliant 44	I am unlovable (I am no good, rotten bastard) 52
	Feel	I am not really interested in people 9	People aren't really interested in me 10		I don't trust people 27	People don't trust me 28		I don't really like people 45	People don't really like me 46	
Too little activity	Act	Under-social 11	Counter-social 12		Abdicrat 29	Submissive 30		Under-personal 47	Counter-personal 48	
	Feel	I am not interested in people 13	People are not interested in me 14		I don't really respect people 31	People don't really respect me 32		I don't like people 49	People don't like me 50	
PATHOLOGICAL INTERPERSONAL RELATIONS	Too Much	Psychotic 17			Obsessive-compulsive 35			Neurotic 53		
	Too Little	Psychotic (Schizophrenia) 18			Psychopath 36			Neurotic 54		

establish and maintain a feeling of mutual respect for the competence and responsib!eness of others. This feeling includes (1) being able to respect others to a satisfactory degree and (2) having others respect the self to a satisfactory degree.

The need for control, defined at the level of perceiving the self, is the need to feel that one is a competent, responsible person.

The interpersonal need for affection is defined behaviorally as the need to establish and maintain a satisfactory relation with others with respect to love and affection. Affection always refers to a two-person (dyadic) relation. "Satisfactory relation" includes (1) a psychologically comfortable relation with others somewhere on a dimension ranging from initiating close, personal relations with everyone to originating close, personal relations with no one; (2) a psychologically comfortable relation with people with respect to eliciting behavior from them on a dimension ranging from always originating close, personal relations toward the self, to never originating close, personal relations toward the self.

At the feeling level the need for affection is defined as the need to establish and maintain a feeling of mutual affection with others. This feeling includes (1) being able to love other people to a satisfactory degree and (2) having others love the self to a satisfactory degree.

The need for affection, defined at the level of the self-concept, is the need to feel that the self is lovable.

This type of formulation stresses the interpersonal nature of these needs. They require that the organism establish a kind of equilibrium, in three different areas, between the self and other people. In order to be anxiety-free, a person must find a comfortable behavioral relation with others with regard to the exchange of interaction, power, and love. The need is not wholly satisfied by having others respond toward the self in a particular way; nor is it wholly satisfied by acting toward others in a particular fashion. A satisfactory balance must be established and maintained.

Inclusion, Control, and Affection Behavior

Thus far these key terms have been discussed only from the standpoint of their status as interpersonal needs. Since the value of the theory is dependent to a large extent on the cogency and clarity of these terms, it is important to describe them as fully as possible. In later chapters many different ways of describing these terms will be introduced, including

1. Examples;
2. Synonyms (Chapter 2);
3. A description of aspects of these behaviors at various levels of personality (Chapter 2);
4. A description of the interconnection between these terms and other terms in the theory, such as "compatibility" (Chapter 6);

5. A description of the relations between these areas and factors found by other investigators (Chapter 3);

6. A description of these areas as applied to literary works (Chapter 9); and

7. A measuring instrument FIRO–B (Fundamental Interpersonal Relations Orientation—Behavior), which measures two aspects of each of the three areas (Chapter 4).

Inclusion behavior is defined as behavior directed toward the satisfaction of the interpersonal need for inclusion.

Control behavior is defined as behavior directed toward the satisfaction of the interpersonal need for control.

Affection behavior is defined as behavior directed toward the satisfaction of the interpersonal need for affection.

In general, *inclusion behavior* refers to association between people. Some terms that connote a relation that is primarily positive inclusion are "associate," "interact," "mingle," "communicate," "belong," "companion," "comrade," "attend to," "member," "togetherness," "join," "extravert." Some terms that connote lack of, or negative, inclusion, are "exclusion," "isolate," "outsider," "outcast," "lonely," "detached," "withdrawn," "abandoned," "ignored."

The need to be included manifests itself as wanting to be attended to, to attract attention and interest. The classroom hellion who throws erasers is often objecting mostly to the lack of attention paid him. Even if he is given negative affection he is partially satisfied, because at least someone is paying attention to him.

In groups, people often make themselves prominent by talking a great deal. Frequently they are not interested in power or dominance but simply prominence. The "joker" is an example of a prominence seeker, very much as is the blond actress with the lavender convertible.

In the extreme, what is called "fame" is primarily inclusion. Acquisition of fame does not imply acquisition of power or influence: witness Marilyn Monroe's attempt to swing votes to Adlai Stevenson. Nor does fame imply affection: Al Capone could hardly be considered a widely loved figure. But fame does imply prominence, and signifies interest on the part of others.

From another standpoint, behavior related to belonging and "togetherness" is primarily inclusion. To desire to belong to a fraternal organization by no means necessarily indicates a liking for the members or even a desire for power. It is often sought for its "prestige value," for increase of "status." These terms are also primarily inclusion conceptions, because their primary implication is that people pay attention to the person, know who he is, and can distinguish him from others.

This last point leads to an essential aspect of inclusion, that of identity. An integral part of being recognized and paid attention to is that the individual be identifiable from other people. He must be known as a specific individual; he must have a particular identity. If he is not thus known, he cannot truly be attended to or have interest paid to him. The extreme of this identification is that he be understood. To be understood implies that someone is interested enough in him to find out his particular characteristics. Again, this interest need not mean that others have affection for him, or that they respect him. For example, the interested person may be a confidence man who is exploring his background to find a point of vulnerability.

At the outset of interpersonal relations a common issue is that of commitment, the decision to become involved in a given relation or activity. Usually, in the initial testing of the relation, individuals try to identify themselves to one another to find out which facet of themselves others will be interested in. Frequently a member is silent for a while because he is not sure that people are interested in him. These behaviors, too, are primarily in the inclusion area.

This, then, is the flavor of inclusion. It has to do with interacting with people, with attention, acknowledgement, being known, prominence, recognition, prestige, status, and fame; with identity, individuality, understanding, interest, commitment, and participation. It is unlike affection in that it does not involve strong emotional attachments to individual persons. It is unlike control in that the preoccupation is with prominence, not dominance.

Control behavior refers to the decision-making process between people. Some terms connoting a relation that is primarily positive control are "power," "authority," "dominance," "influence," "control," "ruler," "superior officer," "leader." Some terms that connote primarily a lack of, or negative, control are "rebellion," "resistance," "follower," "anarchy," "submissive," "henpecked," "milquetoast."

The need for control manifests itself as the desire for power, authority, and control over others and therefore over one's future. At the other end is the need to be controlled, to have responsibility taken away. Manifestations of the power drive are very clear. A more subtle form is exemplified by the current magazine advertising campaign featuring the "influential." This is a person who controls others through the power he has to influence their behavior.

The acquisition of money or political power is a direct method of obtaining control over other persons. This type of control often involves coercion rather than more subtle methods of influence like persuasion and example. In group behavior, the struggles to achieve high office or to make suggestions that are adopted are manifestations of control behavior. In an argument in a group we may distinguish the inclusion seeker from the control seeker in this way: the one seeking inclusion or prominence wants very much to be one of the participants in the argument, while the control seeker wants to be the winner or, if not the winner, on the same side as the winner. The prominence seeker would prefer to be the losing participant; the dominance seeker would prefer to be a winning nonparticipant. Both these roles are separate from the affectional desires of the members.

Control behavior takes many subtle forms, especially among more intellectual and polite people. For example, in many discussion groups where blackboards are involved, the power struggle becomes displaced onto the chalk. Walking to the blackboard and taking the chalk from the one holding it, and retaining possession, becomes a mark of competitive success. Often a meeting is marked by a procession of men taking the chalk, writing something, and being supplanted by another man for a further message. In this way propriety is maintained, and still the power struggle may proceed.

In many gatherings, control behavior is exhibited through the group task. Intellectual superiority, for one thing, often leads to control over others so that strong motivation to achieve is often largely control behavior. Such superiority also demonstrates the real capacity of the individual to be relied on for responsible jobs, a central aspect of control. Further, to do one's job properly, or to rebel against the established authority structure by not doing it, is a splendid outlet for control feelings. Doing a poor job is a way of rebelling against the structure and showing that no one will control you, whereas asquiescence earns rewards from those in charge which satisfies the need to be respected for one's accomplishments.

Control is also manifested in behavior toward others controlling the self. Expressions of independence and rebellion exemplify lack of willingness to be controlled, while compliance, submission, and taking orders indicate various degrees of accepting the control of others. There is no necessary relation between an individual's behavior toward controlling others, and his behavior toward being controlled. The domineering sergeant may accept orders from the lieutenant with pleasure and gratefulness, while the neighborhood bully may also rebel against his parents; two persons who control others differ in the degree to which they allow others to control them.

Thus the flavor of control is transmitted by behavior involving influence, leadership, power, coercion, authority, accomplishment, intellectual superiority, high achievement, and independence, as well as dependency (for decision making), rebellion, resistance, and submission. It differs from inclusion behavior in that it does not require prominence. The concept of the "power behind the throne" is an excellent example of a role that would fill a high control need and a low need for inclusion. The "joker" exemplifies the opposite. Control behavior differs from affection behavior in that it has to do with power relations rather than emotional closeness. The frequent difficulties between those who want to "get down to business" and those who want to get to "know one another" illustrate a situation in which control behavior is more important for some and affection behavior for others.

In general, *affection behavior* refers to close personal emotional feelings between *two* people. Affection is a dyadic relation; it can occur only between pairs of people at any one time, whereas both inclusion and control relations may occur either in dyads or between one person and a group of persons. Some terms that connote an affection relation that is primarily positive are "love," "like," "emotionally close," "positive feelings," "personal," "friendship," "sweetheart." Some terms that connote primarily lack of, or negative, affection are "hate," "dislike," "cool," "emotionally distant."

The need for affection leads to behavior related to becoming emotionally close. An affection relation must be dyadic because it involves strong differentiation between people. Affectional relations can be toward parental figures, peers, or children figures. They are exemplified in friendship relations, dating, and marriage.

To become emotionally close to someone involves, in addition to an emotional attachment, an element of confiding innermost anxieties, wishes, and feelings. A strong positive affectional tie usually is accompanied by a unique relation regarding the degree of sharing of these feelings.

In groups, affection behavior is characterized by overtures of friendship and differentiation between members. One common method for avoiding a close tie with any one member is to be equally friendly to all members. Thus "popularity" may not involve affection at all; it may often be inclusion behavior, whereas "going steady" is usually primarily affection.

A difference between affection behavior, inclusion behavior, and control behavior is illustrated by the different feelings a man has in being turned down by a fraternity, failed in a course by a professor, and rejected by his girl. The fraternity excludes him and tells him, in effect, that they as a group don't have sufficient interest in him. The professor fails him and says, in effect, that he finds him incompetent in his field. His girl rejects him, and tells him, in effect, that she doesn't find him lovable.

Thus the flavor of affection is embodied in situations of love, emotional closeness, personal confidences, intimacy. Negative affection is characterized by hate, hostility, and emotional rejection.

In order to sharpen further the contrast between these three types of behavior, several differences may be mentioned.

With respect to an interpersonal relation, inclusion is concerned primarily with the formation of the relation, whereas control and affection are concerned with relations already formed. Basically, inclusion is always concerned with whether or not a relation exists. Within existent relations, control is the area concerned with who gives orders and make decisions for whom, whereas affection is concerned with how emotionally close or distant the relation becomes. Thus, generally speaking, inclusion is concerned with the problem of *in or out,* control is concerned with *top or bottom,* and affection with *close or far.*

A further differentiation occurs with regard to the number of people involved in the relation. Affection is *always* a one-to-one relation, inclusion is *usually* a one-to-many relation, and control may be either a one-one or a one-many relation. An affectional tie is necessarily between two persons, and involves varying degrees of intimacy, warmth, and emotional involvement which cannot be felt toward a unit greater than one person. Inclusion, on the other hand, typically concerns the behavior and feelings of one person toward a group of people. Problems of belonging and membership, so central to the inclusion area, usually refer to a relatively undifferentiated group with which an individual seeks association. His feelings of wanting to belong to the group are qualitatively different from his personal feelings of warmth toward an individual person. Control may refer to a power struggle between two individuals for control over each other, or it may refer to the struggle for domination over a group, as in political power. There is no particular number of interactional participants implied in the control area.

Control differs from the other two areas with respect to the differentiation between the persons involved in the control situation. For inclusion and affection there is a tendency for participants to act similarly in both the behavior they express and the behavior they want from others; for example, a close, personal individual usually likes others to be close and personal also. This similarity is not so marked in the control area. The person who likes to control may or may not want others to control him. This difference in differentiation among need areas is, however, only a matter of degree. There are many who like to include but do not want to be included, or who are not personal but want others to be that way toward them. But these types are not as frequent as the corresponding types in the control area.

TYPES OF INTERPERSONAL BEHAVIOR

For each area of interpersonal behavior three types of behavior will be described: (1) deficient—indicating that the individual is not trying directly to satisfy the need, (2) excessive—indicating that the individual is constantly trying to satisfy the need, (3) ideal—indicating satisfaction of the need, and (4) pathological.

In delineating these types it is assumed that anxiety engendered by early experiences leads to behavior of the first, second, and fourth types, while a successful working through of an interpersonal relation leads to an individual who can function without anxiety in the area. The developmental origins are dealt with in Chapter 5. For simplicity of presentation the extremes will be presented without qualifications. Actually, of course, the behavior of any given individual could be best described as some combination of behavior incorporating elements of all three types at different times, for instance, the oversocial, undersocial, and social.

Inclusion Types

THE UNDERSOCIAL

The interpersonal behavior of the undersocial person tends to be introverted and withdrawn. Characteristically, he avoids associating with others and doesn't like or accept invitations to join others. Consciously he wants to maintain this distance between himself and others, and insists that he doesn't want to get enmeshed with people and lose his privacy. But unconsciously he definitely wants others to pay attention to him. His biggest fears are that people will ignore him, generally have no interest in him, and would just as soon leave him behind.

Unconsciously he feels that no one ever will pay attention to him. His attitude may be summarized by, "No one is interested in me, so I'm not going to risk being ignored. I'll stay away from people and get along by myself." There is a strong drive toward self-sufficiency as a technique for existence without others. Since social abandonment is tantamount to death, he must compensate by directing his energies toward self-preservation; he therefore creates a world of his own in which his existence is more secure. Behind this withdrawal lie anxiety and hostility, and often a slight air of superiority and the private feeling that others don't understand him.

The direct expression of this withdrawal is nonassociation and inter- action with people, lack of involvement and commitment. The more subtle form is exemplified by the person who for one reason or another is always late to meetings, or seems to have an inordinate number of conflicting en- gagements necessitating absence from people, or the type of person who precedes each visit with, "I'm sorry, but I can't stay very long."

His deepest anxiety, that referring to the self concept, is that he is worthless. He thinks that if no one ever considered him important enough to receive attention, he must be of no value whatever.

Closely allied with this feeling is the lack of motivation to live. Associa- tion with people is a necessary condition for a desire to live. This factor may be of much greater importance in everyday interaction than is usually thought. The degree to which an individual is committed to living probably determines to a large extent his general level of enthusiasms, perserverance, involvement, and the like. Perhaps this lack of concern for life is the ultimate in regression: if life holds too few rewards, the prelife condition is preferable. It is likely that this basic fear of abandonment or isolation is the most potent of all interpersonal fears. The simple fear that people are not interested in the self is extremely widespread, but in scientific analyses it, too, often, is included as a special type of affectional need. It is extremely useful, however, to make clear the distinction between inclusion and affection.

THE OVERSOCIAL

The oversocial person tends toward extraversion in his later interper- sonal behavior. Characteristically, he seeks people incessantly and wants them to seek him out. He is also afraid they will ignore him. His interpersonal dynamics are the same as those of the withdrawn person, but his overt be- havior is the opposite.

His unconscious attitude is summarized by, "Although no one is inter- ested in me, I'll make people pay attention to me in any way I can." His in- clination is always to seek companionship. He is the type who "can't stand being alone." All of his activities will be designed to be done "together." An interesting illustration of this attitude occurs in the recent motion picture, "The Great Man." José Ferrer, as a newspaper man, is interviewing a woman about her reasons for attending the funeral of a television celebrity.

"Because our club all came together," she replies.
"But," Ferrer persists, "why did you come *here?*"
"I came here because the rest came here."
"Were you fond of the dead man?"
"Not especially," she replies, "but we always do things together."

This scene (the dialogue is from memory) nicely illustrates the importance of being together presumably as an end in itself. The interpersonal behavior of the oversocial type of person will then be designed to focus attention on himself, to make people notice him, to be prominent, to be listened to. There are many techniques for doing this. The direct method is to be an intensive, exhibitionistic participator. By simply forcing himself on the group he forces the group to focus attention on him. The more subtle technique is to try to acquire status through such devices as name dropping, or by asking startling questions. He may also try to acquire power (control) or try to be well liked (affection), but for the primary purpose of gaining attention. Power or friendship, although both may be important (depending on his orientation in the other two interpersonal areas), is not the primary goal.

THE SOCIAL

To the individual for whom the resolution of inclusion relations was successful in childhood, interaction with people presents no problem. He is comfortable with people and comfortable being alone. He can be a high or low participator in a group, or can equally well take a moderate role, without anxiety. He is capable of strong commitment and involvement to certain groups and also can withhold commitment if he feels it is appropriate.

Unconsciously, he feels that he is a worth while, significant person and that life is worth living. He is fully capable of being genuinely interested in others and feels that they will include him in their activities and that they are interested in him.

He also has an "identity" and an "individuality." Childhood feelings of abandonment lead to the absence of an identity; the person feels he is nobody. He has no stable figures with whom to identify. Childhood feelings of enmeshment lead to confusion of identity. When a child is nothing but parts of other people and has not had sufficient opportunity to evaluate the characteristics he observes in himself, he has difficulty knowing who he is. The social person has resolved these difficulties. He has integrated aspects of a large number of individuals into a new configuration which he can identify as himself.

INCLUSION PATHOLOGY

Failure to be included means anxiety over having contact with people. Unsuccessful resolution of inclusion relations leads to feelings of exclusion, of alienation from people, of being different and unacceptable, and usually the necessity of creating a phantasy world in which the nonincluded person is accepted. Inclusion, because it is posited to be the first area of interpersonal relations to be dealt with by the infant, has strong narcissistic elements and other close similarities to the description by psychoanalysts of the interpersonal characteristics in the oral stage. Hence a pathological difficulty in the inclusion area leads to the most regressed kind of behavior, that concerned with belonging to people, being a significant individual. This syndrome is very much like the functional *psychoses*. In Ruth Munroe's description of the Freudian explanation of psychoses (66) these points are made clear:

> "The essential feature of Freud's explanation of psychotic conditions may be stated as the greater depth of regression. The adult never lapses back to infancy all of a piece of course ... Freud felt, however, that the truly psychotic manifestations belong to the pre-oedipal period—indeed to the stage of narcissism before the ego has properly developed. The mechanisms of psychoses are the archaic mechanisms of the infant before secure object relations have been established." (p. 288)

The last line of this quotation is especially pertinent to demonstrating the close relations between the Freudian discussion of the psychosis and the area of inclusion. The phrase, "before secure object [interpersonal] relations have been established," certainly bears a close resemblance to the preceding discussion of the problems of becoming included in the social group.

It appears, then, that difficulty in establishing a satisfactory relation with other persons, with regard to inclusion or contact, when difficulty reaches a pathological state, leads to psychosis, especially schizophrenia. This statement does not mean that all conditions now called psychosis are caused by difficulties in the inclusion area, nor does it necessarily mean that all inclusion problems will, if pathological, become psychoses; nor does it even imply that there are "pure" inclusion problems uncontaminated with other areas. It implies only that there is a close relation between disturbance in the inclusion area and psychosis.

Psychosis, especially schizophrenia, appears to be related more to the undersocial pattern than the oversocial. The lack of identity and inability to be alone, if carried to the extreme, would correspond to the pathological extreme of the oversocial.

Control Types

THE ABDICRAT

The abdicrat is a person who tends toward submission and abdication of power and responsibility in his interpersonal behavior. Characteristically, he gravitates toward the subordinate position where he will not have to take responsibility for making decisions, and where someone else takes charge. Consciously, he wants people to relieve him of his obligations. He does not control others even when he should; for example, he would not take charge even during a fire in a children's schoolhouse in which he is the only adult; and he never makes a decision that he can refer to someone else. He fears that others will not help him when he requires it, and that he will be given more responsibility than he can handle. This kind of person is usually a follower, or at most a loyal lieutenant, but rarely the person who takes the responsibility for making the *final* decision. Unconsciously, too, he has the feeling that he is incapable of responsible adult behavior and that others know it. He never was told what to do and therefore never learned. His most comfortable response is to avoid situations in which he will feel helpless. He feels that he is an incompetent and irresponsible, perhaps stupid, person who does not deserve respect for his abilities.

Behind this feeling are anxiety, hostility, and lack of trust toward those who might withhold assistance. The hostility is usually expressed as passive resistance. Hesitancy to "go along" is a usual technique of resistance, since actual overt rebellion is too threatening.

THE AUTOCRAT

The autocrat is a person whose interpersonal behavior often tends toward the dominating. Characteristically, he tries to dominate people and strongly desires a power hierarchy with himself at the top. He is the power seeker, the compete. He is afraid people will not be influenced or controlled by him—that they will, in fact, dominate him.

Commonly, this need to control people is displaced into other areas. Intellectual or athletic superiority allows for considerable control, as does the more direct method of attaining political power. The underlying dynamics are the same as for the abdicrat. Basically the person feels he is not responsible or capable of discharging obligation and that this fact is known to others. He attempts to use every opportunity to disprove this feeling to others and to himself. His unconscious attitude may be summarized as, "No one thinks I can make decisions for myself, but I'll show them. I'm going to make all the decisions for everyone, always." Behind this feeling is a strong distrust that others may make decisions for him and the feeling that they don't trust him. This latter becomes a very sensitive area.

THE DEMOCRAT

For the individual who has successfully resolved his relations with others in the control area in childhood, power and control present no problem. He feels comfortable giving or not giving orders, and taking or not taking orders, as is appropriate to the situation. Unconsciously, he feels that he is a capable, responsible person and therefore that he does not need to shrink from responsibility or to try constantly to prove how competent he really is. Unlike the abdicrat and autocrat, he is not preoccupied with fears of his own helplessness, stupidity, and incompetence. He feels that other people respect his competence and will be realistic with respect to trusting him with decision making.

CONTROL PATHOLOGY

The individual who does not accept control of any kind develops pathologically into a psychopathic personality. He has not been adequately trained to learn the rules of behavior established for respecting the rights and privileges of others. Ruth Munroe (66) says,

"The major Freudian explanation for this condition is that there has been a serious failure of superego development. The parental image has not been adequately internalized in the form of conscience but remains the policeman at the corner—an external force. Truly, the behavior of the psychopath is childish without the limited experience of the child. When the resources of adulthood are used without the inner controls of adulthood the resultant behavior is very likely to be deplorable. Object relations generally are poor of necessity since good early object relations would have led to more adequate superego development." (p. 292)

Affection Types

THE UNDERPERSONAL

The underpersonal type tends to avoid close personal ties with others. He characteristically maintains his dyadic relations on a superficial, distant level and is most comfortable when others do the same to him. Consciously, he wishes to maintain this emotional distance, and frequently expresses a desire not to get "emotionally involved"; unconsciously he seeks a satisfactory affectional relation. His fear is that no one loves him. In a group situation he is afraid he won't be liked. He has great difficulty genuinely liking people. He distrusts their feeling toward him.

His attitude could be summarized by the "formula," "I find the affection area very painful since I have been rejected; therefore I shall avoid close personal relations in the future." The direct technique for maintaining emotional distance is to reject and avoid people to prevent emotional closeness or involvement actively, even to the point of being antagonistic. The subtle technique is to appear superficially friendly to *everyone*. This behavior acts as a safeguard against having to get close to, or become personal with, any *one* person. ("Close" and "personal" refer to emotional closeness and willingness to confide one's most private concerns and feelings. It involves the expression of positive affection and tender feelings.) Here the dyadic relation is a threatening one. To keep everyone at the same distance obviates the requirement for treating any one person with greater warmth and affection.

The deepest anxiety, that regarding the self, is that he is unlovable. He feels that people won't like him because, in fact, he doesn't "deserve" it. If people got to know him well, he believes, they would discover the traits that make him so unlovable. As opposed to the inclusion anxiety that the self is of no value, worthless, and empty, and the control anxiety that the self is stupid and irresponsible, the affection anxiety is that the self is nasty and bad.

THE OVERPERSONAL

The overpersonal type attempts to become extremely close to others. He definitely wants others to treat him in a very close, personal way. His response may be summarized by the formula, "My first experiences with affection were painful, but perhaps if I try again they will turn out to be better." He will be striving in his interpersonal relations primarily to be liked. Being liked is extremely important to him in his attempt to relieve his anxiety about being always rejected and unlovable. Again, there are two behavioral techniques, the direct and the subtle. The direct technique is an overt attempt to gain approval, be extremely personal, intimate, and confiding. The subtle technique is more manipulative, to devour friends and subtly punish any attempts by them to establish other friendships, to be possessive.

The underlying dynamics are the same as those for the underpersonal. Both the overpersonal and the underpersonal responses are extreme, both are motivated by a strong need for affection, both are accompanied by strong anxiety about ever being loved, and basically about being unlovable, and both have considerable hostility behind them stemming from the anticipation of rejection.

THE PERSONAL

For the individual who successfully resolved his affectional relations with others in childhood, close emotional relations with one other person present no problem. He is comfortable in such a personal relation, and he can also relate comfortably in a situation requiring emotional distance. It is important for him to be liked, but if he isn't liked he can accept the fact that the dislike is the result of the relation between himself and one other person —in other words, the dislike does not mean that he is an unlovable person. Unconsciously, he feels that he is a lovable person who is lovable even to people who know him well. He is capable of giving genuine affection.

AFFECTION PATHOLOGY

Neuroses are commonly attributed to difficulties in the area of affection. Ruth Munroe (66) says,

"The early bloom of sexuality, which cannot possibly come to fruition, is called the phallic stage to differentiate it from true genitality leading to mature mating and reproduction. At this period attitudes are formed which are crucial for later heterosexual fulfillment and good relations with people generally. For this reason it is the stage most fraught with potentialities for neurotic distortion." (p. 199)

The discussion of pathology in this chapter should be supplemented with the discussion of the childhood origins of various adult behavior patterns presented in Chapter 5. Combining the early experience and present behavior with the pathological classification will provide a more complete picture of the process of personality development and disintegration.

Summary

To summarize, difficulties with initiating interaction range from being uncomfortable when not associating with people ("can't stand to be alone" —the *oversocial*) to not feeling comfortable initiating interaction ("can't stand being with people"—the *undersocial*). Difficulties with controlling others range from not feeling comfortable controlling the behavior of anyone ("can't tell anyone what to do"—the *abdicrat*) to not feeling comfortable when unable to control everyone ("always have to be in charge"—the *autocrat*). Difficulties with originating close, personal relations range from being uncomfortable when unable to establish a sufficiently close, personal relation ("can't get close enough"—the *overpersonal*) to being uncomfortable when getting too close and personal with someone ("don't like to get emotionally involved with people"—the *underpersonal*).

This description could be stated in psychoanalytic terms with little if any difference in meaning. In the struggle between the id and the superego to determine the individual's behavior the excessive response in each area represents the triumph of the id. The restrained response results from the triumph of the superego. The ideal response represents the successful resolution of the id impulses, the demands of the superego, and external reality; it therefore corresponds to the triumph of the ego.

In each of the nonideal (extreme) types described there are anxiety, hostility, and ambivalence. (One outcome of this analysis is to suggest that each of these widely used terms could be divided profitably into three types.) Anxiety arises from a person's (a) anticipation of a nonsatisfying event (for instance, being ignored, dominated, rejected) and (b) fear of exposure, both to self and others, of what kind of person he "really" is—his inadequate self-concept. The anxiety indicates that these behavior patterns are inflexible, since anxiety usually leads to rigid behavior. The threat involved in changing behavior is too great to allow for much flexibility. Hostility also follows from anxiety; so the hostility, too, may arise in three ways.

Finally, ambivalence is also present in the nonideal behaviors, since the behavior pattern being utilized is necessarily unsatisfactory. In many instances an overpersonal individual, for example, will occasionally become underpersonal, and vice versa. Complete reversals are to be expected more than slight modifications, especially for the extreme behavior patterns. The characterization of a person's behavior can describe only his most usual behavior, not his invariable behavior.

3

The Postulate of Interpersonal
Needs: Plausibility

PLAUSIBILITY

As mentioned in Chapter 1, after the explanation of each postulate a presentation is made of the antecedent probability, or plausibility, of the postulate. Antecedent probability is the likelihood that the postulate is true, based on knowledge that is available prior to a specific predictive test of theorems derived from the postulate. This knowledge may be intuitive, theoretical, introspective, and anecdotal, or it may be based on data gathered in other contexts. Anything bearing on the probability that the theorems may be confirmed by experiment is relevant to antecedent probability.

In this chapter many studies dealing with various aspects of interpersonal behavior are reviewed and interpreted in the light of Postulate 1. An attempt is made to present enough of the study to convey the flavor of the results without involvement in the details of any one example. It is quite possible that the reader will want to disagree with some of the interpretations made for certain studies, although pains have been taken to avoid the Procrustean pitfall of forcing everything to fit the ICA framework. (This designation will be used to indicate the present theory, that is, a framework for understanding interpersonal behavior based on inclusion, control, and affection.)

The primary purpose of this chapter is to demonstrate that a large number of studies of interpersonal behavior could be reasonably interpreted as being consistent with the idea that inclusion, control, and affection are the three basic interpersonal need areas. To the degree that this is true, theorems derived from Postulate 1 have high antecedent probability. In other words, the postulate does not do violence to the information already at hand.

It not only is consistent with it but provides a general framework within which hitherto unrecognized connections are called to observers' attention.

Clearly the worth of the postulate, or truth of the theorems derived from it, are not solely dependent on the argument made here. If, after reading this chapter, the reader feels it is more likely that Postulate 1 will lead to true theorems, then this review has increased the antecedent probability of the postulate for that reader.

Supplementing this chapter is a forthcoming book by Hare (47) which includes an application of the present theory to a wider scope of literature on small groups. It therefore could be said to constitute a plausibility argument for Postulate 1.

A by-product of this literature review is a widening of the conception of inclusion, control, and affection. By showing how the concepts of other investigators are translatable, the new terms take on richer and clearer meaning.

The matrix presented in Table 2–1 will be used to show the relations within the ICA framework among the studies to be reviewed. The numbers of the cells relevant to each formulation will be inserted into the text. These cells designate the closest approximation to the aspect of interpersonal behavior under discussion. However, as a rule there is less than complete overlap between a factor described by another author and one of the ICA need areas. Usually inclusion, control, or affection is *emphasized* in the description, although elements from the other areas may appear. It is always the area emphasized that is of interest in establishing the parallelism of the investigation with the ICA framework. This relation is similar to that of rotated axes in factor analysis (91). Table 3–1 summarizes the literature that will be discussed in the chapter, and lists the terms used by the authors that are felt to approximate inclusion, control, and affection.

Parent-Child Relations

The child typically experiences interpersonal relations first with his parents. If the needs for inclusion, control, and affection are present in all persons, it should be possible to find behavior in these areas appearing in parent-child relations.

BALDWIN, KALLHORN, BREESE

In 1945 Baldwin, Kallhorn, and Breese (8) performed a large-scale study of the patterns of parent behavior. They began by doing an empirical study based on five different ratings of 125 cases. Subjects were infants through fourteen years old, above the national average in IQ, education, and economic status of parents. Using a modification of factor analysis suggested by Sanford, they found "three central syndromes" of parental behavior. These syndromes were labeled, "democracy in the home, acceptance

Table 3–1. Summary of Studies Finding Aspects of the Three Fundamental Interpersonal Needs

	AUTHOR	INCLUSION	CONTROL	AFFECTION
PARENT-CHILD RELATIONS	1. Baldwin, Kallhorn, Breese (1945)	Indulgence	Democracy in the home	Acceptance
	2. Champney (1941)	Stimulative-inactive	Freedom-control	Approving-deprecating
	3. Sewell, Mussen, Harris (1955)	Parent-child interaction	Promotion of independence	Permissive feeding
PERSON-ALITY TYPES	4. Fromm (1947)	Withdrawal-destructive	Symbiotic relatedness	Love relatedness
	5. Freud (1931)	Narcissistic type	Obsessional type	Erotic type
	6. Horney (1945)	Moving away from people	Moving against people	Moving toward people
GROUP BEHAVIOR	7. Kaiser group (1957)	Intensity	Dominance-submission	Affiliation hostility
	8. Couch, Carter (1954)	Individual prominence	Group-goal facilitation	Sociability
	9. Bion (1949)	Fight-flight	Dependence	Pairing
MISCEL-LANEOUS STUDIES	10. Benne, Sheats (1948)	Individual	Task	Maintenance
	11. Swanson (1951)	Participation	Influence	Being liked
	12. Back, *et al* (1951)	Group prestige	Task direction	Personal attraction
	13. Corsini, Rosenberg (1955)	Actional	Intellectual	Emotional
	14. Jenkins, Lippitt (1951)	Extracurricular activity	Power	Friendliness
	15. Varon (1953)	Status	Independence	Expressing feelings
	16. Glueck (1950)	Cohesiveness	Discipline	Affection

of child, and indulgence." The authors describe the syndromes in terms of the variables that formed them.

The authors' syndrome "indulgence" corresponds to the inclusion area, with a slight emphasis on excessive amount (enmeshed). The first two items reflect excessive attention; the last two express well the interaction aspect.

"*Indulgence* seems to describe best the following syndrome of variables.

> General protectiveness
> General babying
> Child-centeredness of the home
> Acceptance of Child
> Solicitousness for welfare
> Duration of contact with mother
> Intensity of contact with mother"

[Matrix cells 4, 6, 10] (p. 14)

The syndrome "democracy in the home" corresponds to the control area. The concepts of guidance and fostering of independence and responsibility are readily apparent in their listing.

"*Democracy in the home* is the title given to the following cluster of variables listed in the order of their importance in the syndrome.

> Justification of policy
> Democracy of policy
> Non-Coerciveness of suggestions
> Readiness of explanation
> Direction of criticism (approval)
> Clarity of policy
> Understanding of the child
> Non-Restrictiveness of regulations"   [22, 24, 28] (p. 14)

The syndrome "acceptance of child" corresponds to the affection area. The word "affection" is used directly in the third item, and the first four items together show a strong emphasis on the emotional closeness and affectional aspects of the parent-child relation.

"*Acceptance of the child* ...

> Rapport with the child
> Affectionateness toward child
> Direction of criticism (approval)
> Effectiveness of policy
> Child-centeredness of the home
> Non-Disciplinary friction"   [40, 42, 46] (p. 14)

It is interesting to note the appearance of child-centeredness on this list as well as on the first one, though it is a little lower here. Its presence perhaps reflects a relation between inclusion and affection. Child-centeredness in the syndrome with affectionateness, approval, and rapport has a different meaning from child-centeredness in a syndrome with duration and intensity of contact with mother.

CHAMPNEY *

Part of the basis for the Baldwin study was the earlier work of Champney (24). Champney used what he called an "arm-chair factor analysis" to find the "basic factors of parent-child behavior." He arrived at six factors:

> Freedom-control
> Stimulative-inactive
> Maladjusted-harmonious
> Approving-deprecating
> Emotional-rational
> Socialized-individualized   (p. 536)

* The following seven lists and footnote are from H. Champney, "The Variables of Parent Behavior," *Journal of Abnormal and Social Psychology*, 36, 1941, 525–542.

Two of these factors seem not to be factors of parent-child behavior in the sense of interpersonal interaction but are more descriptive of general characteristics of the home and the relation of the home to outsiders. Interpersonal relations between parent and child are not clearly implied.

Maladjusted–Well adjusted

Home is erratic, discordant, disorganized, tense, neurotic, unpleasant.	Home is organized, harmonious, relaxed, characterized by sense of humor.

Socialized–individualized

The home is characteristically friendly, sociable, outgoing, hospitable, tolerant, generous, cooperative.	The home is characteristically reclusive, aloof, isolated; atmosphere within the home, characterized by privacy, private property, individual rights and duties. (p. 535)

Hence only four of Champney's factors are directly relevant to this analysis in that they are dimensions of interpersonal behavior.

Champney's factor of "stimulative-inactive" corresponds closely to inclusion. He uses the terms "attention" and "ignored" and stresses amount of interaction.

Stimulation-neglect

Child-centered home; child constantly subject to attention, affection, suggestion, concern, action. [10]	Adult-centered home; child left to own devices, neglected, ignored, unstimulated. [6] (p. 535)

For "child-centered home" there is an example of emphasis on one area, that is, inclusion, but an element of another type, "affection," is present.

"Freedom-control" corresponds even in name to the control area. Here the aspects of independence and excessive guidance and interference with the child's decision making are stressed:

Freedom-arbitrary control

Child free to choose, decide, originate, reject; never subject to arbitrary or autocratic control. [22, 28]	Child restrained strictly within the bounds of autocratic despotism. Obedience demanded. [24] (p. 535)

Champney's factor of "approving-deprecating" corresponds to the affection area. The emphasis is again on positive feeling, approval, encouragement, and the interesting idea of facilitation.

Approving-deprecating

Child is typically, praised, encouraged, approved, accepted, facilitated. [40]	Child is typically blamed, discouraged, disapproved, rejected, inhibited. [42] (p 535)

A further indication that the last two of the above items are similar to our affection and control is this footnote of Champney's:

> His [Symond's] two factors, dominance–submission and acceptance–rejection, seem to correspond closely with what we have called freedom-control and approving-deprecating. (p. 535)

Champney's remaining factor appears to be irrelevant:

Rational-non-rational

Attitude toward child is logical, organized, analytical, intellectual.	Attitude is expedient, prescriptive, authoritarian, emotional. (p. 535)

There are three bases for rejecting this factor. (1) The "nonrational" aspect is almost identical with control (authoritarian versus "autocratic despotism" and the like). (2) The distinction between opposite ends of the factor seems to be on the ground of a questionable value judgment; namely, rationality is good and emotionality is bad or, at best, like authoritarianism. To be sure, the other factors also have implicit valuations, but they also contain clear behavior criteria. This factor of rational–nonrational is contaminated with control, valuation, and an aspect of method rather than content. (3) The Baldwin *et al.* study, which factor-analyzed Champney's scales, did not retain this factor.

SEWELL, MUSSEN, AND HARRIS *

A third study, by Sewell, Mussen, and Harris (79), though not as helpful as the above two, is nevertheless worth mentioning for the expansion of the areas it affords. A factor analysis was carried out on thirty-eight child-training practices derived from interview ratings on 162 five- and six-year-old rural Wisconsin children and their families of unbroken middle-class homes. The factor analysis, which included some oblique factors, lent itself to reorganization and reinterpretation in the following way.

Factors 3 and 4 correspond to the opposite ends of the inclusion area. (They have the highest negative correlation, —.42, of all factors.) Factor 4 would probably be better named "Ignores child."

* The following quotations are from W. Sewell, P. Mussen, and G. Harris, "Relationships among Child Training Practices," *American Sociological Review*, 20, 1955, 137–148.

Factor 3 has been tentatively identified as the *parent child interaction factor,* since the following variables are significantly loaded with it.

Loading	Variable	
.61	Much activity with father	
.50	Much activity with mother	
.50	Much activity with parents	
.22	Success in bowel training rewarded	
−.32	Short duration confined to playpen	[4,10]

Factor 4 is essentially a *non-punitive treatment factor.* ...

Loading	Variable	
.63	Ignore child's neglect of jobs	
.56	Spanked few times	
.36	Ignore masturbation	
.26	Ignore child's disobedience of mother	[6, 24] (p. 144)

Factor 5 corresponds to the control area.

Factor 5, tentatively identified as *promotion of independence factor.* ...

Loading	Variable	
.43	Take child on picnics	
.37	Child has own spending money	
.32	Non-evasion of child's questions about sex	
.29	Ignore child's fighting	
−.41	Infant fed on demand	
−.35	Night feeding stopped at late age	
−.33	Infant slept with mother	[22] (p. 144)

Their factor 1, "permissiveness in feeding," corresponds to our affection area with some inclusion.

Loading	Variable	
.80	Short duration of bottle feeding	
.76	Long duration of breast feeding	
.48	Infant usually held when bottle fed	
.30	Infant fed on demand	
.23	Infant slept with mother	[40, 4] (p. 144)

All other factors seem to be eliminable on straight statistical grounds, such as very low factor loadings, or through combination with the above variables.

In summary, it would seem unwarranted to say that this study supported our theme as directly as did that of Baldwin *et al.* or the Champney projects. It does seem clear, however, that the three variables do appear rather unequivocally.

SUMMARY OF PARENT-CHILD RELATIONS STUDIES

From the studies reported, our three need areas as applied to parent-child relations look something like this:

Inclusion is also called parent-child interaction, stimulation, and, in the extreme, indulgence. The positive end of inclusion in parent-child relations is characterized by a child-centered home, with the child constantly subject to attention, concern, and action, a high level of activity, and intense and frequent contact with both parents. The negative end is characterized by an adult-centered home where the child is left to his own devices, neglected, ignored, understimulated; interaction with parents is low even for spankings, and disapproved activities will be ignored, including neglect of jobs, masturbation, and disobedience.

Control is called democracy, control, and promotion of independence. The positive end of control includes freedom to choose, decide, originate, reject—freedom from arbitrary control in general. More specifically, the parents characteristically justify their policies, decide things democratically, readily explain (including child's questions about sex), take child on picnics, give him his own spending money, and do not interfere in his fights. The negative aspect shows the child restrained strictly within the bounds of autocratic despotism, his obedience is demanded, suggestions are given coercively, and regulations are restrictive.

Affection is called affectionateness, approval and affectionateness, and acceptance of the child. The positive side seems to involve behavior that is affectionate, accepting, approving, encouraging, facilitating. The negative aspect shows the child blamed, discouraged, disapproved, rejected, and inhibited, as well as not receiving affection.

Personality Types

Before an examination of certain specific typologies of prominent personality theorists, it is of interest to study the major, broad lines of disagreement among the psychoanalytic giants, Jung, Adler, and Freud. The *major theoretical emphasis* of each man that set him apart from the other two might be characterized as follows. For Jung, the primary explanatory area was the relation of the individual to the world and to history, his "life energy" and its characteristic modes of expression, intraversion and extraversion. Adler emphasized the "will to power" and the overcoming of feelings of inferiority. For Freud, the libidinal impulses, centering around sex and affectional feelings, were most significant. Of course, each man was aware of the other areas, but it appears that in terms of central concepts Jung emphasized inclusion, Adler emphasized control, and Freud gave primacy to affection.

If Postulate 1 is correct, a classification of personality types should include types emphasizing each interpersonal need area. Although some authors emphasize different aspects of personality (for example, Horney describes the undersocial at great length but does not have much to say about the oversocial [9, 5]), and others combine two or more areas (to illustrate, Fromm's "love relatedness" includes elements of control, although it is clearly affection in emphasis), there seems to be an impressive overlap in several important classifications of personality.

FROMM *

The aspect of Fromm (39) most closely related to our interpersonal needs is what he calls "orientation in the process of socialization." Fromm delineates just three kinds of "interpersonal relatedness."

One type of relatedness he calls "withdrawal-destructiveness," which corresponds to inclusion behavior. He is emphasizing undersocial and oversocial behavior.

> "[Withdrawal-Destructiveness] ... relatedness is one of distance. ...
> The feeling of individual powerlessness can be overcome by withdrawal from others who are experienced as threats. ... withdrawal becomes the main form of relatedness to others, a negative relatedness. ... Its emotional equivalent is the *feeling of indifference* toward others, often accompanied by a compensatory feeling of self-inflation. ... can, but need not, be conscious ... covered up by a superficial kind of interest and sociability.
>
> "Destructiveness is the *active form of withdrawal;* the impulse to destroy others follows from the fear of being destroyed by them. ... it is the energy of *unlived life* transformed into energy for the destruction of life." [9, 11, 5] (p. 109, 110; italics added)

Of particular interest is the reference to the "feeling of indifference." This feeling could be interpreted as an identification with those who were indifferent to him (see Chapter 5). Fromm's reference to being destroyed will become a recurrent theme in this review of the literature. His treatment stresses the aspect of self-preservation. Being ignored is, in a social sense, tantamount to not existing or to being destroyed. Dynamically, the anxiety developed in the area of inclusion is basic to the existence of the organism itself. Freud and Bion also give prominence to the terms "existence" and "self-preservation."

Another type of relatedness, which Fromm calls "symbiotic," corresponds to the control area. Fromm emphasizes in all his types the escape from "aloneness" and freedom. In this type the emphasis is on a power relation and freedom. Fromm mentions the other dimensions but stresses that their manifestations occur *in the service* of the power drive.

> "In the *symbiotic* relatedness the person is related to others but loses or *never attains* his *independence;* he avoids the danger of aloneness by becoming part of another person, either by being "swallowed" by that person or by "swallowing" him. The former is the root of what is

---

* The following three quotations are from *Man for Himself,* by Erich Fromm. Copyright, 1947, by Erich Fromm. Reprinted by permission of Rinehart & Company, Inc.

clinically described as masochism. Masochism is the attempt to get rid of one's individual self, to escape from freedom, and to look for security by attaching one self to another person. ... [This dependency may be] rationalized as sacrifice, duty, or love. ...

"The impulse to swallow others, the *sadistic,* active form of symbiotic relatedness, appears in all kinds of rationalizations, as love, overprotectiveness, "justified" domination, "justified" vengeance, etc. ... All forms ... go back to the impulse to have complete mastery over another person. ... Complete domination over a powerless person is the essence of active symbiotic relatedness. ... the benevolent domination which often masquerades as "love" is an expression of sadism too. While the benevolent sadist wants his object to be rich, powerful, successful ... he *tries to prevent* ... *his object* [*from becoming*] *free and independent* ... thus ceas[ing] to be his.

.   .   .   .   .

"... the *symbiotic relationship* is one of *closeness* to and intimacy with the object ... at the expense of freedom and integrity. ..." [23, 27] (p. 107–109; italics added)

The references to the autocrat and abdicrat are quite clear.

One kind of relatedness which corresponds to affection Fromm calls "love." The relation refers to close ties. Fromm speaks only of the successful expression of this relation (the personal type).

"Love—is the productive form of relatedness to others and to oneself. It implies responsibility, care, respect, knowledge, and the wish for the other person to grow and develop. It is the expression of intimacy between two human beings under the condition of the preservation of each other's integrity." [37] (p. 110)

Actually, this type implies a person who has successfully resolved his relations with the people in the areas of control and inclusion, as well as affection. Again, however, the emphasis is on affection.

In summary, Fromm discusses both the autocrat and abdicrat reactions to a control difficulty, the undersocial and oversocial in the inclusion area, but discusses only the well-adjusted response to the affection area (personal) and combines it with the well-adjusted response to the inclusion and control areas (social, democrat). He does not explicitly discuss the two extreme responses to the affection problem, namely, underpersonal and overpersonal. [41, 45]

FREUD

In Freud's introductory comment in *Libidinal Types* (37) he states rather well the object of his classification schema, an object that applies equally well to the ICA typology. He says that these types must not coincide with a specific clinical picture; "on the contrary, they should embrace all the variations which fall within the category normal." Freud acknowledges that "these libidinal types are not the only possible ones," an assertion that appears to be true, but if our analysis is correct, the libidinal types each *do* emphasize one of the three interpersonal need areas.

Freud's *narcissistic* type corresponds to the inclusion area. This is the least worked out of the three libidinal types, all of which were, unfortunately, only perfunctorily discussed by Freud. The main point of correspondence between the narcissistic type and inclusion is expressed by the concept of self-preservation. As mentioned in the discussion of Fromm's withdrawal-destructive type, the reactions to difficulties in the inclusion area (being ignored) seem to center around some mechanism of self-preservation of social existence. Freud discusses a type that might be described as a milder, more acceptable form of Fromm's destructive type.

> "*Narcissistic* ... no tensions between ego and super–ego ... no preponderance of erotic needs; the main interest is focused on self preservation; the type is independent and not easily overawed. The ego has a considerable amount of aggression available, one manifestation ... being a proneness to activity; where love is in question, loving is preferred to being loved. ... it is on them that their fellow-men are especially likely to lean; they readily assume the role of leader, give fresh stimulus to cultural development or break down existing development." [1, 43] (p. 249)

The reference to activity fits well with the manifestation of inclusion found in the group behavior in which inclusion is related to amount of participation of activity.

Freud's *obsessional* type corresponds to the control area. He emphasizes the anxiety derived from incorporating a strong authority figure similar to the autocrat.

> "*Obsessional* ... its distinct characteristic is the supremacy ... [of] the super-ego, which is segregated from the ego with great accompanying tension. Persons of this type are governed by the anxiety of conscience instead of by the dread of losing love; they exhibit ... an inner instead of an outer dependence; they develop a high degree of self-reliance, and from the social standpoint they are the true upholders of civilization ... in a conservative spirit." [7, 33, 21] (p. 248)

This last aspect regarding upholding civilization is strikingly similar to an aspect of the factor discovered in group behavior (see Carter below), called *group goal facilitation*. In both these cases the emphasis is on the social helpfulness of behavior in this area which accepts the dictates of the authority. This acceptance serves to elaborate the guidance aspect of the control area.

Freud's *erotic* type corresponds to the affection area. He describes the overpersonal, whose primary and uppermost concern is to be loved.

"*Erotic* ... Loving, but above all things being loved, is for them the most important thing in life. They are governed by the dread of loss of love, and this makes them peculiarly dependent on those who may withhold their love from them." [37, 38, 41] (p. 248)

In summary, Freud's libidinal types seem to correspond asymmetrically to ICA types. He discusses the overpersonal in the affection area, omitting the underpersonal (and the personal that Fromm deals with); the autocrat in the control area, omitting the abdicrat; and a mixture of the undersocial and nonanxious social in the inclusion area, omitting the oversocial.

HORNEY *

In the framework which Horney (49) finds useful in approaching the area she calls "neurotic trends," she feels we must "gain a clearer perspective of the essential moves (a child makes) ... to cope with the environment." She, too, feels that three main lines crystallize for describing the movement a child makes to come to terms with his environment.

Horney's "moving away from people" corresponds to the area of inclusion. Her description details one reaction to this situation, undersocial and the desire to avoid obligation and intimate contact.

"[*Moving away from people*.] When he moves away from people he wants neither to belong nor to fight, but keeps apart. He feels he has not much in common with them, they do not understand him anyhow. (p. 43)

.   .   .   .   .

"... solitude ... detachment ... estrangement from people ... estrangement from the self ... a numbness ... as to what one is, what one loves, hates, desires, hopes, fears, resents, believes. ... detached persons have in common ... their capacity to look at themselves with a kind of objective interest. ... (p. 73–74)

"What is crucial is their inner need to put emotional distance between themselves and others. ... not to get emotionally involved with others in any way, whether in love, fight, co-operation, or competition. ... superficially, they may "get along" with people. ...

"All the needs and qualities they acquire are directed toward this major need of not getting involved. (p. 75)

.   .   .   .   .

"... His independence ... has a negative orientation; it is aimed at not being influenced, coerced, tied, obligated. (p. 77)

"... Timetables constitute a threat. ... Other person's expecting him to do certain things or behave in a certain way makes him uneasy

* The following three quotations are from K. Horney, *Our Inner Conflicts* (New York: W. W. Norton & Company, Inc., 1945), pp. 42–43, 63, 73.

and rebellious. ... To conform with accepted rules of behavior or traditional sets of values is repellent to him. He will conform outwardly ... but in his own mind he stubbornly rejects all conventional rules and standards. (p. 78)

.   .   .   .   .

"... the detached person becomes panicky if he can no longer safeguard his emotional distance from others ... the reason his panic is so great is that he has no technique for dealing with life. ... the detached person can neither appease nor fight, neither co-operate nor dictate terms, neither love nor be ruthless. ... [He must] escape and hide." [9, 45, 12] (p. 91–92)

Horney's descriptions are especially mixed with respect to the ICA framework. In this description, control and especially affection play an important role, although it seems that inclusion is the primary focus.

Horney's "moving against people" corresponds to the control area. The emphasis is on power, with love being unimportant. Horney's description of this type is lengthy and many-faceted, but she seems to be talking mainly about the autocrat.

"[*Moving against people.*] When he moves against people he accepts and takes for granted the hostility around him, and determines, consciously or unconsciously, to fight. He implicitly distrusts the feelings and intentions of others toward himself. He rebels in whatever ways are open to him. He wants to be the stronger and defeat them, partly for his own protection, partly for revenge. (p. 42–43)

.   .   .   .   .

"... His attitude is sometimes quite apparent, but more often it is covered with a veneer of suave politeness, fairmindedness and good fellowship. (p. 63)

.   .   .   .   .

"His needs stem ... from his feeling that the world is an arena where ... only the fittest survive and the strong annihilate the weak. ... *his primary need becomes one of control over others.* Variations in the means of control are infinite. There may be an outright exercise of power, there may be indirect manipulation through oversolicitousness or putting people under obligation. He may prefer to be the power behind the throne. ... (p. 64; italics added)

"Concomitantly he needs to excell, to achieve success, prestige, or recognition in any form. Strivings in this direction are partly oriented toward power, in as much as success and prestige lend power in a competitive society. ...

"... Love, for him, plays a negligible role. [Love objects are for exploitation to outdo others.]" [23, 24] (p. 65)

In this description again we see mention of the other areas but *in the service of* power and domination.

Horney's "moving toward people" corresponds to the affection area. Her statement seems to be descriptive of the overpersonal.

"[*Moving toward people.*] When moving toward people he accepts his own helplessness, and in spite of his estrangement and fears tries to win the affection of others and to lean on them. Only in this way can he feel safe. ... (p. 42)

. . . . .

"... marked need for affection and approval and an especial need for a 'partner.' ... they all center around a desire for human intimacy. (p. 50)

. . . . .

"If we understand the structure of the compliant type we can see why love is so all important to him. ..." [41, 37] (p. 59)

In summary, Horney describes the undersocial in the area of inclusion, the autocrat in the control area, and the overpersonal in the affection area.

SUMMARY OF PERSONALITY TYPES

In the inclusion area Horney stresses the undersocial, whereas Fromm, and to some extent Freud, discuss both the withdrawn and what Fromm calls the destructiveness (similar to oversocial) aspects of this area. Freud emphasizes the well-adjusted (social) aspect somewhat more than Fromm and Horney.

The undersocial is described as follows: main interest is self-preservation; withdrawal from others who are experienced as threat; withdrawal is a negative relatedness; feeling of indifference toward others; wants to keep apart; detachment from others and from self; inner need is to keep emotional distance between themselves and others; not to get involved with others in any way; major need is not getting involved. The oversocial is described as active form of withdrawal; the impulse to destroy others following from the fear of being destroyed by them; the energy of the unlived life transformed into energy for the destruction of life; ego has a considerable amount of aggression available; a proneness to activity; can break down existing cultural development.

In the control area Freud, Horney, and Fromm all describe the autocrat. The autocrat is described by supremacy of superego, governed by anxiety of conscience; upholders of civilization in a conservative spirit; fundamental impulse is to have complete mastery over another person, tries to prevent object from becoming free and independent and cease to be his, determined to fight; wants to be the stronger and defeat them; primary need is one of control over the other either by outright exercise of power or indirect manipulation; needs to excel for purposes of attaining power. Fromm describes the abdicrat as one who escapes from freedom by attaching himself to another person, who loses or never attains his independence.

The personality types primarily concerned with the area of affection are of two kinds. Freud and Horney describe the overpersonal with an emphasis on the other-to-self aspects. The characteristics of the overpersonal include believing that the most significant thing in life is being loved; being governed by dread of loss of love; being peculiarly dependent on withholders of love; showing marked need for approval and affection, especially need for a partner; central need is a desire for human intimacy; love is all important. Fromm describes the personal type who is able to operate effectively in the affection area. His characteristics are as follows: wish for the other person to grow and develop; feeling of responsibility, care, respect for, and knowledge of, other; expression of intimacy between two human beings under the condition of the preservation of each other's integrity. Types corresponding to the underpersonal are not explicitly described. This category is often included in descriptions of other types.

Group Behavior

If Postulate 1 corresponds with our experience, behavior in the three interpersonal need areas should be observable in the interaction of groups. In other words, all behavior that is interpersonal should have reference to one or more of the three need areas, and measures of such behavior should basically resolve into measurements of different responses in those three areas.

Several studies directed toward the analysis of interpersonal behavior in a group shall be presented and an attempt made to show how all the analyses performed in these studies converge into three types of behavior having to do primarily with inclusion, control, and affection.

LEARY AND THE KAISER GROUP

In a stimulating series of articles culminating in Leary's book (58), Leary and the Kaiser group, working at the Kaiser Foundation Hospital in Oakland, California, have presented an analysis of interpersonal behavior based on examination of interview protocols, test records, group therapy meetings, and other material. These observers arrive at three concepts in their final classification: dominance-submission, affiliation-hostility, and the intensity of each behavior. The first two classifications are quite clearly related to our affection and control areas. Sample terms used to describe them:

> "*Affiliation-Hostility.* ... Effusive, affectionate, friendly, warm, affiliative, praising, approving; unfriendly, hostile, irritable, critical, pugnacious, condemning." [41, 39, 45]
> "*Dominance-Submission.* ... Autocratic, bossy, dictatorial, lead-

ing, forceful, masterful, able to give orders; weak, submissive, spineless, obedient, meek, docile, deferent." [23, 21, 27] (pp. 150, 151, 158)

Intensity is discussed as follows:

"[There are] ratings of intensity on a three point scale for each interpersonal mechanism. ... A rating of "3" indicates an ... interaction ... of high intensity; ... a rating of "1" indicates an interaction of but low or mild intensity. A zero rating of an interpersonal mechanism represents the absence of a discernible or ratable amount of activity of that type. The dimension of intensity is important in defining normal or generally well-adjusted behavior as opposed to abnormal extremes. Generally, consistent display of interpersonal mechanisms of 3 or 1 ratings of intensity would indicate inappropriate or rigid social behavior, while 2 ratings represent for the most part flexibility or social adaptiveness." (p. 152)

The concept of a "consistent display of rating 3 behavior" corresponds to the oversocial in the inclusion area [5], while consistent rating 1, regardless of type of behavior, corresponds to the social [9].

CARTER

Carter (23) attempts to answer the question, "What are the characteristics which can be evaluated by observing people interacting?" He states, "It will be contended that in assessing the behavior of individuals participating in small groups or situational tests, probably only three or at most four independent dimensions of behavior can be evaluated." It may be added that this situation is not accidental. If Postulate 1 is correct, the theoretical considerations leading to it provide sound dynamic reasons why *exactly* three types of behavior are discernible.

Carter proceeds to discuss the results of eight independent analyses of group situations which differed in size, kind of task, and leadership structure, performed by Couch and Carter. He then describes his three factors, which he feels are supported by the other studies.

Factor 1 corresponds to the inclusion area. The positive end of the factor is close to the oversocial and stresses a detailed description of the kinds of behavior that would be engaged in by someone seeking to be noticed and recognized.

"Factor I: *Individual Prominence*—the dimension of behavior which is interpreted as indicating the prominence of that individual as he stands out from the group. The behavior associated with the traits of aggressiveness, leadership, confidence, and striving for individual recognition seems to have a common element that is interpreted as the member's attempting to achieve individual recognition from the group." [5, 6, 15] (p. 495)

Carter's second factor, "group facilitation," corresponds to the control area. Extreme autocrats and abdicrats would usually interfere with the attainment of group goals, while democrats would facilitate them.

> "Factor II: *Group Goal Facilitation*—the dimension of behavior which is interpreted as being effective in achieving the goal toward which the group is oriented. Efficiency, adaptability, cooperation, etc., all seem to have the common element which facilitates group action in solving the task." [21] (p. 495)

Factor III corresponds to the affection area.

> "Factor III: *Group Sociability*—the dimension of behavior which is interpreted as indicating the positive social interaction of an individual in the group. The traits heavily loaded in this factor—sociability, striving for group acceptance and adaptibility—all have a common element which represents a friendly interpersonal behavior pattern of the individual toward other group members." [39] (p. 495)

B I O N *

Bion (16), a psychoanalytically oriented group therapist, is concerned with the problem of understanding under what basic assumptions a group is operating. He feels that there are three basic assumptions, which he calls dependence, pairing, and fight-flight.

With regard to the area of inclusion Bion's analogous "basic assumption" is *fight-flight,* which he describes as the group's main technique of self-preservation.

> "... the group seems to know only two techniques of self-preservation; fight or flight. The frequency with which a group, when it is working as a group, resorts to one or the other of these two procedures, and these two procedures only, for dealing with all its problems, made me first suspect the possibility that a basic assumption exists about becoming a group. Clinical observation gives as much reason for saying that the basic assumption is that the group has met for fight or flight, as for saying it has met to preserve the group. The latter is a convenient hypothesis for explaining why the group, which shows itself intolerant of activities that are not forms of fight or flight, will nevertheless tolerate the formation of pairs. Reproduction is recognized as equal with fight or flight in the preservation of a group." [5, 9, 6, 8, 1] (p. 15)

Reference to becoming a group suggests the emphasis on the process of formation and the problem of "in-or-out" which was mentioned in Chapter 2 as being characteristic of the inclusion area.

* The following three quotations are from W. Bion, "Experiences in Groups: III, IV," *Human Relations,* 2, 1949, 13–22.

Paralleling the control area, Bion talks about the *dependent* basic assumption. Here the relation between Bion and ICA is quite direct.

"... It is the basic assumption that the group has met together to obtain security from one individual on whom they depend." (p. 17)

"The group concentrates at first on establishing this idea of doctor and patients as firmly as it can; it conforms to a strict discipline, imposed *ad hoc,* being careful to limit conversation severely to topics which are not important except in so far as they support the view that patients are talking to a doctor. ..." (p. 295)

"... The dependent group with its characteristic elevation of one person. ... Benefit is felt no longer to come from the group, but from the leader of the group alone. ..." [19] (p. 296)

Parallel to the basic dimension relating to expressions concerning the affection area, Bion describes the basic assumption of *pairing.* He makes clear an essential element of the affection area, the dyadic relation:

"... Some patterns of behavior were recurring and, in particular, one that went like this: two members of the group would become involved in a discussion; sometimes the exchange between the two could hardly be described but it would be evident that they were involved with each other, and that the group as a whole thought so too. ... Whenever two people begin to have this kind of relationship in the group—whether these two are man and woman, man and man, or woman and woman— it seems to be a basic assumption, held both by the group and the pair concerned, that the relationship is a sexual one. ... the group seems prepared to allow the pair to continue their exchange indefinitely.

"... The emotions derived from the basic assumption [are] that two people can be met together only for one purpose, and that a sexual one.

.   .   .   .   .

"... If my observation of the basic assumption of the group is correct, it is not surprising that ... sex [occupies] a central position with other emotions more or less secondary." [37, 38] (p. 14, 15)

Miscellaneous Studies

The next several studies do not support the ICA framework as directly or clearly as those presented above. However, there is considerable basis for assuming a large overlap of concepts, and it is of value to consider these studies as an aid to indicating the wide variety of areas where the ICA framework is applicable.

BENNE AND SHEATS

Benne and Sheats (11), basing their study mainly on their experience at the National Training Laboratory workshop at Bethel, attempted to present a list of roles found in groups. They classified roles into three main types, which correspond respectively to inclusion, control, and affection.

1. Individual roles: Participation here is directed toward the satisfaction of the participant's individual needs, which are not relevant either to the group task or to the functioning of the group as a group. [6, 8]

2. Group task roles: Participant roles are related to the task which the group is undertaking; their purpose is to facilitate and coordinate group effort in the selection and definition of a common problem and in the solution of that problem. [19]

3. Group building and maintenance roles: These roles are oriented toward the functioning of a group as a group; they are designed to alter or maintain the group way of working, to strengthen, regulate, and perpetuate the group as a group. [39]

SWANSON

Swanson (88) correlated scores from the Blacky test with a large number of behavioral measures. Just three of these measures were significantly related to Blacky scores. This result supports Carter's observation that there are perhaps only three distinguishable types of group behavior. Corresponding respectively to inclusion, control, and affection are Swanson's measures of participation [3], influence [21], and liking received [40].

BACK

Back (6) and many in the Michigan school describe three bases for group cohesion. These bases for cohesion correspond respectively to the areas of inclusion, control, and affection. Back's corresponding terms (phrased in connection with inculcating groups with varying amounts of cohesion):

1. *Group Prestige.* ... cohesiveness was produced ... by *stressing the value of belonging to the group.* ... selection for this particular group [was] an important achievement. The rarity of this achievement ... varied to create different strength of cohesiveness.

   Low: "... lab section instructor told us you would be particularly good material for a good group. ... had some idea of putting people together who were congenial, but that didn't work out because of schedule difficulties."

   High: "... putting congenial people together didn't work out because of schedule difficulties. ... you have all the qualifications which have been set up to be good in this task: you two should be about the best group we have had." (p. 13)

2. *Task Direction.* ... the *outcome of the task was stressed.* The experiment was introduced as a test.

   Low: "... you will have the best chance to show your ability and get a high score in the test—you know, we had some idea of putting

people together who were congenial. But that didn't work. ..."
High: "... test shows how well you can use your imagination. ...
special prize group. ... we had some idea of putting people together who were congenial, but that didn't work out. ..." (p. 12)

3. *Personal Attraction.* [Degree to which the two group members are personally attracted toward each other.]

Low: "We tried to find a partner with whom you could work best. ...
you probably will like him."
High: "You'll like him a lot. ... you should get along extremely well."
(p. 12)

CORSINI AND ROSENBERG

Using an extensive review of the literature on group therapy, Corsini
and Rosenberg (29) attempted to classify all the terms used by various authors as "expressions of dynamics." They reduced them all to nine classes
of mechanisms. Then they state, "The nine classes found appear to reduce
to three still more general factors. An *intellectual* factor consisting of uni-
versalization, intellectualization, and spectator therapy appears. Also an
emotional factor including acceptance, altruism, and transference evolves.
And there is an *actional* factor of reality testing, interaction, and ventila-
tion." (p. 409) These correspond, respectively, to the control, affection, and
inclusion areas. The intellectualizing aspect of control mentioned in Chapter
2 is highlighted by this parallel.

JENKINS AND LIPPITT

In Jenkins and Lippitt's analysis (51) of questionnaire data of children,
their teachers, and parents, three themes appeared in more than one of the
between-group relations. Between adults and children there was a common
interest in *social and extracurricular activities*. In the teacher-student and
parent-child relations, *power* and *control* were stressed. The teachers were
most concerned with *friendliness* in all the relations.

These three kinds of interpersonal relations correspond to inclusion
(social and extracurricular activities), control (power and control), and affection (friendliness).

VARON

Varon (92) discusses issues that recur in group therapy sessions.

"In any situation in which two or three persons are gathered, there may
well be problems of status, if it is only that status of the best story-
teller. There may be problems about expressing feeling. ... similarly,
there is the issue of conformity vs. rebellion vs. independence, whether
to do as is expected, rebel against it, or do as one pleases."

The recurrent problems correspond to our areas of inclusion (status), control (independence), and affection (expressing feelings).

GLUECK AND GLUECK

In Glueck and Glueck's attempt to predict the background factors leading to delinquency (40), five factors proved useful. The Glueck's five factors were apparently chosen by picking up social factors which had highest correlation with "failure" scores, that is, number of boys followed who became delinquent. These factors are as follows:

1. Discipline of boy by father   [24]
2. Supervision by mother   [24]
3. Affection of father for boy   [42]
4. Affection of mother for boy   [42]
5. Cohesiveness of family   [6, 10]

Cohesiveness is related to the inclusion area, discipline and supervision to control, and affection from mother and father to the affection area.

This completes the brief survey of some selected studies in the area of interpersonal relations. The purpose of the survey was to establish high antecedent probability or plausibility for Postulate 1.

There is one further study that could be considered a direct test of a theorem following directly from Postulate 1. This study constitutes a test of the theorem and is therefore relevant to evidential probability.

EVIDENCE

Theorem 1–1.   If a representative battery of measures of interpersonal behavior is factor analyzed, the resulting factors will reasonably fall into the three need areas, inclusion, control, and affection.

This project was undertaken by the author in connection with an experiment on small group behavior which is described in Chapter 7. A total of seventy measures was administered to sixty Harvard freshmen. These measures were intended to cover all the need areas, parental behavior (as remembered and now perceived by the subject), and all levels of personality except overt behavior. (See Appendix B)

Parental behavior was covered by Slater's *Parental Role Preference* (PRP) questionnaire (82).

The unconscious levels of personality are covered by the *Blacky* (B) projective test based on Freud's psychosexual stages. The preconscious and conscious levels were covered by Edward's *Personal Preference Schedule* (PPS), which is based on fifteen of Murray's needs; the *Interpersonal Checklist* (IPC), based on the Kaiser scheme; Guilford's *Rhathymia* (R) and *Cyclothymia* (C) scales; the California *F–scale* (F); the author's FIRO–1

(Fundamental Interpersonal Relations Orientation); and the Blacky *Defense Preference Inquiry* (DPI), designed to measure preferred mechanisms of defense.

To tap the attitude area at the conscious level, Bales' *Value Profile* (VP) was administered. A cluster analysis, using the method of the B-coefficient suggested by Holzinger and Harman (48) revealed six clusters. One cluster was made up entirely of Blacky scales (oral eroticism, anal eroticism, oedipal intensity, masturbation guilt, sibling rivalry, positive ego ideal, total anxiety). This factor was interpreted to be an artifact of the Blacky scales and/or the scoring techniques used. No other scales fit onto this factor, and there was no readily apparent commonality among the particular scales selected from Blacky. Further, the cluster included half of all the Blacky scales, indicating that for this sample the differentiations on Blacky scales were not very great. The remaining five clusters, the scales which constituted them, and our interpretation will now be presented.

In order to give an estimate of how well each scale fits in the cluster a figure (equal to the ratio of the mean correlation between the scale and all other scales in the cluster, to the mean correlation between the scale and all scales not in the cluster) is presented. A ratio of 1.15 was established as the cutting point for exclusion of items from a cluster.

Cluster 1. *I am a High Participator in a Group.*
Correlation
Ratio

3.52	I'm a high group participator (FIRO–1).
3.27	I participate in group discussions (FIRO–1).
2.70	I participate in informal discussions (FIRO–1).
2.24	I make suggestions in a group (FIRO–1).
1.70	I talk about myself in a group (FIRO–1).
1.35	I am a dominant (initiating) person (IPC).

This cluster is interpreted to be in the inclusion area, perception of the relation of self to others. This cluster corresponds to cells 3, 5, and 7 in Figure 2–1.

Cluster 2. *I Want People to Take Good Care of Me.*
Correlation
Ratio

3.31	I like to get credit for a good idea (FIRO–1).
3.13	It's important for me to be liked (FIRO–1).
2.36	I like people to help me (Succorance) (PPS).
2.31	I don't like to do things by myself (Autonomy) (PPS).

This cluster is interpreted to be in the area of inclusion, at the conscious level, comprising the evaluation of the relation of others toward the self. On the matrix this is cells 1, 4, 6, 8, 10.

Cluster 3. *I Do Things the Way They Shoud Be Done.*
Correlation
Ratio

3.44	I am dependent on rules and authority (FIRO–1).
3.40	I think groups that follow rules are more efficient (FIRO–1).
2.34	I feel better in a group that follows rules (FIRO–1).
2.11	I am not intraceptive (PPS).
1.60	I use the defense of projection (DPI).
1.44	I have a need for orderliness (Order) (PPS).
1.27	I value the acceptance of authority (VP).
1.15	I have anxiety about anal retention (B).

This cluster is interpreted to be in the control area, perception of the relation of self toward others. These statements correspond to cells 19, 24, 28, 34.

Cluster 4. *I am Friendly toward People.*
Correlation
Ratio

3.27	I am personal (FIRO–1).
3.27	I like groups where people get personal (FIRO–1).
3.30	I like to talk about myself in a group (FIRO–1).
2.02	I initiate personal discussion (FIRO–1).
1.41	I don't have anxiety over sibling rivalry (B).
1.30	I do not value individualism (VP).
1.28	I like to have many friends (Affiliation) (PPS).
1.26	I'm not aggressive (PPS).

This cluster is interpreted to be in the affection area, perception of relation of self to others. This corresponds to cells 39, 41, 45.

Cluster 5. *I Have Anxiety.*
Correlation
Ratio

1.98	My father was a strong disciplinarian (PRP).
1.92	I have anxieties over oral eroticism (B).
1.92	I have high anxiety generally (B).
1.88	I have anxiety about castration (B).
1.36	I differentiate between people (FIRO–1).

This cluster reflects fear and anxiety over punishment in both affection and control. It is much weaker than the other clusters (all have four items with a higher correlation ratio than the highest in this cluster), and possibly it resulted from a statistical quirk and would disappear with a replication. What sense can be made of it indicates that it is more a personal than an interpersonal cluster.

Thus it seems that the clusters fit the theoretical framework without too much difficulty (except cluster 5), and there seem to be no major areas missing. This fact indicates that the framework is adequate for an analysis of a fairly diverse set of measures.

4

The Measurement of the Fundamental Interpersonal Relations Orientations: FIRO–B

Thus far an extensive description of the three interpersonal needs has been presented, with a reinterpretation of some studies to illustrate the plausibility and universality of these needs. In this chapter a measuring instrument designed to measure an individual's orientations to these interpersonal needs is introduced. The term "need area" will be used to mean the class of all behavior directed toward the satisfaction of a specific interpersonal need.

This questionnaire, the FIRO–B, is the key measuring instrument for the development of the present theory. Because of its importance, FIRO–B will be presented in a formal manner in accordance with the standard procedures for presentation of a new psychological test or questionnaire (4). This procedure allows both for demonstrating the relation of the measure to the theoretical framework and to subsequent empirical results, and for a complete presentation of the psychometric properties of the instrument.

The FIRO–B is the product of a long evolution. Before FIRO–B was developed, the following forms were used in one or more studies:

1. FIRO–Q. A Q-sort form of ninety-six items.
2. FIRO–1. Fourteen cumulative (Guttman) scales.
3. FIRO–2. Four forced-choice paragraphs.
4. FIRO–3. Theoretically derived items. To be used later for development of a different measure (FIRO–F).
5. FIRO–4. Refinement of FIRO–2.

6. FIRO–5B3. Six Guttman scales, similar to FIRO–B.

Although the form of FIRO used in various studies differed, the underlying theory on which the forms were based remained essentially the same. For this reason all forms will be considered as early forms of the present instrument FIRO–B. Failings in the early forms are considered in assessing results, but it is assumed that few basic changes in results occurred because of the form used.

DESCRIPTION

Name

The measuring instrument is called "FIRO–B," which stands for "Fundamental Interpersonal Relations Orientation—Behavior." The title simply represents the thing being measured, how an individual characteristically relates to other people. The "B" stands for the aspect of personality (see Chapter 2) being explored—behavior. It is expected that other forms measuring other aspects of the FIRO will follow. FIRO–F (for feelings) is now being developed, and others that will measure unconscious orientations are contemplated. The title of the test does not reveal its purpose, is reasonably easy to remember, and is nonthreatening.

Development

The primary purposes for developing FIRO–B are (1) to construct a measure of how an individual acts in interpersonal situations, and (2) to construct a measure that will lead to the prediction of interaction between people, based on data from the measuring instrument alone. In this second regard FIRO–B is somewhat unique among personality tests. It is designed not only to measure individual characteristics but to measure specifically characteristics that may be combined in particular ways (see Chapter 6) to predict relations between people.

For this form of FIRO it was decided to concentrate on how a person *behaves* rather than how he feels. Since the prediction of interaction is a proposed aim for FIRO–B, it is reasonable to assess what behavior the individual *expresses* toward others (*e*), and how he *wants* others to behave toward him (*w*). A matching of *e*'s and *w*'s for groups of people seems likely to give information about compatible interaction.

FIRO–B therefore is designed to measure the individual's behavior toward others (*e*) and the behavior he wants from others (*w*) in the three areas of interpersonal interaction. This measure leads to six scores: expressed inclusion behavior (e^I), wanted inclusion behavior (w^I), expressed control behavior (e^C), wanted control behavior (w^C), expressed affection behavior (e^A), and wanted affection behavior (w^A). (Whenever a measure refers to a specific need area it will be indicated by an *I*, *C*, or *A* as a superscript.) Table 4–1 presents the basic statement of the content of the *e* and *w* aspects of each need area.

TABLE 4–1. Schema of Interpersonal Behaviors

DIMENSION	EXPRESSED BEHAVIOR	WANTED BEHAVIOR
Inclusion	I initiate interaction with people.	I want to be included.
Control	I control people.	I want people to control me.
Affection	I act close and personal toward people.	I want people to get close and personal with me.

By making the expressed and wanted aspects of each dimension the axes of a Cartesian plot, all possible types of orientation toward interpersonal relations in this framework may be represented geometrically. (The terms in each quadrant of Figure 4–1 describe the person who falls at the extreme point in that quadrant.)

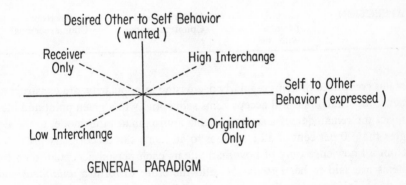

GENERAL PARADIGM

FIGURE 4–1. General Schema for Describing Interpersonal Behavior

Application of this general paradigm to each need area can be seen in Table 4–2.

After the schema were used, the next task was to construct items that would measure the six interpersonal aspects adequately. Of the several techniques available for composing psychological scales the one that appeared most appropriate was the Guttman technique for cumulative scale analysis (44). It appeared to be an especially appropriate technique for measuring specific orientations, as opposed to techniques more appropriate to exploratory studies.

The technique of scale analysis has been described at length elsewhere (44); thus there is no great benefit in going into detail here. In general terms,

TABLE 4–2. Descriptive Schema and Appropriate Terminology for Each Interpersonal Need Area

			I initiate interaction with others	
			Low	*High*
	I	*High*	Undersocial	Oversocial
	want		Social-compliant	Social-compliant
INCLUSION	to be			
	in-	*Low*	Undersocial	Oversocial
	cluded		Countersocial	Countersocial

			I try to control others	
			Low	*High*
	I	*High*	Abdicrat	Autocrat
	want		Submissive	Submissive
CONTROL	to be			
	con-	*Low*	Abdicrat	Autocrat
	trolled		Rebellious	Rebellious

			I try to be close and personal	
	I		*Low*	*High*
	want	*High*	Underpersonal	Overpersonal
	others		Personal-compliant	Personal-compliant
AFFECTION	to be			
	close &	*Low*	Underpersonal	Overpersonal
	personal		Counterpersonal	Counterpersonal
	with me			

scales comprised of items regularly decreasing in popularity, are constructed; hence any individual will accept items sequentially to a given point and then reject the remainder. If a series of items approximates this model to the degree that 90 per cent of all responses to all items can be correctly predicted from a knowledge only of how many items each person accepted, then the items are said to be *reproducible* and therefore to form a *unidimensional* scale. "Unidimensionality" means that all items are measuring the same dimension.

The respondents are assigned scale scores equal to the number of items accepted. For each of the six dimensions it was decided to construct a nine-item scale. This number has the virtues of (a) providing sufficient length for acceptable reliability (stability) of the scale, (b) providing sufficient categories for dividing respondents into as many classes as desired, (c) keeping the questionnaire reasonably short (fifty–four items) and brief, (d) keeping scoring uniform among scales and in single digits for computational ease.

The scales were developed on about 150 subjects gathered from the Boston area colleges (Massachusetts Institute of Technology, Massachusetts State Teachers College, Harvard, Boston University) and a military group (Air Force reserve unit). They were then cross-validated to ensure that the scales maintained the required characteristics of acceptable Guttman scales.

For the cross-validation study a population of about 1,500 subjects was used, made up primarily of about 1,000 Harvard freshmen, 230 Radcliffe freshmen, and various students from the Harvard Business School and colleges in the Boston area. The results of this procedure are presented in Table 4–3. Because of revision of certain scales the number of subjects used for developing each scale varies. In each table the results of the total sample of approximately 1,500 are given for

1. Per cent of respondents accepting each item (the item "marginal").
2. Per cent of respondents receiving each scale score.
3. Items and the answer categories; the categories scored as "accepting" the item are in italics (each item is dichotomized into accept-reject at a point determined by the distribution of responses).

TABLE 4–3. FIRO–B Scales

Scale e^I. Expressed Behavior of the Self in the Inclusion Area

Item Number	Per Cent Accepting	Scale Score	Per Cent Receiving Scale Score	
1	95	0	01	
2	89	1	03	
3	84	2	04	
4	86	3	07	
5	65	4	18	
6	56	5	16	
7	44	6	20	
8	13	7	19	
9	16	8	10	
		9	03	$N = 1,615$

Items — Scale e^I

1. I try to be with people.
   usually　*often*　*sometimes*　occasionally　rarely　never
2. I join social groups.
   usually　*often*　*sometimes*　*occasionally*　rarely　never
3. I tend to join social organizations when I have an opportunity.
   usually　*often*　*sometimes*　*occasionally*　rarely　never
4. I try to be included in informal social activities.
   usually　*often*　*sometimes*　occasionally　rarely　never
5. I try to include other people in my plans.
   usually　*often*　sometimes　occasionally　rarely　never
6. I try to have people around me.
   usually　*often*　sometimes　occasionally　rarely　never
7. When people are doing things together I tend to join them.
   usually　*often*　sometimes　occasionally　rarely　never
8. I try to avoid being alone.
   usually　often　sometimes　occasionally　rarely　never
9. I try to participate in group activities.
   usually　often　sometimes　occasionally　rarely　never

Scale w^I. Behavior Wanted from Others toward Self in Inclusion Area

Item Number	Per Cent Accepting	Scale Score	Per Cent Receiving Scale Score
1	71	0	15
2	75	1	06
3	70	2	04
4	70	3	05
5	67	4	06
6	64	5	05
7	62	6	08
8	36	7	19
9	31	8	15
		9	19

$N = 1,582$

Items — Scale w^I

1. I like people to include me in their activities.

   usually   *often*   sometimes   occasionally   rarely   never

2. I like people to invite me to things.

   usually   *often*   sometimes   occasionally   rarely   never

3. I like people to invite me to join their activities.

   usually   *often*   sometimes   occasionally   rarely   never

4. I like people to invite me to participate in their activities.

   usually   *often*   sometimes   occasionally   rarely   never

5. I like people to invite me to things.

   most people   many people some people a few people one or two people nobody

6. I like people to invite me to join their activities.

   most people   many people some people a few people one or two people nobody

7. I like people to include me in their activities.

   most people   many people some people a few people one or two people nobody

8. I like people to ask me to participate in their discussions.

   most people many people some people a few people one or two people nobody

9. I like people to invite me to participate in their activities.

   most people many people some people a few people one or two people nobody

---

Scale e^C. Expressed Behavior of the Self in Control Area

Item Number	Per Cent Accepting	Scale Score	Per Cent Receiving Scale Score
1	79	0	11
2	69	1	12
3	61	2	11
4	52	3	12
5	55	4	12
6	21	5	17
7	24	6	08
8	16	7	06
9	13	8	05
		9	06

$N = 1,554$

Items — Scale e^C

1. I try to be the dominant person when I am with people.
   usually   often   sometimes   occasionally   rarely   never
2. I try to take charge of things when I am with people.
   most people   many people   some people   a few people   one or two people   nobody
3. I try to have other people do things I want done.
   usually   often   sometimes   occasionally   rarely   never
4. I try to influence strongly other people's actions.
   usually   often   sometimes   occasionally   rarely   never
5. I try to influence strongly other people's actions.
   most people   many people   some people   a few people   one or two people   nobody
6. I try to have other people do things the way I want them done.
   usually   often   sometimes   occasionally   rarely   never
7. I try to have other people do things the way I want them done.
   most people   many people   some people   a few people   one or two people   nobody
8. I take charge of things when I'm with people.
   usually   often   sometimes   occasionally   rarely   never
9. I try to take charge of things when I'm with people.
   usually   often   sometimes   occasionally   rarely   · never

---

Scale w^C. Behavior Wanted from Others toward Self in Control Area

Item Number	Per Cent Accepting	Scale Score	Per Cent Receiving Scale Score
1	93	0	02
2	85	1	04
3	84	2	08
4	63	3	16
5	65	4	18
6	19	5	23
7	22	6	11
8	12	7	09
9	16	8	04
		9	05 $N = 1,574$

Items — Scale w^C

1. I let other people decide what to do.
   usually   often   sometimes   occasionally   rarely   never
2. I let other people decide what to do.
   most people   many people   some people   a few people   one or two people   nobody
3. I let other people take charge of things.
   most people   many people   some people   a few people   one or two people   nobody
4. I let other people strongly influence my actions.
   most people   many people   some people   a few people   one or two people   nobody
5. I let other people strongly influence my actions.
   usually   often   sometimes   occasionally   rarely   never

6. I let other people control my actions.

   usually   often   sometimes   occasionally   rarely   never

7. I am easily led by people.

   usually   often   sometimes   occasionally   rarely   never

8. I let people control my actions.

   most people   many people   some people   a few people   one or two people   nobody

9. I am easily led by people.

   most people   many people   some people   a few people   one or two people   nobody

---

Scale e^A. Expressed Behavior of the Self in the Affection Area

Item Number	Per Cent Accepting	Scale Score	Per Cent Receiving Scale Score
1	95	0	01
2	64	1	13
3	72	2	11
4	52	3	27
5	44	4	10
6	29	5	12
7	21	6	06
8	24	7	05
9	11	8	09
		9	06

$N = 1,467$

Items — Scale e^A

1. I try to be friendly to people.

   most people   many people   some people   a few people   one or two people   nobody

2. My personal relations with people are cool and distant.

   most people   many people   some people   *a few people   one or two people   nobody*

3. I act cool and distant with people.

   most people   many people   some people   *a few people   one or two people   nobody*

4. I try to have close relationships with people.

   usually   often   sometimes   occasionally   rarely   never

5. I try to have close, personal relationships with people.

   usually   often   sometimes   occasionally   rarely   never

6. I try to have close relationships with people.

   most people   many people   some people   a few people   one or two people   nobody

7. I try to get close and personal with people.

   most people   many people   some people   a few people   one or two people   nobody

8. I try to have close, personal relationships with people.

   most people   many people   some people   a few people   one or two people   nobody

9. I try to get close and personal with people.

   usually   often   sometimes   a few people   one or two people   nobody

Scale w^A. Behavior Wanted from Others toward Self in Affection Area

Item Number	Per Cent Accepting	Scale Score	Per Cent Receiving Scale Score
1	90	0	05
2	72	1	11
3	72	2	05
4	64	3	07
5	64	4	08
6	34	5	28
7	35	6	08
8	34	7	07
9	17	8	09
		9	11 $N = 1,467$

Items — Scale w^A

1. I like people to act friendly toward me.
   most people   many people   some people   a few people   one or two people   nobody

2. I like people to act cool and distant toward me.
   usually   often   sometimes   occasionally   *rarely   never*

3. I like people to act distant toward me.
   usually   often   sometimes   occasionally   *rarely   never*

4. I like people to act cool and distant toward me.
   most people   many people   some people   a few people   *one or two people*   nobody

5. I like people to act distant toward me.
   most people   many people   some people   a few people   *one or two people*   nobody

6. I like people to act close toward me.
   most people   many people   some people   a few people   one or two people   nobody

7. I like people to act close and personal with me.
   usually   often   sometimes   occasionally   rarely   never

8. I like people to act close and personal with me.
   most people   many people   some people   a few people   one or two people   nobody

9. I like people to act close toward me.
   usually   often   sometimes   occasionally   rarely   never

These scales constitute FIRO-B. When the test is given to most populations, no instructions are provided. The questionnaire can usually be given to a group of one hundred within fifteen minutes. The scale score (the number of items accepted for each scale) ranges from 0 to 9. Each respondent's FIRO-B result is expressed as a set of six single-digit numbers presented in the order, e^I, w^I, e^C, w^C, e^A, w^A. Various characteristics of validity and reliability of FIRO-B will now be discussed.

VALIDITY

Content Validity

Content validity is determined by showing how well the content of the test samples the class of situations or the subject matter about which conclusions are to be drawn. If the theory underlying the use of Guttman scales is accepted, then content validity is a property of all legitimate scales.

If all the items are measuring the same dimension, and if they are of descending popularity, then they must represent a sample of items from that dimension. Any other item in that dimension fits between (or beyond) scale items according to the percentage accepting the item (its marginal), and an individual's response to the new item is at least 90 per cent reproducible (that is, predictable) from his scale score. This implies that any sample of items in this dimension would rank respondents in essentially the same way; therefore the sampling of the universe of items yields a satisfactory content validity.

Concurrent Validity

Concurrent validity is evaluated by showing how well test scores correspond to measures of concurrent criterion performances or status. This validity area refers to studies which attempt to demonstrate differences, on the basis of the new measuring instrument, between already existent groups or between people with already known attitudes. Studies presented include an investigation of FIRO-B and political attitudes, FIRO-B and occupational choice, and FIRO-B and conformity behavior. These studies represent several different areas where there was an opportunity to measure concurrent validity.

FIRO–B is supposed to be measuring orientations toward interpersonal relations. Since the interpersonal orientations developed early in life are so deeply rooted and have been a part of the personality so long, they should be related to all situations in which the interpersonal element is significant. This category includes most important aspects of adult life. The assumption underlying the relation between interpersonal orientations and other aspects of life is that all contacts with other people repeat to a certain extent contacts with people (especially parents) in the past (see Chapter 5 for a fuller discussion). In some areas a person's relations with other people were resolved unsatisfactorily; for example, he was unloved or dominated, and therefore his attempts at resolving this dissatisfaction are carried into present relations with people. As described in Chapter 5, these attempts may be classified as either (a) trying to achieve from people what could not be achieved in the past, or (b) withdrawing from interaction in the unsatisfactory area so as not to repeat the dissatisfaction. Any behavior may be described as the resultant of "here-and-now" reality considerations and "there-and-then" unresolved childhood relations. For example, dissatisfaction with army life may be due to realistically harsh treatment, as well as dislike of having to obey any orders from anyone because one's father was an overly severe disciplinarian.

This formulation implies that virtually every choice made and opinion formed by an adult has to some degree the interpersonal element. In the choice of occupation there are great differences in the interpersonal characteristics in various jobs. Jobs may be classified according to their interpersonal requirements (see Chapter 8). For example, the essence of a salesman's job, ordinarily, is wide and frequent contact with people, or high inclusion. The politician's role involves high control in that when in office he exercises power over a large number of constituents, but he also may be voted out by them; therefore his constituency has a kind of collective control over him. The expectations for a military officer as far as his relations to subordinates is concerned, may be described as low affection, exemplified by the "no fraternization" dictum interposed between officer and enlisted man. Since specific interpersonal elements characterize most occupations, any measuring instrument that purports to measure orientations toward interpersonal relations may be expected to reveal differences between people in different occupational roles.

Another area in which data supporting the concurrent validity of FIRO–B may be expected is that of political attitudes. A careful examination of these attitudes reveals strong interpersonal overtones in virtually every conflict in which political opinions diverge. The issue of segregation in the south, although vastly complex, is a good example of a social problem primarily in the inclusion area. Differences between exponents of each side of the segregation issue rarely involve either questions of whites liking Negroes ("some of my best friends," and so on) or questions of respecting Negroes; usually the issue is inclusion or exclusion. Inclusion problems also play a prominent role in the recent widespread discussion regarding community development. The growth of suburbia has raised an issue between those who seek to create a "community" in which everyone is very active and there is stress on common activites, and those who wish to be left alone and not obligated to associate with people unless they so desire (94).

Discussion about democracy and authoritarianism, about building up military strength, or about the President's treatment of a rebellious governor, basically concern how people should relate to each other with respect to the control area. Should the government decide or should the states? Should the President exercise his authority ("use his influence") or should he let Congress or the governor decide for themselves?

Questions of affection often arise in such political issues as our obligations to our allies. What differences are there in our behavior toward "friendly" and "unfriendly" nations? How do we behave when an ally does something of which we don't approve? Also the issue of "cronyism," the relations and obligations of the President to his friends, and the issue of using the Fifth Amendment to protect "friends" have come in for protracted discussion in recent years. These issues, too, are heavily weighted with affectional elements.

As with occupations, it seems reasonable to expect that an individual's orientations toward his own interpersonal relations will parallel closely his attitudes toward the interpersonal elements of external affairs such as political events. When a person is confronted with a large, sweeping issue involving, for the most part, factors with which he has no firsthand information, he must try to place the situation in a familiar framework which he can understand and toward which he can react. Certainly one such framework is the interpersonal. Utilizing this structure brings the problem into familiar setting and makes familiar responses appropriate to new situations. It could then be expected, for example, that Nasser's defiance of the powerful Western powers would not be unlike a child's defiance of his powerful parent. Advocates of harsh discipline and punishment for the child should tend to favor stern measures, perhaps force, for dealing with Nasser.

For another example, when the United States has differences with an old ally such as England, the attitudes adopted toward the resolution of these differences may be quite similar to those adopted toward the treatment of friends. If having friends or allies is very important to an individual, his attitude may be toward conciliation of differences. If being close and friendly creates some anxiety in an individual, he may wish to use the incident to keep more distance between ourselves and our allies. This analogy, of course, does not imply that these are the only reasons for reaching these decisions. This illustration is only to exemplify the manner in which interpersonal orientations may influence larger social and political attitudes. Clearly, the full determinants of these attitudes present a far more complicated picture.

In all these examples the emphasis is on rather specific political attitudes rather than on doctrinaire positions. Reference is to particular political opinions rather than, say, whether the individual is a Republican or a Democrat, a conservative or a liberal. The global positions are usually so multidetermined and often so internally contradictory that they are too complicated to understand from the interpersonal standpoint alone. Specific issues, on the other hand, are much clearer and therefore easier to understand. For example, the factor of hereditary choice of political party (56), which is found to be such a strong determinant, indicates that at the least the social scientist would have to examine the respondent's relation to his parents in addition to the content of his choice, in order to understand choice of political party.

Complexity arises when in specific instances there are competing and contradictory interpersonal values. For example, on the issue of the Supreme Court deciding that FBI data introduced as testimony must be made available to the accused (Jencks Case, 1957), there are two aspects of the control problem. If one believed in upholding authority figures, he would support the FBI's rights over the accused, but he would also uphold the Supreme Court's decision over the FBI. Thus a dilemma arises, demonstrating the necessity of carefully analyzing all of the interpersonal aspects of the issue.

POLITICAL ATTITUDES

An exploratory project was done by McElheny (60) under the supervision of the author on the relation between FIRO scores and political attitudes. Political attitude scales were constructed to measure significant aspects of political events with emphasis on interpersonal aspects. A random listing of items on the various political scales presented issues typical of everyday political discussions. The items concerned political issues pertinent in the 1956 Presidential election and at the same time involved a definite interpersonal element.

Sample: McElheny used eighty-three subjects, Harvard undergraduates drawn from the following subpopulations: executive and policy committees of the Harvard Young Democratic Club, business and editorial staffs of the Harvard daily newspaper, a group of conservatives suggested by a leading undergraduate conservative, and members of a class of volunteer case aid workers. Their background characteristics: *Religion*—Protestant (29 members), Jewish (24), Catholic (12), Greek Orthodox (1), none or agnostic (12), no report (2); *Father's income*—ranged from $4,000 to $150,000, with a median of $15,000; *Parents' political affiliation*—Republican (33), Democrat (22), Independent Democratic (2), Independent (10), others (4). The attempt was made to balance liberal and conservative elements and active and nonactive interests in politics in general.

Procedure: The experimental procedure was as follows: The instruments used were FIRO–4 (for 50 subjects) and FIRO–5B3 (for 33 subjects), plus original questionnaires intended to measure the political opinions of the subjects. These instruments were administered to the sample of 83. The political questionnaire was constructed for the following general areas: the office and duties of the President, the Middle East, segregation in the South. The final questionnaire comprised four Guttman scales:

1. POLITICAL INDIVIDUAL SIGNIFICANCE scale (Reproducibility = .94); (Hypothesized to be related to inclusion)
2. POLITICAL AUTOCRAT scale (Reproducibility = .91); (Related to FIRO expressed control, e^c)
3. POLITICAL ABDICRAT scale (Reproducibility = .91); (Related to FIRO wanted control, w^c)
4. POLITICAL PERSONAL scale (Reproducibility = .91); (Related to FIRO affection)

A series of chi-square tests were made between the FIRO scores and political variables. The predicted outcome was that the four FIRO scales would correlate significantly with their respective political scales as indicated, and, furthermore, that these four correlations would be the only significant ones of the sixteen possible correlations.

The political scales were administered to the sample of eighty-three. Guttman scaling was done for half the sample and then cross-validated on the other half. As discussed later regarding FIRO–B, Guttman scaling provides a type of built-in equivalence (split-half) reliability, as well as content validity. No data are available on the stability (test-retest) of the political scales. That the results of this experiment were, on the whole, positive, affords a certain indication of the reliability of the political scales.

Results: The first hypothesis predicted a relation between the FIRO measure of inclusion ("participation," GH of FIRO–4, e^I and w^I of FIRO–5B3) and the political significance scale. An examination of this scale indicates why such a prediction is consistent with the theory.

Political Individual Significance Scale
(Reproducibility $= .94$)

1. Nasser is one of those little men who get pushed into the limelight by events.
2. When the President faces a new and unknown situation, he should have confidence in his ability to think up some solution to the problem, and if that doesn't work, admit it and try another solution.
3. The reason Southern Negroes are making such a fuss over segregation in bus transportation is that they dislike it as a symbol of exclusion.
4. Nasser's policies probably all come from a desire to win fame for himself.
5. The President must love being famous.
6. Any man who gets to be President is pretty special.

Each item was presented with six answer categories ranging from strongly agree to strongly disagree. Each item was dichotomized and one point scored for each item "accepted." Scores ranged from 0 to 6.

TABLE 4–4. Relation to FIRO Inclusion Scale and Attitude toward Personal Significance in Politics

		Individual Political Significance		
		High	*Low*	
FIRO Inclusion	*High*	22	15	$\chi^2 = 3.19$
				$p < .05$
	Low	13	21	

To a statistically significant degree, those scoring high on the FIRO inclusion scale—liking to associate with people—tended to feel that the individual is significant in politics. (See Table 4–4.) This result is particularly consistent with cell 15 of Table 2–1. The significance level for this and other predicted relations was computed by one-tail tests, since the direction of results was predicted. All chi-squares are corrected for continuity where appropriate. No other political scale was significantly related to FIRO inclusion, and no other FIRO scale was significantly related to the Political Individual Significance Scale.

The second hypothesis predicted a relation between the Political Autocrat scale and the FIRO expressed control scale (control–superior–C–D on FIRO–4; e^C on FIRO–5B3). (See Table 4–5.) Again the items on the political scale will illustrate why this relation was posited.

Political Autocrat Scale
(Reproducibility = .91)

1. When there is a conflict between what the President feels is right and what the people feel is right, it is the President's duty to go ahead on his own.
2. The President should have the power to remove any administrative official who opposes him.
3. Israel attacked Egypt this fall because she felt that unless she stopped Egyptian commando raids, her independence would be destroyed.
4. If the Israelis and Egyptians and the other Arab countries don't make peace within a reasonable time, the United States should send troops to the area to keep order.
5. It may not have been the smartest thing to do, but I can't help admiring the British and French for their taking responsibility and trying to stop Nasser last fall.

TABLE 4–5. Relation between FIRO Control Scale and Attitudes toward Political Autocratic Behavior

		Political Autocrat		
		High	Low	
FIRO	High	22	14	$\chi^2 = 3.16$
Control				$p < .05$
	Low	14	21	

To a significant degree, those high on FIRO control—liking to control others—tended to support autocratic behavior in politics. Again, this was the only relation for either scale that even approached significance.

The third hypothesis stated that the Political Abdicrat scale would be related to the FIRO wanted control (control subordinate, EF on FIRO–4; w^o on FIRO–5B3) scale. Again the consistency of this prediction with the theory is demonstrated by the items in the political scale.

Political Abdicrat Scale
(Reproducibility = .91)

1. The Supreme Court's desegregation decision three years ago did not go far enough. The Court should have decreed the end of all segregation immediately. There is no compromise with the law. (Negative item)
2. Gradually bringing the South around to giving up segregation is the best way. Local customs can't be changed overnight.
3. The President should make it a policy not to delegate responsibility unless it is absolutely necessary. (Negative item)
4. When government officials disagree with the President, they should have the right to tell the press their side of the story, even if it might embarrass the President.
5. If the Israelis and Egyptians don't make peace within a reasonable length of time, the United States should send some troops to the area to keep order. (Negative item)
6. When a problem comes up, the President should make a policy to leave it to his subordinates until it is absolutely necessary for him to deal with the problem personally.
7. The President, when he is working with his advisers, should play down his position as leader.

TABLE 4–6. Relation between FIRO Wanted Control and Attitudes toward Political Abdicratic Behavior

		Political Abdicrat		
		High	Low	
FIRO	High	23	13	$\chi^2 = 6.23$
Control				$p < .01$
	Low	12	23	

To a significant degree, those scoring high on FIRO wanted control—wanting to be controlled by others—tended to have the attitude that political power should be abdicated or minimized. (See Table 4–6.) This, too, was the only significant relation for either variable.

The fourth prediction was not statistically significant, but the minuscule trend was in the right direction. The hypothesis stated a relation between the Political Personal Scale and FIRO Personal Scale (Personal, AB of FIRO–4; $e^A + w^A$ on FIRO–5B3). The political items are shown in the scale below.

Political Personal Scale
(Reproducibility = .91)

1. The President should not make close personal friends of the men he works with officially on the job. (Negative item)
2. It is important for the President to be a good speaker, but it isn't necessary for him to be too warm with the people he meets individually.
3. The President should not care very much how popular he is. (Negative item)
4. The President would break down on his job if he didn't have close personal friends he can relax with, play sports with, and with whom he can forget about being President for a while.
5. America has been friendly to both the Arab countries and Israel because America needs all the friends she can find.

Table 4–7 presents the relation between the FIRO measure of affection and attitude toward political friendship.

TABLE 4–7. Relation between FIRO Affection Measure (e^A and w^A) and Attitudes toward Political Friendship

		Political Personal		
		High	*Low*	
FIRO	*High*	20	16	$\chi^2 = 0.35$
Personal				not significant
	Low	17	18	

Neither scale was significantly related to any other scale.

Thus three of the four predicted relations were significant at the .05 level or better. The probability of this occurrence, when three of the only four significant relations of sixteen possible relations are selected correctly, is less than .01.

The result of this study is very encouraging for the hypothesis that interpersonal relations orientations are significantly related to specific political attitudes. Despite its exploratory nature, this study provides a degree of concurrent validation for the FIRO–B (as the refined successor to 4 and 5B3) for the discrimination of individuals with divergent political attitudes.

OCCUPATIONS

Since occupations do have strong interpersonal elements, as mentioned earlier in this chapter, an empirical investigation into average FIRO scores should reveal significant differences in plausible, or easily understood, directions. FIRO–4 was administered to several different occupational groups and the results explored to detect reasonable differences. Several groups were used and their mean scores on each scale divided at the median for all occupational groups. Hence each group was scored *high* or *low* on each FIRO–4 scale. The following occupational groups were used for this exploration:

1. *Air Force Senior Officers* (N=864), a group of colonels and lieutenant colonels at a command training school.
2. *Industrial Supervisors* (N=39), a group of male (except one) foremen (aged 26–55) in a large Detroit automotive plant.
3. *Public School Administrators* (N=40), a group of relatively progressive administrators from one county in Maryland. They were of both sexes and about 30–45 years old.
4. *Student Nurses* (N=60), a group of young (17–20), female, recent high school graduates, just beginning nursing training at a large Boston hospital.

In Table 4–8 are the results of the questionnaire administrations (no prediction was made for inclusion, since it did not seem relevant in its FIRO–4 form):

TABLE 4–8. Scores on FIRO–4 of Various Occupation Groups

	Affection	Expressed Control	Wanted Control
Officers	Low	High	High
Supervisors	High	High	High
Teachers	High	Low	Low
Nurses	High	Low	Low

Perusal of the results reveals them to be on the whole reasonable. That officers and supervisors should be high on control and officers low on affection seems congruent with stereotypes of their roles. Beyond speculative interest, interpretation is risky. For one thing, interpretation is complicated by the fact that it is difficult to distinguish whether certain personality types are attracted to certain occupations or whether practicing the occupation determines the orientation. This problem could yield to empirical investigation. At any rate, the result above indicates that with a more refined measure, namely, FIRO–B, and a more careful analysis of the interpersonal properties of various occupations, it may well be possible to demonstrate the types of people (in FIRO–B types) who perform in various occupations.

Another similar study was performed using FIRO–B. Three Harvard groups were given the questionnaire—virtually the entire freshman class at Harvard; at Radcliffe (all girls); and one course at the Harvard Business School consisting of sixty-one graduate students being trained for industrial leadership. Their mean scores are shown in Table 4–9.

TABLE 4–9. Mean Scores of Three Groups on FIRO–B Scales

FIRO–B	MEAN SCORE		
	Business School	Harvard Freshmen	Radcliffe Freshmen
Expressed Inclusion	5.60	5.49	4.61 ••
Wanted Inclusion	6.16	5.56	5.37
Expressed Control	5.46 ••	4.11 ••	2.86 ••
Wanted Control	4.87	4.55	4.73
Expressed Affection	4.11	4.24 •	3.67 •
Wanted Affection	5.22	4.80	4.96
$N =$	63	1012	228

•• = Significantly different from other two scores at .01 level.
• = Significantly different from each other at .01 level.

Thus the Business School students, as expected, are very much higher on controlling and influencing others, and somewhat higher on inclusion. In general, on interchange with people, that is, the desire to have extensive relations with people, they score much higher than either freshman group (total of all scores = 31.42, to 28.75 for Harvard freshmen and 26.20 for Radcliffe freshmen). This result seems consistent with the stereotype of the businessman. A sex difference appears strikingly in e^c, expressed control, where both male groups are significantly higher than the female (Radcliffe) group.

CONFORMITY

In recent years there has been a great interest in studies of conformity behavior inspired primarily by the experiments of Asch (5). In these experiments the subject is put under social pressure to respond incorrectly because all the other members of his group respond incorrectly. This situation is clearly one with a strong emphasis on interpersonal relations and therefore should be explicable in terms of FIRO–B scores. Those who do conform to the group when subjected to the social pressure should score differently in an easily explicable way on FIRO–B than those who do not conform. An experiment was performed to test this prediction.

From the Harvard experiment described in Chapter 7 several conformity or opinion-change experiments were derived. These were later analyzed by Bunker (21) and the author. The experiments were as follows:

Subjects: Sixty Harvard freshmen, randomly selected.

Procedure: During the course of the Harvard experiment (see Chapter 7) four discussion problems were presented to each of twelve five-man groups. The problem was read to the group by the experimenter, and then each subject wrote his individual response to the problem. The group next discussed the problem for from twenty to forty minutes with the instruction to reach a "group decision," a purposely ambiguous phrase to allow them freedom to structure their discussions as they wished. After the discussions, the experimenter returned and the subjects filled out their individual opinions. The group-selected spokesman then presented the group decision to the experimenter.

The problems included in the study are called Traffic, Cheat, Child, and Group, and are presented in Appendix B. For each problem an objective answer sheet was presented so that change of opinion due to discussion could be noted. For the analysis, subjects were divided into changers (those who changed on one or more problems) and nonchangers (those who changed on no problems). Ninety-five per cent of the changes of opinion were in the direction of conformity, that is, toward majority opinion. The category of changer-nonchanger was then compared to FIRO–1 scales. Two significant results and one interesting trend were found. No other FIRO–1 scales were significantly related to change.

TABLE 4–10. Change of Opinion and FIRO–1 Scales

		Changed Opinion		
		Yes	*No*	
FIRO–1 Scale G	*High*	10	24	$\chi^2 = 12.83$
(I Participate				$p < .001$
in Group	*Low*	26	10	
Discussions.)				

		Changed Opinion		
		Yes	*No*	
FIRO–1 Scale	*High*	18	16	$\chi^2 = 2.95$
SR (I Like				$p < .05$
Strict Rules.)	*Low*	8	18	

		Changed Opinion		
		Yes	*No*	
FIRO–1 Scale	*High*	13	11	$\chi^2 = 1.91$
A (It Is				$p < .10$
Important for	*Low*	13	23	
Me to Be Liked.)				

This result indicates that people who do not change are high participators, who say it's not important for them to be liked. Those who change tend to like strict rules. This configuration suggested the possibility of looking for personality types made up of patterns of scores from all three interpersonal need areas to explain opinion changes. By finding all those high on participation and low on need to be liked, and on liking for rules ($-A, +G, -SR$), and comparing these with the opposite pattern—wanting to be liked, like strict rules, and low participation ($+A, -G, +SR$), clear-cut differences were obtained (Table 4–11).

TABLE 4–11. Opinion Change for Two Personality Types

		Changed Opinion		
		Yes	*No*	
Personality	$-A, +G, -SR$	1	10	Fisher exact test
Type (FIRO–1)				$p < .01$
	$+A, -G, +SR$	7	3	

Thus, although only 21 cases of 60 fall into these personality categories, 17 of these are in the predicted direction. This discovery led to a further investigation of personality types and conformity behavior.

Cohen (27) administered FIRO–4 with several other personality measures to a group of fifty Harvard students from all classes in an experiment replicating and extending the Asch experiment. He kindly made a portion of his data available to us. Since FIRO–4 had different scales from FIRO–1, a transformation was made with the following:

	FIRO–1	FIRO–4
	A	Affection
Scale	SR	Control (expressed and wanted)
	G	Inclusion

Table 4–12 shows the results of the analysis made of the Bunker data applied to the subjects in Cohen's experiment.

TABLE 4–12. Replication of Bunker Pattern Result on Cohen Data

	Opinion Change	
	Yes	*No*
−A, −C(s), +I	1	4
+A, +C(s), −I	3	1

The number is too small to be significant (nine cases of fifty), but the direction is the same. Table 4–13 shows the result of combining this finding with the Bunker data.

TABLE 4–13. Combining Bunker and Cohen Data for All Subjects Fitting Certain FIRO Personality Types

	Opinion Change		
	Yes	*No*	
−A, −C, +I	2	14	Fisher exact test $p < .01$
+A, +C, −I	10	4	

This combining of data assumes the validity of the transformations made from FIRO–1 scales to FIRO–4. By combining, twenty-four out of thirty cases, or 80 per cent, are in the desired direction, a result significant at the .01 level.

It was not possible to generalize this approach to include more of Cohen's subjects. Although the result obtained is interesting, it includes relatively few subjects (27 per cent of both samples) and is not amenable to generalization to the majority of people. It is hoped that FIRO–B will provide a better measure for pursuing the personality characteristics of conformity. The evidence so far seems to indicate most strongly that those who profess little need to be liked, who don't like to be governed by rules, and who express themselves freely tend not to change their opinions when under social pressure.

Predictive and Construct Validity

Predictive validity is evaluated by showing how well predictions made from the test are confirmed by evidence gathered at some subsequent time. Construct validity is evaluated by investigating what psychological qualities a test measures, for example, by demonstrating that certain explanatory concepts account to some degree for performance on the test. Essentially it is a validation of the theory underlying the test.

Since FIRO–B is designed to test a theory, virtually every study in this book is relevant to predictive validity. In Chapter 5 the relation of childhood interpersonal atmospheres to FIRO is explored for what may be called "construct concurrent validity." In Chapter 7 predictions which are based on the theory underlying FIRO and which utilize the measuring instrument itself are tested. These are tests of "construct predictive validity."

In addition to these studies, Hampton (46) related responses to FIRO–1 to observed behavior. Further information about the relation of successive revisions of FIRO–B is necessary for better understanding of these and other studies.

RELIABILITY

Coefficient of Internal Consistency

The coefficient of internal consistency is the measure based on internal analysis of data obtained on a single trial. Essentially this measure indicates the degree to which the items are homogeneous, or measuring the same thing. The most usual test for internal consistency is the split-half method, the correlation between scores on two halves of the test.

Since the scales of FIRO–B are all Guttman scales, reproducibility is the appropriate measure of internal consistency. If the items have the cumulative property, their unidimensionality is established.

Reproducibility, according to Guttman, is a more stringent criterion than internal consistency, since it requires not only unidimensionality—that all items measure the same dimension—but also that the items occur in a certain order. The usual criterion for reproducibility is that 90 per cent of all responses are predictable from knowledge of scale scores. As mentioned above, the scales were developed on about 150 subjects and the reproducibility computed for the remainder of the sample (Table 4–14).

The number of subjects varied, owing to the evolution of the scales. Some were altered when they proved unsatisfactory, and then readministered with unaltered scales. Subjects were, as described above, mostly college stu-

TABLE 4–14. Reproducibility of FIRO–B Scales

Scale	Reproducibility	Number of Subjects
e^I	.94	1615
w^I	.94	1582
e^C	.93	1554
w^C	.94	1574
e^A	.94	1467
w^A	.94	1467
Mean	.94	1543

dents with a small population of Air Force personnel. The reproducibility for all scales is very high and consistent over all samples. These reproducibility scores are the coefficients of internal consistency for FIRO–B.

Coefficient of Equivalence

The coefficient of equivalence is the correlation between scores from two forms given at essentially the same time. There is at present only one form of FIRO–B; thus no such coefficient is calculable. However, the remarks under content validity are applicable here. To the extent that the theory underlying Guttman scaling is accepted, the items on any one scale represent a sampling of the universe of items, and therefore theoretically there should be a high correlation between FIRO–B and an alternate form. Empirically, however, no data are available.

Coefficient of Stability

Coefficient of stability refers to the correlation between test and retest with an intervening period of time. For FIRO–B this is an important measure, since interpersonal orientations are presumably stable traits. FIRO–B was administered to college students at one-month intervals. Two unsatisfactory scales (e^A and w^A) were replaced with earlier versions of the same scales. These two were then given to a smaller sample of Harvard students with a one-week interval (Table 4–15).

TABLE 4–15. Stability (Test-Retest) of FIRO–B Scales

Scale	Stability	No. of Subjects	MEAN Test	MEAN Retest	STANDARD ERROR Test	STANDARD ERROR Retest
e^I	.82	126	5.21	5.00	1.90	2.19
w^I	.75	126	3.88	3.42	3.20	3.30
e^C	.74	183	3.14	2.94	2.22	2.19
w^C	.71	125	4.44	4.58	1.91	2.13
e^A	.73	57	3.42	3.19	2.43	2.71
w^A	.80	57	3.95	3.54	2.74	2.88
Mean	.76					

Although it is difficult to find stability data for many personality tests, and therefore to have a standard for acceptance of a scale, an inspection of the data led to the selection of .70 as a satisfactory coefficient of stability. This figure in itself is not very helpful, since it conveys little useful information. Therefore the stability will be described in a different way so that a somewhat clearer picture of the degree of invariance of the measures will be presented.

Usually the score a person makes on FIRO–B will be used to classify him for some purpose. It is of interest, therefore, to consider how many people retain the same classification on the retest that they attained on the test. To demonstrate the degree of stability of FIRO–B scales, a case derived from the stability population is presented in which a group is tested and divided into three approximately equal groups, and assigned the names "high," "middle," and "low." The same classification is made for the retest (Table 4–16).

TABLE 4–16. Distribution of Respondents Test-Retest of FIRO–B (by Per Cent)

e^I		Retest			e^C		Retest			e^A		Retest		
		Low	*Md*	*Hi*			*Low*	*Md*	*Hi*			*Low*	*Md*	*Hi*
	Low	57	37	06		*Low*	64	26	10		*Low*	83	06	11
Test	*Md*	13	54	33		*Md*	34	46	20		*Md*	24	52	24
	Hi	00	08	92		*Hi*	10	31	59		*Hi*	11	06	83
	$N = 126$					$N = 126$					$N = 57$			

w^I		Retest			w^C		Retest			w^A		Retest		
		Low	*Md*	*Hi*			*Low*	*Md*	*Hi*			*Low*	*Md*	*Hi*
	Low	71	27	02		*Low*	67	29	04		*Low*	78	17	05
Test	*Md*	33	45	23		*Md*	10	63	27		*Md*	33	28	39
	Hi	02	31	67		*Hi*	00	50	50		*Hi*	05	10	85
	$N = 126$					$N = 126$					$N = 57$			

ALL SCALES COMBINED

		Retest		
		Low	*Md*	*Hi*
	Low	70	24	06
Test	*Md*	24	50	27
	Hi	04	26	70

Seventy per cent of the highs and lows remain in that category on the retest, whereas half of the middles retain that status. The probability of an individual's jumping from a high to a low, or a low to a high, is extremely slight—about 10 per cent.

In Chapter 6, when the technique for combining FIRO–B scale scores to predict compatibility is presented, stability measures are given for that specific application. That figure is of even more immediate usefulness than the general measure presented here.

INTERCORRELATION OF SCALES

The intercorrelation between FIRO–B scales obtained from a sample of 108 subjects, all college students, is shown in Table 4–17.

TABLE 4–17. Intercorrelations among FIRO–B Scales

	e^I	w^I	e^C	w^C	e^A	w^A	
e^I		.62	.15	.12	.46	.31	
w^I			.10	.13	.49	.48	$r_{.05}=.20$
e^C				.25	.17	.00	$r_{.01}=.26$
w^C					−.02	−.15	
e^A						.70	$N = 108$
w^A							

Table 4–17 indicates significant correlation between e and w for inclusion and affection, and a somewhat smaller significant correlation between the scales of I and A. The correlation is small enough so that predictions about specific individuals would be somewhat hampered by reducing the number of scales. It is important to be aware of the fact that FIRO–B contains nonindependent scales, but it seems at this point to be advantageous, from the standpoint of the theoretical meaning of each scale, to retain them in this form.

The emphasis on differentiation of roles in the control area (Chapter 2), as opposed to the other two areas, is here given empirical support. How one expresses himself in the inclusion and affection areas is similar to how one would like to be acted toward; this is not so in the control area. In that area there is a clear differentiation between how one would like to be acted toward and how one tries to act toward others.

This section completes the presentation of FIRO–B. Several empirical applications are presented in subsequent chapters. Most of these applications utilize an earlier form of FIRO–B, but the principles underlying the construction of the instrument have remained essentially the same.

5

The Postulate of Relational
Continuity

Postulate 2. *The Postulate of Relational Continuity.* **An individual's expressed interpersonal behavior will be similar to the behavior he experienced in his earliest interpersonal relations, usually with his parents, in the following way:**

> *Principle of Constancy:* **When he perceives his adult position in an interpersonal situation to be similar to his own position in his parent-child relation, his adult behavior positively covaries with his childhood behavior toward his parents (or significant others).**
>
> *Principle of Identification:* **When he perceives his adult position in an interpersonal situation to be similar to his parent's position in his parent-child relation, his adult behavior positively covaries with the behavior of his parents (or significant others) toward him when he was a child.**

EXPLANATION

"An individual's expressed interpersonal behavior" may be interpreted to be the e introduced in the last chapter, that is, the characteristic way in which he expresses himself in an interpersonal situation with regard to the three interpersonal need areas.

Before the general significance of the postulate is discussed, a diagram may help to clarify its meaning (Fig. 5–1).

The first diagram schematizes the relation of the parent and child. In the second diagram the child-become-adult perceives that he occupies a

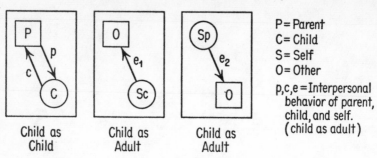

Child as   Child as   Child as
Child   Adult   Adult

FIGURE 5–1. Schema for Postulate of Relational Continuity

role similar to the one he had as a child (Sc). In the third diagram he perceives that he occupies a role similar to the one his parent occupied toward him (Sp). The Postulate of Relational Continuity specifies the relations between e_1, e_2, p, and c. To demonstrate the postulate, all possibilities for e_1 and e_2 (the term e will be used to designate both e_1 and e_2) are enumerated:

1. e covaries positively with c.
2. e covaries negatively with c.
3. e does not covary with c.
4. e covaries positively with p.
5. e covaries negatively with p.
6. e does not covary with p.

The term "covaries" means "varies concomitantly in a statistically significant sense." It is to be interperted as a statistical concept measured by the appropriate statistical measure, for example, product-moment correlation, chi-square, rank-order correlation.

The Principle of Constancy asserts that for e_1, possibility (1) is true; that is, e_1 covaries positively with c. The Principle of Identification asserts the truth of (4) for e_2; that is, e_2 covaries positively with p. It should be noted that the Principle of Constancy implies that (2) and (3) are false but is noncommittal about (4), (5), and (6). Similarly, the Principle of Identification implies that (5) and (6) are false, and is noncommittal about (1), (2), and (3).

Briefly, then, the postulate states that a person will behave interpersonally as he did when he was a child when he feels that he is in a position similar to his childhood position (for instance, "I treat him just as I treated my mother"), but when he feels that his role is more similar to his parents' role he will behave as they did toward him (for instance, "He treats his children just as his parents treated him").

One difficulty at present in the formulation of Postulate 2 is the classification of adult roles as perceived to be more parentlike or more childlike. Several factors aid in determining whether a certain adult role is more like parent or like child, such as the formal designation of adult roles, for example, boss–employee, officer–enlisted man, which approximate the parent-child relation in the control area. In addition, there is some evidence that in the affection and inclusion areas there is a considerable similarity between parent and child behavior; for instance, the unloving parent frequently has an unloving child. These factors minimize the errors in classifying adult roles as parentlike or childlike. However, the problem of classification of roles is an area where more work is required before Postulate 2 can be stated with exactness.

This postulate is by no means new. It is essentially a restatement of a fundamental aspect of psychoanalytic and other psychodynamic theory. The idea that present perceptions and behaviors are traceable to childhood experiences is quite widely accepted. The contribution intended by the present formulation is the specification of this general principle in three ways: (1) the general principle of continuity from childhood to adulthood holds *in particular* for interpersonal behavior; (2) an individual's *most common* reaction to a childhood interpersonal relation is to continue to prefer personal relations like those he has experienced; (3) the particular *areas* in which these continuities occur are inclusion, control, and affection.

PLAUSIBILITY

These three points provide a good framework for presenting specific plausibility arguments. But before a detailed discussion of these, a few comments are appropriate on the plausibility of the who'e concept of the effect of infantile experience on adult personality. In asserting this relation we are of course following the psychoanalysts quite closely. One of the cornerstones of Freud's position was the systematic relation between early childhood experiences and specific aspects of adult life. A great deal of present-day psychotherapy is based on this notion. In fact, the concept is so widely accepted that it has virtually lost its identity with Freudianism. The effect of childhood experiences on adult life is accepted in the present theory in the sense analogous to the construction of a tall building. The foundation and lower stories are the most important parts of the building because if any flaw exists in them it is transmitted to the entire structure. In order to correct the flaw the structure must be "unbuilt" down to the bottom and then rebuilt. In contrast, if a structural flaw occurs at the top floor, only that floor must be repaired. Similarly, the earlier an important experience occurs, the more impact it will have on subsequent development and the more difficult it will be to alter.

Now to consider the points of specification:

The General Principle Holds in Particular for Interpersonal Behavior

One area where the effect of childhood experience is observable in adult behavior is that of interpersonal behavior. The way in which people interact with and perceive others depends, as do most other characteristics, on their past experience. People learn to interact just as they learn any skill. One must learn how people initiate activity toward the self, how they respond to various activities of the self, how the self feels in response to various behaviors of others, how and why others reward and punish, love, ignore, and so forth. All these activities are complex and vitally important events, and must be learned. After the earliest learning the resultant responses of the individual become reinforced or nonremembered to various degrees by continued interaction with others. Unless some highly dramatic event intervenes, such as psychotherapy or a severe traumatic experience, the reinforced earliest learned interpersonal responses should be discernible in adult behavior.

The Early Interpersonal Relations Continue Throughout Life

The second major facet of this proposition is the notion of relational continuity, which means that the interpersonal relation one experienced early in life continues to be the model for interpersonal behavior throughout adult life. The model includes the behavior expressed as a child and the behavior observed in the parent. There are several reasons why this situation serves as a model.

One reason is psychological economy. In the same way that it is easier to use the language one learns in growing up than to change to an unfamiliar and untried language, it is easier to continue to use the same models of interpersonal behavior. Experiencing a new situation requires a learning of unfamiliar situational characteristics and an unlearning of the familiar, giving rise to all the uncertainty attached to unfamiliarity. The individual does not know how new interpersonal behavior will satisfy needs. Trying unfamiliar interpersonal orientations is in many ways a more severe threat than holding on to known, though unsatisfactory, orientations. For example, if an individual comes from a home in which there is low affection interchange, it is very uncomfortable for him to find himself in a situation where there is the opposite expectation—people who take the initiative in expressing affection effusively and expect the same in return. Theoretically, he would be disturbed by the large amount of interchange of affection and would feel incapable of accepting it or reciprocating.

In addition, to adopt different interpersonal behaviors usually involves, to some degree, rejection of those persons, usually the parents, who behave in the rejected ways. Thus, if one desires to change from a conformist, law-abiding, slightly authoritarian mode of relating (control area) to a less conforming, liberalized mode, it is necessary to reject in some form the conformist parent in whom the original behavior was observed. This rejection, because it is usually extremely difficult, acts as a strong deterrent to noncontinuity of interpersonal behavior.

There is a similarity between the Principle of Identification and the generalized psychoanalytic notion of identification with the aggressor. One response to the inability to express and accept negative feelings toward a parental figure is to assuage the guilt arising from these feelings by becoming "like" the parent figure, often in precisely those traits that are detested in the parent. For example, if the parent is meticulous and demanding, the individual often is amazed to find that these infuriating characteristics are exactly those he is exhibiting toward his own children. Hence both the essentially cognitive factors of learning a new interpersonal orientation and the essentially emotional factors involved in rejection of significant others lead to the phenomena of relational continuity.

This postulate asserts only the *most common* response to a childhood situation. Certainly there are many instances of rebellion against the earlier situation. Data, however, ruled against the importance of such a response. This notion of rebellion was included in an earlier formulation of Postulate 2 as another possible response to the early parental situation, but the evidence reported later in this chapter seemed to indicate that the rebellious response, although very likely existent, is not nearly so frequent as anticipated, and apparently is completely dwarfed by the continuity responses—constancy and identification. Therefore, until more sensitive measures are devised for detecting the rebellion response, it will not be included in the postulate.

The Particular Areas Where Relational Continuity Occurs Are Inclusion, Control, and Affection

Perhaps the newest aspect of this formulation of the principle involves the specification of *the particular* aspects of interpersonal behavior that follow the Postulate of Relational Continuity. Although it is often stated that there is a relation between early childhood experiences and later adult behavior, it is not often stated exactly what aspect of childhood experience leads to which adult behaviors.

According to Postulate 1, interpersonal behavior can be usefully classified into the area of inclusion, control, and affection. By observation of the parent-child relation *in these areas* it should be possible to make predictions to the corresponding areas of adult behavior. Observations are focused on specific aspects of interpersonal behavior rather than on the diffuse mass of behavior observable. For example, behavior in the area of parental affection is relevant to the prediction of behavior in the area of affection between friends, sweethearts, and so on. Therefore the problem of liking among pairs of peer group members, to illustrate, is a relevant area of generalization.

First the type of behavior in the parent-child relations that leads to orientations in each interpersonal need area will be described. Then a brief description will be presented of the various types of difficulties in the relation, and the "ideal" relation between parent and child will be more fully described. Next will be described the adult behavior that is the most likely result of each type of parent-child relation. This description specifies not only what type of adult behavior is likely to arise from a childhood interaction but, in some instances, also which role the child is most likely to perceive as his in an adult relation.

INCLUSION BEHAVIOR

The child's need for inclusion requires a satisfactory relation regarding interaction and association with people. The parent satisfies this need by spending a satisfactory amount of time interacting with the child. A popular child's book called, *Who Will Play with Me?* (89) exemplifies this area. The book tells of a small child, Linda, looking for a playmate. Linda goes to her mother, father, sister, and friend, only to find they are all busy. She then amuses herself by creating paper dolls to play with. Finally her family and friends finish their work and all offer to play with Linda together. This development illustrates the distinction between affection and inclusion. The author stresses that not playing with Linda was a matter of relative importance—the problem was priority of certain activities rather than lack of love. The central importance of playing together for the young child highlights the need for association or interaction even with playmates the child may not like or may fight with.

In addition to the *amount* of playing or interacting with the child, the *quality* of interaction between parent and child plays a central role in inclusion behavior. In order to feel *he* is really being interacted with, the child requires undivided attention and needs to feel that he is being acted toward *as a unique person*. In the absence of this attention it is difficult for the child to feel that he is important enough to be interacted with. If he is treated like "a child" rather than like a specific person, it is difficult for him to feel the importance that is implied by being interacted with.

Inclusion-behavior is characterized by a great deal of contact and interaction between parent and child, with the parent expressing a wide range of emotion in the interaction. He exhibits a wide range of behavior appropriate to his feelings, both originating behavior toward the child and showing behavior in response to the child's behavior. He gets to know well and to understand his child. A continuum of inclusion in terms of parental attitudes would involve the following (from little inclusion behavior to much inclusion behavior): ignore, notice, acknowledge, pay attention to, interact with, be interested in, get to know, get to know well, understand.

As discussed in Chapter 9, inclusion behavior parallels the oral stage of the Freudians. While the psychoanalysts emphasize the dominant erogenous zone for a particular developmental stage, the emphasis here is on the dominant interpersonal relation. At the oral stage the primary relation between parent and child is inclusion and contact. The child has little comprehension of control or discipline, and only a dawning understanding of an affectional, or love, relation.

Difficulties with inclusion behavior in the parent-child relation come when the parent "abandons" the child or "enmeshes" the child. "Abandon" refers to lack of sufficient attention or contact, and has to do with both the quantity and quality of the contact, as described above. "Enmesh" refers to the opposite difficulty, the parent always including the child in every activity, at the expense of the child's privacy. According to the principles both of constancy and identification, abandoned children would tend to become undersocial and enmeshed children to become oversocial.

The ideal relation between parent and children in the inclusion area is between the two extremes of abandoned and enmeshed. The parent interacts widely and frequently with the child and takes an active interest in his activities but also allows the child freedom to be alone, away from interaction with people. This condition constitutes the optimal relation in the inclusion area for the parent and child. Such a relation tends to develop children who are comfortable either in the presence or absence of others, the type that has been called "social."

CONTROL BEHAVIOR

The child's need for control is the need for a satisfactory relation with people regarding control and power. Behavior relevant to this need centers on the making of decisions. Problems of discipline and guidance have as their focus the question of who will make decisions and in what way. The child must be *taught* how to make sound decisions, and he must also be *allowed* to make them. Hence all parent-child behavior centering on discipline, control, power, decision making, setting limits, teaching of rules, authority, guidance, giving direction, fostering independence, and so forth is control behavior.

The Freudian anal stage is comparable to the parent-child control behavior, again with the difference that the psychoanalysts emphasize the dominant erogenous zone, whereas the present approach emphasizes the dominant interpersonal relation. The chief importance of the anal stage is the appearance of bargaining power for the child. He has something (feces) others want dealt with in a specific way. Concurrent with this event, all the problems of socialization, discipline, and learning occur. Thus rather clearly the dominant interpersonal area is control. Inclusion is still important, but has taken a secondary position. Affection relations are still undeveloped at the time control behavior is dominant.

Difficulties with control behavior in the parent-child relation occur when the parent "dominates" the child or when the parent forces the child to make all his own decisions even before he is capable of assuming this responsibility unaided ("undirected"). According to the principle of identification, children who are dominated tend to become autocrats, while those who are undirected tend to become abdicrats. The principle of constancy might indicate somewhat different predictions. The results reported below suggest that identification is the stronger principle in this instance.

The ideal relation between parent and child in the control area lies between the two extremes of dominated and undirected. The parent develops the child's ability to make responsible decisions on his own, and allows him to make them; yet at the same time he makes necessary decisions for the child, for example, about crossing the street. This relation constitutes the optimal relation in the control area between parent and child. It tends to develop a child who is democratic in his interpersonal dealings when he becomes an adult; that is, he can feel comfortable either controlling or not controlling, and either being controlled or not being controlled.

AFFECTION BEHAVIOR

The child's need for affection is the need for a satisfactory relation with people regarding affection and love. Behavior relevant to this area centers around feelings of warmth, emotional acceptance, and love, and coldness, emotional rejection, and hate. It differs from inclusion behavior in that the stress is on the emotional feeling rather than on the amount of interaction.

For example, a father may spend a great deal of time with his son and even take an interest in his work, and still lack a feeling of love and warmth. Perhaps he wants the son to develop into a famous man so that glory will be reflected on himself, whereas actually he has little feeling for the child as an individual. An example of the reverse relation is expressed by the phrase, "mother loved me, but she never really knew me, or took an interest in my work." Perhaps the mother was occupied by her chores and her own problems and could not devote more time to her children, but her emotional feeling of love and warmth was communicated.

Affection is the dominant interpersonal relation during the Freudian phallic and oedipal stages. This stage includes the dawning of sexual and affectional feelings toward specific others, and requires more maturity than was theretofore available, since its essence is the giving up of the narcissistic concentration on the self so important for successful development in earlier stages, and giving part of the self to another. These feelings and relations certainly suggest that at this stage the interpersonal relation focuses on affection.

(The parallel to the psychosexual stages has important implications for the theory of temporal sequences of the appearance of the interpersonal needs. This topic is discussed at length in Chapter 9. The purpose of this section is simply to delineate the types of behavior occurring in the parent-child relation regardless of the time at which they occur.)

Difficulties in the affection area occur when the parent is "smothering" or "unloving." "Smothering" refers to giving the child too much love. The "doting mother" is a common phrase used to describe this idea. The so-called "overprotective" mother probably more closely parallels the dominating mother of the control area, although often the type may be both dominating and smothering. The unloved child tends to develop into a underpersonal adult, while the smothered child tends to develop into the overpersonal adult, following both principles of the Postulate of Relational Continuity.

The ideal relation between parent and child in the affection area lies between the unloving and the smothering relations. The parent gives ample affection and love to the child but not so much that the child feels overwhelmed and incapable of assimilating—and perhaps reciprocating—the love. This ideal type of relation in childhood usually leads to an adult who is capable of establishing and maintaining a close, personal relation with another person, and who also can feel comfortable in a more emotionally distant relation. This ideal type is called personal.

It should be stressed that for most parent-child interaction these three areas usually occur simultaneously. The areas are to be construed as dimensions along which any single interaction may be described. Table 5–1 summarizes these parent-child relations and the most usual resultant adult behaviors.

TABLE 5–1. Summary of Parent-Child Relations and the Resultant Adult Behavior

This Type of Parental Behavior toward Child		is Called	and Leads to This Type of Behavior by the Child
TOO MUCH	Inclusion	Enmesh	Oversocial
	Control	Dominate	Autocratic
	Affection	Smother	Overpersonal
TOO LITTLE	Inclusion	Abandon	Undersocial
	Control	Undirect	Abdicrat
	Affection	Unlove	Underpersonal
IDEAL	Inclusion	Include	Social
	Control	Respect	Democrat
	Affection	Love	Personal

Some theorems that follow from Postulate 2, the Postulate of Relational Continuity, will now be presented, together with some empirical findings. These data, as well as the remainder to be presented below, resulted primarily from a series of studies made at Harvard in the general area of small-group behavior during 1955 and 1956 and continuing at the present time.

EVIDENCE

Theorem 2–1.   There is a positive covariation between reports made by an adult of his childhood relations with his parents and his present behavior in the areas of inclusion, control, and affection.

Empirical investigations testing Theorem 2–1 were carried out in the following manner. Concurrent with the small-group experiment described in Chapter 7, a series of 74 personality measures and 34 measures of behavior were made on sixty subjects, all Harvard freshmen. These measures covered projective material, defense mechanisms, values, personality characteristics, and perceptions of parental behavior. For testing Theorem 2–1 these data were analyzed to discover the relations of all other scales to the parental perception scales. The parental scale used in this study was Slater's Parental Role Preference (PRP) questionnaire. This study will be called the *PRP Study*.

Encouraged by several positive results from the PRP study, the investigators devised a new questionnaire (see Appendix B) called the POP (Perception of Parents), which measures the perception the respondent has of the interpersonal relations between himself and his parents during his childhood in the areas of Attention, Discipline, and Warmth. (Different names are used for the areas of parent-child interaction corresponding, respectively, to inclusion, control, and affection.) This questionnaire was administered to a group of about 150 Harvard students of varied backgrounds and interests. Also administered was FIRO–2. These questionnaires were given to a large sample to check the tendencies revealed by the PRP study. This study will be called the POP study.

The PRP Study

Subjects: Sixty randomly selected Harvard freshmen.

Procedure: In the PRP study the instrument used for assessing childhood experiences was Slater's Parental Role Preference questionnaire, which measures several characteristics of the perception of parents. The measures of primary interest are Slater's two main (cluster-analyzed) factors. These he calls "inhibitory demands and discipline (discipline)" and "emotional supportiveness and warmth (warmth)"; these are measured separately for both father and mother.

With this instrument as a measure of parental relations, several other measures pertinent to testing the relational continuity principle for each of the three needs were explored (see Appendix B for description of these measures).

1. *To test participation (inclusion) attitudes:*
   Observer rating, "Participation"
2. *To test control (control) attitudes:*
   California F–scale, "Authoritarianism"
   Observer rating, "Attempts to be influential"
3. *To test personal (affection) attitudes:*
   FIRO scale A, "It's important for me to be liked"
   Interpersonal Checklist (IPC) scale, "Affiliation-Hostility"
   Observer rating, "Attempts to promote personal feelings"
   Observer rating, "Attempts to be liked"

All of the above measures were related to reports of parental behavior in the predicted direction, with the use of the chi-square test. In order to benefit from a comparison of the PRP study with what is essentially a replication, the POP study, the results of both studies will be presented jointly after the POP study has been described.

The POP Study

Subjects: One-hundred-fifty Harvard students from an elementary course in social relations.

Procedure: To test the results of the PRP study, two questionnaires were administered, FIRO–2 and POP. Each subject received a score of 1 (low) to 6 (high) on four variables: (1) undersocial (nonparticipant in groups) to oversocial (overly high participant in groups); (2) abdicratic (weak) when in superordinate role to autocratic (dominating) when in superordinate role; (3) autocratic (rebellious) when in subordinate role to abdicratic (submissive) when in subordinate role; (4) underpersonal (avoid close personal relations) to overpersonal (always seek close personal relations). The first is a measure of the inclusion area, the next two represent control, and the last one, affection.

The questionnaire used to measure parent-child relations is the POP (Perception of Parents). First, to find the gross relations between the scales, correlations were run (Table 5–2).

TABLE 5–2. Intercorrelations of FIRO and POP Scores

	Pers.	Sup.	Sub.	Par.		Warm.	Disc.	Att.
FIRO Personal		.08	.10	.29	POP Warmth		.09	.61
FIRO Superordinate			.25	.10	POP Discipline			.08
FIRO Subordinate				.05	POP Attention			
FIRO Participant								

$$r_{.01} = .18$$

The high correlation between warmth and attention on the POP is difficult to interpret. It could mean that the first wording attempted in framing the test was not sufficient to describe each area without contaminating it with aspects of the other. Or it could mean that although these two areas of interpersonal relations are logically distinguishable they are empirically correlated. This point is discussed at the conclusion of this chapter. To decide between these alternative interpretations, the first must be eliminated before the second is accepted. Thus further clarification of the distinction between attention and warmth in the home is required. Since the studies of Baldwin, Kallhorn, and Breese (8) and Sewell, Mussen, and Harris (79), who used factor analytic-type techniques, showed distinguishable factors, there are good indications that the fault lies in the POP measuring instrument.

RESULTS OF TWO STUDIES ON RELATIONAL CONTINUITY

In all scales, including FIRO–2 and POP, all variables are dichotomized at the mean and subjected to chi-square or Fisher exact test analysis. All probabilities reported are for predicted relations (one-tail test) unless noted, since Theorem 2–1 specifies the direction of the relation.

Since both the PRP and POP measuring instruments are designed primarily to test the behavior of the parent rather than the child, all results in these studies are primarily relevant to the Principle of Identification.

Inclusion. In the area of inclusion the primary prediction is between the amount and quality of interaction between parent and child and the degree of participation or withdrawal in group interaction by the child-now-adult. Since the time of this study the conception of the relation of participation to inclusion has been somewhat altered. Participation is closely related to attitudes toward inclusion, but it also seems to be related to the other areas (see Chapter 2). However, since participation does approximate an important aspect of the inclusion area, the results now reported are useful.

Unfortunately, the PRP questionnaire does not have a scale comparable to the inclusion variable; hence in the PRP study it was necessary to construct an index of PRP scales to approximate parental interaction. The best indicator of ignored children seemed to be children low on *both* warmth received and discipline received (see Table 5–17). This group shall be called the negative group on "parental attention." Since the behavior of the parent and that of the child are assumed to be similar in this situation, in that both are low in participation, the results based on this measure are relevant to the Principle of Constancy as well as the Principle of Identification.

The division of subjects according to parental attention (shown by PRP) was compared to the observers' rating on participation (Table 5–3). Throughout the PRP study behavior ratings on each group were made by from two to five graduate student research assistants. The total of about thirty ratings per group were then combined to form a composite score. See Appendix B for rating sheet.

TABLE 5–3. Relation between Parental Attention (PRP) and Group Participation

		Parental Attention (PRP)		
		High	Low	
Participation	High	34	3	$\chi^2 = 5.08$
(Observers)				$p < .02$
	Low	16	7	

Thus, although the numbers are too low to allow a great deal of confidence in the result, the direction of the result is clearly consistent with Theorem 2–1. The matter of sample size, as well as a more direct measure of parental attention, was dealt with in the POP study. The pertinent result in the POP study is the relation between parental attention (divided at midpoint of POP scale) and participation (Table 5–4).

TABLE 5–4. Relation between Parental Attention (POP) and Participation (FIRO–2)

		Parental Attention (POP)		
		High	Low	
Participation	High	22	47	$\chi^2 = 2.70$
(FIRO–2)				$p < .05$
	Low	15	60	

To summarize these data conveniently, both tables will be combined (Table 5-5). Combining is justified because (1) both tables are presumably measuring the same variables; (2) the tables utilize different populations; (3) the trends are so similar that combination will not mask or neutralize any effect found in either table.

TABLE 5-5. Summary of Relation between Parental Attention (PRP and POP) and Group Participation (Observers and FIRO-2)

		Parental Attention		
		High	Low	
Participation	High	56	50	χ^2(combined)$=9.35$
				$p<.01$
	Low	31	67	

This highly significant result supports Theorem 2-1 in the inclusion area with respect to parental situation involving both high attention and low attention. *In the area of inclusion, Theorem 2-1, derived from the Postulate of Relational Continuity, is confirmed for the parental situation of both high attention and low attention.*

Control. In the control area the Principle of Identification asserts that the strongly disciplined child identifies with the parent and expresses autocratic behavior when in a parentlike role. The parentlike role is approximated by the FIRO-2 Control-Superordinate scale, which refers to behavior in the superordinate position. The same principle would indicate that the undisciplined child would express abdicratic behavior in the superordinate role. Unfortunately, neither the PRP nor the POP studies measured the behavior of the *respondent* when he was a child (only the behavior he recalls of his parents); thus the Principle of Constancy and the FIRO-2 Control-Subordinate scales cannot be tested.

The PRP study did not include FIRO-2, but two other measures proved relevant. The California F-scale measures authoritarianism, an attitude very similar to the autocratic response discussed here (Table 5-6).

TABLE 5-6. Relation of Parental Discipline (PRP) to F-Scale Score

		Parental Discipline (PRP)		
		High	Low	
Authoritarianism	High	23	5	$\chi^2=5.66$
(F-scale)				$p<.01$
	Low	17	15	

Thus those who were more disciplined as children have more authoritarian attitudes, as Theorem 2-1 would predict.

The second pertinent measure was a behavior rating made by observers. This rating was called, "Attempts to influence decisions." Theorem 2-1 indicates that since strong discipline is an extreme form of strong influence the same positive relation would hold (Table 5-7).

TABLE 5–7. Relation between Parental Discipline (PRP) and Attempts to Be Influential in Groups

		Parental Discipline (PRP)		
		High	*Low*	
Attempts to	*High*	26	8	$\chi^2 = 3.39$
Be Influential				$p < .05$
(Observers)	*Low*	14	12	

Again the theorem is confirmed.

In the POP study, parental discipline was compared with the FIRO–2 measure of the Control-Superordinate role as a role in which authority should be exercised fully (Table 5–8).

TABLE 5–8. Relation of Parental Discipline (POP) and Autocratic Behavior in the Superordinate Role

		Parental Discipline (POP)		
		High	*Low*	
Autocratic	*High*	47	35	$\chi^2 = 4.89$
Behavior				$p < .05$
(FIRO–2)	*Low*	24	38	

The follow-up study on the larger sample confirms the previous result. Again it will be convenient for interpretive purposes to combine Table 5–8 with the closest PRP measure, the PRP–F–scale relation (see Table 5–9).

TABLE 5–9. Summary of Relation between Parental Discipline and Attitudes toward Autocratic Behavior (PRP and POP Studies)

		Parental Discipline		
		High	*Low*	
Autocratic	*High*	70	40	χ^2(combined) $= 8.19$
Behavior	*Low*	41	53	$p < .01$

The combined chi-square is significant beyond the .01 level of confidence. From this summary table it can be seen that the relation is relatively symmetrical, though there is a somewhat stronger tendency for dominated (strongly disciplined) children to be autocratic than for undirected (mildly disciplined) children to be abdicratic. *In the area of control Theorem 2–1 derived from the Postulate of Relational Continuity is strongly confirmed, especially when the parental situation is one of high discipline.*

Affection. In the affection area the primary relation hypothesized is that between amount and quality of affection received as a child, and attitudes and behavior regarding close personal relations in a group situation.

There were two measures used in the PRP study to measure attitudes about the self with regard to friendship and liking, the FIRO A scale ("It's important for me to be liked") and the Interpersonal checklist (IPC) "Affection-Hostility" dimension as described by the self (Table 5–10).

TABLE 5–10. Relations between Parental Warmth (PRP) and Attitudes toward Self as Friendly

| | | Parental Warmth (PRP) | | | | Parental Warmth (PRP) | |
		High	Low			High	Low
Affection	High	15	15	"Want to	High	11	11
(IPC)	Low	8	22	be liked."	Low	12	26
				(FIRO–1)			
		$\chi^2 = 3.45$				$\chi^2 = 2.00$	
		$p < .05$				$p < .10$	

The relation holds for the IPC, and the tendency is in the predicted direction for the A scale of FIRO–2. The behavior rating, "Attempts to be liked," is also relevant to the affection area (Table 5–11).

TABLE 5–11. Relations between Parental Warmth (PRP) and Attempts to Be Liked

| | | Parental Warmth (PRP) | | |
		High	Low	
Attempts to	High	12	14	
Be Liked				$\chi^2 = 1.19$
(Observers)	Low	11	23	$p < .15$

In the POP study the pertinent relation was that between the warmth of the parent as measured by POP and the attitude toward close personal relations as measured on FIRO–2 (Table 5–12).

TABLE 5–12. Parental Warmth (POP) and Attitudes toward Closeness (FIRO)

| | | Parental Warmth (POP) | | |
		High	Low	
Personal	High	23	30	
(FIRO–2)				$\chi^2 = 6.89$
	Low	21	71	$p < .01$

Again, with the same justification, the chi-square tables for the POP study and for the A scale of FIRO–1 will be combined. The FIRO–1 measure was chosen, even though its chi-square value was lower than the IPC dimension, because it seemed to be more similar to the FIRO–2 scale (Table 5–13).

TABLE 5–13. Summary Table of Relation between Parental Warmth and Attitudes toward Close Personal Relations (POP and PRP Study)

| | | Parental Warmth Received | | |
		High	Low	
Desire for	High	34	41	
Personal				χ^2(combined)$=8.60$
Closeness	Low	33	97	$p < .01$

Again the result is highly significant. The most interesting result of these explorations relates to the lower right cell. The Principle of Identification seems to be very strongly supported for these situations in which there was little parental warmth. The "unloved" child has a strong tendency to exhibit underpersonal perceptions and attitudes. When there is emotional warmth, the tendency to like close personal relations is only slightly greater (54 per cent) than the tendency not to like them. This asymmetry seems to support the identification with the aggressor explanation discussed earlier. *In the area of affection, Theorem 2–1, derived from the Postulate of Relational Continuity, is strongly confirmed, especially when the parental situation is low in warmth.*

This concludes the presentation of the measures that fall directly into the framework of the theory being proposed. In each interpersonal need area Theorem 2–1 was decisively confirmed. On the whole, there were very few relations which were significant other than the ones presented above.

Unpredicted Significant Relations. In the area of affection the only significant relation other than those presented was between attention and personal in the PRP study. The relation was in the same direction as that between warmth and personal, and significant beyond the .01 level. This relation is easily accounted for in terms of the correlation of .61 between the warmth and attention variables on the POP.

In the control area there were no other relations found.

In the inclusion area, the result of the correlation between warmth and attention again manifested itself, as warmth was significantly related to participation in the POP study ($p < .01$). However, the most interesting unpredicted result in the PRP study was the following (Table 5–14).

TABLE 5–14. Relation of Parental Discipline to Group Participation (PRP and POP)

		Parental Discipline (PRP)			Parental Discipline (POP)			Parental Discipline (Combined)	
		High	Low		High	Low		High	Low
Participation (Observers)	High	28	9	High	40	29	High	68	38
	Low	12	11	Low	31	44	Low	43	55
		$\chi^2 = 3.44$ $p < .10$ (unpredicted)			$\chi^2 = 3.98$ $p < .05$ (unpredicted)			$\chi^2 = 8.23$ $p < .01$ (unpredicted)	

This result leads to interesting speculation on whether discipline itself is a factor in participation, or whether the contact between parent and child implied in discipline is the prime contribution. One explanation for this result is that hostility, which is generated by discipline, leads to participation. This explanation does not seem so plausible, however, as one that focuses on the interaction between parent and child. Many techniques of discipline involve increased interaction (for example, spanking, yelling, lecturing) and imply great involvement by the parent. Lack of discipline may imply lack of interest and attention, and it is this aspect that could affect the child's interaction with others in exactly the same way that other types of parental inattention do (see Chapter 2).

This last explanation can be easily tested by including in the POP questionnaire the distinction between "interaction increasing" discipline, such as spanking, lecturing, and the like, and "interaction decreasing" discipline, such as being sent to room, leaving the table, not allowed out with playmates, and so on. The prediction would be made that for a constant value of the attention variable the "interaction decreasing" disciplined persons are less active in groups than the "interaction increasing" disciplined persons.

CONCLUSIONS

1. As can be observed from Table 5–15 below, Theorem 2–1 is well confirmed and therefore provides evidence that the Postulate of Relational Continuity is a useful one, especially the Principle of Identification. These tables, which combine PRP and POP samples, all yield a chi-square significant beyond the .01 level. They summarize the relations between all three pairs of childhood adult variables in the primary interpersonal need areas. The entries have been converted to percentages of total N for ease of comparison across need areas. The total N is about 210.

TABLE 5–15. Summary of Relations between Parent Behavior and Adult Attitudes and Behavior in the Three Primary Interpersonal Need Areas (Converted to Percentages)

	Parental Attention			Parental Discipline			Parental Warmth		
	High	*Low*			*High*	*Low*		*High*	*Low*
Partici-	*High* 27	25	Autocratic	*High*	34	20	Personal *High*	17	20
pation	*Low* 15	33	Behavior	*Low*	20	26	Closeness *Low*	16	47
	$\chi^2 = 9.27$			$\chi^2 = 8.01$			$\chi^2 = 9.69$		
	$p < .01$			$p < .01$			$p < .01$		

All the major hypotheses were well confirmed. Several results seem to help clarify the whole picture and are suggestive of further refinements and experiments. The tables were all presented in the simplified fourfold table form for two main reasons: (a) the test instruments were largely new and crude and did not warrant a statistical technique of great precision; (b) the theory is new, in this form, and the first question to be answered is simply, "Are the relations posited actually present?"

2. Interpretation of a questionnaire about childhood deserves further discussion. The problems involved in using a perception of a childhood relation as evidence for the actual childhood relation itself require a consideration of the significance of parent-child relations. What is it about the relation that affects later perceptions and behavior of the child? Three points of reference toward the parent-child situation may be utilized: (a) the parent's perception of the relation, (b) the child's perception, and (c) the "real" situation (that is, the perception of trained observers). Since we are concerned with the effect of the parent-child relation on the child's later development, it seems that we are mainly interested in the child's perception, al-

though of course knowledge of the other two perceptions would be very useful for further analysis.

The next pertinent question is, "Is the important variable the child's perception of the event at the time it occurs, shortly thereafter, or considerably later, when he has reached adulthood?" This question leads to questions regarding the mechanism posited to account for relational continuity. Table 5–16 illustrates the various approaches to obtaining information about the parent-child relation:

TABLE 5–16. Data Sources for Parent-Child Relation

		SOURCE OF REPORT		
		Parent (*P*)	Child (*C*)	Observer (*O*)
TIME	Concurrent (*N*)	*NP*	*NC*	*NO*
OF	Immediately Following (*F*)	*FP*	*FC*	*FO*
REPORT	Much Later (Adulthood) (*L*)	*LP*	*LC*	*LO*

Since the conscious perceptions and behaviors of the adult are hypothesized to arise from the unconscious feelings about the self, and the feelings of others toward the self, the main interest is with the unconscious perceptions and interpretations made by the child during the interaction with the parent. Relevant are the child's feelings—mainly the unconscious feelings—about such questions as "Does your parent treat you as if you're a lovable person?" or "Does your parent really feel you are important enough for him to spend his time with?" How is this information best obtained? Direct observation of the parent-child interaction (Cell *NO* in Table 5–16) and subsequent interviews (*FP, FC*) may elicit this information. Immediate superficial questioning (*NP, NC*) may not. Questioning the child after he has become an adult (*LC*) may elicit the desired information because his response may be the resultant of the unconscious childhood perceptions now filtered to retain only the most significant memories. But it is also possible that the adult has need to distort his childhood memories. Perhaps projective techniques (*LC*) would break through this conscious distortion.

Since the best technique is not easy to decide upon, the most practical, reasonable measure was selected—a questionnaire given to the adult about his childhood (*LC*—the POP and PRP). There is always a check of the validity of this choice. If the questionnaires about parent-child relations are measuring the desired variables they should correlate with present behavior, according to the theory, or the theory is wrong. A positive result lends some weight to both the theory and the measure, and a negative result leaves at least those two areas for reinvestigation.

Table 5–16 suggests many other ways of measuring the parent-child phenomena at issue here, and therefore many other ways to test theorems derived from the Postulate of Relational Continuity. It is hoped that results obtained from all of these data sources will converge.

3. The Postulate of Relational Continuity is meant only to account for the largest portion of the relation between childhood interpersonal behavior and group behavior. Obviously, there are many modes of response to a given childhood interpersonal situation. The mechanisms of defense, which have not been discussed, represent a whole series of techniques for handling interpersonal frustrations. The only contention involved in the relational continuity postulate is that the *most common response* is to continue relating interpersonally in the same way in which one starts out. The evidence presented in this chapter seems to provide strong support for this notion.

4. The Postulate of Relational Continuity, aside from being an important postulate in the theory, gives support to the choice of the three interpersonal needs, that is, to Postulate 1. It demonstrates that these are powerful predictive variables which, aside from having intuitive reasonableness and generality as demonstrated by the variety of studies in which they appear, are also empirically meaningful. They can be related from contexts occurring at vastly different time points (childhood to adulthood).

FUTURE RESEARCH

One of the most promising avenues of elaboration of the Postulate of Relational Continuity lies in the combination of need areas. Any particular parent-child interaction has some elements in each of the three areas. In this sense, these areas may be considered the basic categories in terms of which any given behavior may be described. Taking a child on a picnic, for example, has implications for inclusion, for affection, and, before the day is done, for control. This fact suggests a type of result that could be pursued with profit. By a combination of the two scales of the PRP (discipline and warmth) the characteristics of the people falling in each cell—for example, high discipline–low affection—may be investigated.

The most fruitful handling of the differentiation between mother and father proved to be the following: for each person the higher score (of mother's and father's) on discipline and the lower score on affection were used. The rationale for this choice was that the child would be most affected by the stronger disciplinarian and the least affectionate parent. This assumption was partially borne out by results reported above, which indicate that low affection and high discipline seem to have the strongest influence on adult development. This result is consistent with the explanation presented above, based on the notion of identification with the aggressor. It can be assumed that both strong discipline and lack of affection rouse considerable hostility in the child toward the offending parent. Since hostility toward the parents to whom so much is owed and on whom so much depends is not culturally approved, feelings of guilt and fear are roused in the hostile child. The guilt is assuaged by identifying with the parent and acting as he does. The mechanism does not operate in this fashion when there are no strong negative feelings for which to compensate; hence the most direct effect of parental behavior occurs when that behavior is punitive and depriving. This fact suggests that the Postulate of Identification holds better when the parental behavior is extremely negative, that is, harsh discipline, emotional rejection. Thus the subjects were divided into the cells shown in Table 5–17 (division of the subjects was made by partitioning the standard scores into four parts by dividing the scores at the mean, and one standard deviation above and below the mean).

TABLE 5–17. Classification of Subjects According to PRP Measures of Parental Warmth and Discipline

| | | PARENTAL WARMTH (LESS WARM PARENT) | | | |
		Very Warm	*Warm*	*Cool*	*Very Cool*
	Strong Discipline	Very warm, strong discipline	Warm, strong discipline	Cool, strong discipline	Very cool, strong discipline
PARENTAL DISCIPLINE	*Moderate Discipline*	Very warm, moderate discipline	Warm, moderate discipline	Cool, moderate discipline	Very cool, moderate discipline
(MORE DISCIPLINARY PARENT)	*Little Discipline*	Very warm, little discipline	Warm, little discipline	Cool, little discipline	Very cool, little discipline
	No Discipline	Very warm, no discipline	Warm, no discipline	Cool, no discipline	Very cool, no discipline

Since there were sixty subjects and sixteen cells, the number of subjects in any one cell was usually small. However, several suggestive results emerged from these small samples.

Members who fell in the cell representing the combination, "very warm, moderate discipline," had a definite tendency to concentrate on behavior in the area of positive affection. There were only three persons in this cell, but all three were very consistent with respect to the affection area and not similar in any other area. Their mean scores (McCall T–scores are used throughout, where mean is 50 and standard deviation, 10) on several measures of affection behavior are shown in Table 5–18. A score of 55 or above and 45 or below is significantly different from 50 at the .01 level.

TABLE 5–18. Mean Scores of "Very Warm–Moderate Discipline" Subjects on Various Measures (McCall T-scores)

1. Attempts to Be Liked (Sociometric Rating)	59
2. Attempts to Promote Personal Feelings (Sociometric)	56
3. Attempts to Promote Personal Feelings (Observer)	63
4. Attempts to Be Liked (Observer Rating)	61
5. Succeeds in Promoting Personal Feelings (Observer)	63

It appears that individuals from a very warm, moderately permissive home try to foster the warm climate in a group situation. This fact gives support to the notion, stated in the extreme, that smothered children become overpersonal adults.

In the cell representing "very cool, strong discipline" homes (eight subjects) another interesting picture emerges (Table 5–19). (Only measures are given in which at least seven of the eight scored the same direction above or below the mean.)

TABLE 5–19. Mean Scores of "Very Cool–Strong Discipline" Subjects on Various Measures (McCall T-scores)

1. Need for Affiliation (PPS)	45
2. Need for Succorance (PPS)	44
3. Need for Abasement (PPS)	45
4. Need for Autonomy (PPS)	57
5. Use of Projection (DPI)	59
6. Use of Regression (DPI)	55
7. Punitive Social Attitudes (Discussion Tasks)	72% vs. 46% (for other subjects)
8. Tendency to Change Opinion through Discussion (Discussion Tasks)	3% vs. 17% (for other subjects)

The description of these subjects from homes in which there were much discipline and little warmth, revolves around rejection of personal contact and personal dependence, and the strong need to be self-reliant. Together with this occur rather punitive attitudes toward others (the discussion tasks, listed in Appendix B, measured disciplinary vs. permissive attitudes in a variety of "real-life" situations.)

It is interesting to compare this picture with the more extreme situation found in Nazi concentration camps (15) and other situations where identification with the aggressor is found. These internees were subjected to an adult experience similar to that of these experimental subjects in the sense of having had a repressive home life, and the reaction seems to have been to identify with this treatment. In addition, the use of denial, so common in the affection area, operates here very strongly. The underpersonal reaction to lack of affection and emotional dependence is avoided. It is interesting to note that the above were the only measures (of over 100) on which these subjects were similar. This result, which is consistent with that of the first group described, indicates that the cells of Table 5–17 may describe individuals whose adult behavior converges only in a limited area; for example, the "very warm, moderate discipline" children were alike only in affection. This result supports the identification principle in that unloved children become underpersonal and dominated children become autocratic.

If we move to the left of this cell we find an interesting and theoretically reasonable change. The "cool, strong discipline" cell shows the characteristics (five subjects) listed in Table 5–20.

TABLE 5–20. Mean Scores of "Cool–Strong Discipline" Subjects on Various Measures (McCall T-scores)

1. Authoritarianism (F Scale)	62
2. Individualism (VP)	55
3. Use of Avoidance (DPI)	43
4. Punitive Social Attitudes (Discussion Task)	75% vs. 46% (for other subjects)

The interesting difference from the previous group is that as warmth changes from "very cool" to "cool" the problems in the affection area that loomed so large before are now not in evidence. Since the home life of the group differs in that this group received more affection, relational continuity seems to receive added confirmation. Instead of concern over affection come a heightened authoritarianism and general concern in the control area. This group seems to offer a purer illustration that dominated children tend to become autocratic, but home life was not sufficiently lacking in warmth to cause consistently underpersonal behavior.

In the above report of results, mention was made of a derived measure of attention to correspond to the area of inclusion. It is assumed that the lower three right-hand cells best approximate "little attention": "very cool, little discipline," "very cool, no discipline," "cool, no discipline." In all three cases it seems that little attention of any kind was paid to the child. When these three cells were taken together ($N = 6$), the measures (shown in Table 5–21) proved striking (no measure is reported in which at least five of the six subjects did not fall on the same side of the mean):

TABLE 5–21. Mean Scores of "Little Attention" Subjects on Various Measures (McCall T-scores)

1. Participation (FIRO–1)	41
2. Dominance (IPC, Self-description)	43
3. Participation (Observer Ratings)	44
4. Use of Intellectualization (DPI)	57

Here the tendency reported above is more extensively substantiated. The strong tendency for these people who lacked attention in their home is to be low participators, and low in dominance. The defense of intellectualization is probably part of the introverted pattern. This pattern gives support to the idea that abandoned children become withdrawn adults.

These results are obviously only suggestive, but on the whole they are very promising and congruent with the rest of the theory. They indicate that a concerted research effort on the different home atmospheres, in terms of the three need areas, should be fruitful for predicting adult interpersonal behavior.

PART II

Interaction

of Individuals

6

The Postulate of Compatibility: Measurement

Postulate 3. *The Postulate of Compatibility.* **If the compatibility of one group, h, is greater than that of another group, m, then the goal achievement of h will exceed that of m.**

Up to this point discussion has centered around the individual's orientations to interpersonal relations. This chapter introduces the section on the interaction of individuals. The next four chapters deal with various aspects of this interaction. The discussion in Chapter 7 first focuses on the relation between the interpersonal orientations of individual group members and their feelings and behavior toward one another. Then these orientations are related to more general characteristics, such as productivity and cohesiveness, of the entire group. The relation between the ICA framework and such concepts as "role," "sanction," and "norm" is described in Chapter 8. A conception of the developmental process through which all interpersonal relations pass is presented in Chapter 9.

The central concept used in the theoretical explanation of the interaction of the individuals is "compatibility." This chapter presents a definition of compatibility of any two or more persons. The postulate of compatibility is discussed in the succeeding chapters as well as in this one.

EXPLANATION

Compatibility is a property of a relation between two or more persons, between an individual and a role, or between an individual and a task situation, that leads to mutual satisfaction of interpersonal needs and harmonious coexistence. Since this term is central to the ensuing theoretical development, it must be given a more precise definition. This process of making an already used term more precise has been called "explication" by Carnap (22):

> "By the procedure of explication we mean the transformation of an inexact, prescientific concept, the *explicandum,* into a new exact concept, the *explicatum.*"

This procedure applies to "compatibility," a term which has acquired many meanings through past usage; it is now to be transformed into a more exact term. The criteria for determining the adequacy of the new term, the explicatum, are given by Carnap as (1) similarity to the explicandum, (2) exactness, (3) fruitfulness, (4) simplicity. These criteria form the basis for the introduction of the term "compatibility."

The definition of "compatibility" should be similar to the explicandum; that is, it should retain most of the usual meanings of "compatibility." "Compatibility" is defined by Webster as "being capable of co-existing in harmony." It is best explicated sociometrically by the relation "works well with." Compatibility does not necessarily imply liking. It is probable that often liking and compatibility are linked, but it is rather simple to recognize dyads (two people) who work well together without any particular liking, and dyads who like each other but don't work well together effectively.

Exactness of the definition is a criterion that is met by defining particular types of compatibility in mathematical terms based on scale scores derived from FIRO–B. For any dyad a precise compatibility score may be assigned, and the reliability (stability) of that score may be determined. Evidence for the fruitfulness of defining "compatibility" as is done on the following pages must await presentation of the data which follow in the next chapter. Even now, however, there is some demonstrated fruitfulness in that this definition allows the term to be used in a theory and related to several other terms in the theory. Simplicity is a criterion met by the fact that the mathematical operations used to define "compatibility" are no more complicated than addition and subtraction, and that the conceptions are kept simple and straightforward. The use of only three major variables also aids in simplifying the concept.

In order to develop the various types of compatibility it is necessary to consider more closely the two measures yielded by FIRO–B in each area, expressed behavior (e), and behavior wanted from others (w), and the diagrams presented in Chapter 4.

There are two main types of compatibility. These can be understood best by considering the diagonals of the diagram below. The high-interchange quadrant represents those who prefer a great deal of exchange of the "commodity" (interaction, power, love) relevant to the area. The low-interchange quadrant includes those who wish to avoid exchange of the appropriate commodity, those who neither initiate nor want to receive inclusion, control, or affection. In order to be compatible, two people should be similar with respect to the interchange variable (this point is discussed at greater length in the

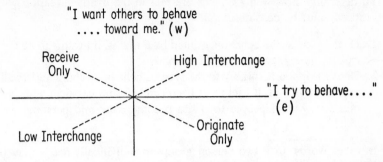

FIGURE 6–1. General Schema for Interpersonal Behavior Measured by FIRO–B

section on plausibility, p. 116). Compatibility based on similarity along this diagonal is called *interchange compatibility* and symbolized by xK (for "exchange," a close synonym).

The other diagonal goes from those who desire only to initiate or originate behavior to those who wish only to receive it, for example, the autocratic-undirected and the abdicratic-dominated. On this diagonal, two people should complement each other, that is, be equidistant from the center in opposite directions, in order to be compatible. Compatibility based on complementarity along this diagonal is called *originator compatibility* and symbolized as oK.

A similar measure derived from the major axes rather than the diagonals is based on the assumption that the expressed behavior of one member of a dyad must equal the wanted behavior of the other member, and vice versa. This is called *reciprocal compatibility,* and symbolized as rK. It differs from originator compatibility (oK) in certain interesting ways, the significance of which is still under study.

Reciprocal Compatibility (rK)

The theory thus far presented describes each individual as desiring a certain optimal relation between himself and others in each need area. For the dyad this theory means that a person wants to act a certain way toward the other, and wants to be acted toward in a certain way. If the responses of people to self-description questionnaires are considered a reasonably accurate picture of their behavior—as the evidence presented later seems to indicate—then the measure of how well two people will satisfy each other's needs follows directly. By comparing A's description of how he likes to be acted toward with B's description of how he likes to act toward people, and vice versa, a measure of mutual need satisfaction emerges. Of course, there is one important assumption underlying this statement. A could describe the behavior he desires in other persons along an infinite number of dimensions. The important ones are assumed to be inclusion, control, and affection, those measured by FIRO–B.

To determine how well *i*'s needs are met in the dyadic situation with *j*, two aspects must be considered:

1. Does *j* express the behavior wanted by *i*; that is, if *i* wants to be controlled, does *j* tend to control people?
2. Does *j* respond favorably to the type of behavior *i* characteristically expresses; that is, if *i* tends to become close and personal with people, does *j* want people to try to become close and personal with him?

In other words, in a two-person group an individual's needs may be frustrated if the other person does not satisfy them ("He doesn't give me what I want") or if the individual is not able to express his preferred behavior toward this person ("I can't act the way I like to when I'm with him").

Reciprocal compatibility (*rK*) may be indicated quantitatively by letting e_i and e_j stand for the score on the expressed behavior ("I try to act toward others") for the first and second members of the dyad, respectively, and w_i and w_j, the score of the behavior wanted from others ("I like people to act toward me ..."), for the two members of the dyad. A comparison is made between the way member *i* likes to be acted toward (w_i) and the way member *j* likes to act toward others (e_j), and similarly between w_j and e_i. The smaller the discrepancy between each pair of scores, the better will each person satisfy the needs of the other. Hence a measure of the reciprocal compatibility of persons *i* and *j* is given by

$$rK_{ij} = |e_i - w_j| + |e_j - w_i|.$$

Absolute measures are used, since at this point the main concern is with the size rather than the direction of differences. The name for this type of compatibility is derived from the fact that it reflects the degree to which members of a dyad reciprocally satisfy each other's behavior preferences.

Originator Compatibility (oK)

Originator compatibility is based more directly on the originate-receive axis. Individual scores falling along this diagonal are interpreted as follows:

1. In the inclusion area, a preference for applying, joining, or always being in interpersonal activities but not wanting to be asked in by others (originate only), as opposed to never actively participating but waiting to be asked or invited to join (receive only).
2. In the control area, a preference for always dominating and controlling the actions of others and strongly resisting their influence (originate only), as opposed to always being influenced and never being influential (receive only).
3. In the affection area, a preference for loving over being loved (orig-

inate only), as opposed to the passive role of being loved without loving (receive only).

For two people to operate effectively together, their preferred behavior regarding originating and receiving should be complementary.

Originator compatibility in each area occurs when

1. People who very actively initiate group activities work with those who want to be included in such activities (inclusion).
2. Those who wish to dominate and control the activities of others work with those who want to be controlled (control).
3. Those who wish to give affection work with those who want to receive affection (affection).

Conflict arises when there is disagreement regarding preference of who shall originate relations and who shall receive them. For each need area (I,C,A) there are two types of conflict: between two originators, *competitive originator incompatibility,* and between two receivers, *apathetic originator incompatibility.* (All examples given use extreme cases for clarity of presentation. In any interpersonal relation there is a scale of attitudes toward these problems, and differences often revolve around shades of gray rather than black and white.)

1. In the inclusion area, the competitive conflict is between two persons each of whom wants to "select his own company." Each wants only to join the activities he wishes but not to have others join him. The apathetic conflict is between two persons; both want to be included, but neither will act to join the other. (oK^I)

2. In the control area, the competitive conflict is between two persons each of whom wants to be dominant and run the activities but does not want to be told what to do. This situation is exemplified by the familiar power struggle. The apathetic conflict in this area is between two submissive people each of whom wants to be told what to do but neither of whom will take the initiative in doing it. This situation arises with a boss who cannot make decisions and an employee with no "initiative." (oK^C)

3. In the affection area, the competitive conflict is between two who desire to originate close relations but not to receive them. An example is the Don Juan for whom pursuit is an end in itself and reciprocation is threatening. The apathetic conflict is between two who want to be liked but do not want to initiate it. An example is the two coworkers secretly fond of each other but neither ever initiating a personal relation. (oK^A)

To obtain a measure of originator compatibility (oK) a score for each individual, to express his degree of preference for initiating and not receiving, is obtained. The simplest measure of this preference is the difference between the expressed and wanted aspects of a given need area, that is, $(e_i - w_i)$.

Highest compatibility occurs when the two persons' scores are complementary. Complementarity of two scores is measured by adding algebraically two originator scores. If they are exactly complementary, that is, have the same value with opposite signs, their scores will add to zero. If both persons prefer to originate rather than receive, the sum of their scores will be positive, reflecting competitive incompatibility. If both prefer receiving, the sum of their scores will be negative, indicating apathetic incompatibility. For the computation of originator compatibility, therefore, the sign is retained to indicate competitive or apathetic types of incompatibility. Hence the originator compatibility of persons i and j is given by

$$oK_{ij} = (e_i - w_i) + (e_j - w_j),$$

with the sign of oK_{ij} positive if $[(e_i - w_i) + (e_j - w_j)]$ is greater than zero, and negative if it is less than zero.

Interchange Compatibility (xK)

A third type of compatibility highlights a different aspect of the dyadic relation. The situations covered by reciprocal and originator compatibility refer to need satisfactions by a specific person. The measures are most appropriate for dyads. It is also useful to speak of a general context or "atmosphere" in which a relationship exists. *Interchange* refers to the mutual expression of the "commodity" of a given need area. For example, high affection interchange refers to a situation in which all participants exchange a good deal of affectional behavior and feelings, such as in a close family situation. Low control interchange refers to a situation in which there is little controlling of the behavior of others by anyone, as in a laissez-faire schoolroom situation or a Quaker meeting. High inclusion interchange refers to a situation in which there is a great deal of contact between persons, as in a submarine or in a jury session. Preferred amount of interchange is a characteristic of both an individual and a group. The dimension high interchange–low interchange for an individual has these characteristics:

1. In the area of inclusion, high interchange means high interaction with others in terms of general activities, a desire to associate with others and to have them associate with the self, as opposed to being separated from them and being alone (low interchange).

2. In the area of control, high interchange means a preference to be both influenced or controlled by others and to influence or control their actions, as opposed to neither influencing nor being influenced by others (low interchange).

3. In the area of affection, high interchange means a preference for close personal relations both toward people and from them toward the self, as opposed to maintaining affectional distance (low interchange).

With regard to the interchange axis, two individuals' scores should be similar for maximum compatibility, since interchange, like atmosphere, is something that must be mutually shared in order to satisfy the members of the dyad. In the three need areas, interchange compatibility means

1. In the area of inclusion, people must agree on how involved they like to become with other persons, varying from always with others to always alone.

2. In the area of control, people must agree on how much of an authority structure they will operate under, varying from entirely structured to entirely unstructured.

3. In the area of affection, people must agree on the same degree of closeness of personal feelings, of expression of confidences, and so forth, varying from close and intimate to very cool and distant.

Incompatibility of the interchange variety (xK) arises when members of the dyad disagree on the amount of interchange in a particular area of interpersonal relations. Specifically,

1. In inclusion, the conflict is between the joiner and participator who always likes to do things "together" (high interchange) and the withdrawn person who prefers to be by himself (low interchange). The introvert-extravert distinction is relevant here. (xK^I)

2. In control, the conflict is between the conformist and the rebel. The one who wants to follow the rules from above and enforce the rules below (high interchange), with the one who wants to do neither (low interchange). The former is very much like the authoritarian, while the latter resembles the anarchist. (xK^C)

3. In affection, the conflict is between the affectionate, expressive person who likes others to be the same (high interchange) and the more reserved, distant individual who prefers that others keep their emotional distance (low interchange). It occurs when one person likes to be personal, intimate, and confiding, while the other does not want to discuss personal matters. This problem often arises in the marital situation. (xK^A)

To measure interchange compatibility, one further assumption must be made. The amount of interchange an individual desires may be measured by combining his scores on both the expressed and wanted scales. The major diagonal is thus assumed to be a direct measure of interchange. That is, each individual's score is the point on the graph obtained by projecting both the expressed and wanted scale scores onto the major diagonal. Analogous to the situation with originator compatibility, this value is conveyed by the sum of the two scores $(e_i + w_i)$. This value for an individual is called his *interchange score*.

Since the more similar two persons' scores are on this diagonal the more compatible the persons are, to measure compatibility one score is simply subtracted from the other. Further, since the direction of the difference is not important, the absolute value of the difference is sufficient. Hence the interchange compatibility score for two persons, i and j, is given by

$$xK_{ij} = |(e_i + w_i) - (e_j + w_j)|.$$

The interpretation of xK is analogous to rK and oK; the smaller the value of xK, the greater the interchange compatibility. It appears likely that this type of compatibility will be even more relevant for groups larger than two. (For larger groups a measure of dispersion is used to assess compatibility.) Since an individual entering a larger group usually finds it difficult to relate directly to one person, he must interact with the group as a whole. The atmosphere of the group may be described in terms of the amount of interchange occurring in each need area; hence his satisfaction would be determined to a large extent by the atmosphere into which he enters. This fact suggests, incidentally, that the often used term "group atmosphere" may be explicated by the concept of interchange. That is, what may be usually meant by group atmosphere is the degree to which there is inclusion interchange (amount of contact and interaction), control interchange (giving and taking orders, advice, and the like), and affection interchange (expressions of closeness, intimacy, and emotional involvement with one another) present in the group.

Need Compatibility (nK)

The final type of compatibility depends on the *relative importance* of the interpersonal need areas. It is different from the other types of compatibility, in that it deals with the relations *among* interpersonal need areas rather than examines relations *within* areas. When people get together, one of their primary problems is to decide what they are going to do and to discuss together how they are going to do it. For example, if one person is overpersonal he will be deeply interested in interacting in the affection area. But if a second person has no special problems in the personal area, and is autocratic and must prove his capabilities, he may be impatient with affection interchange and desire control interchange. The measure of this type of compatibility has not yet been worked on extensively; therefore no formulas will be offered. The ASIA questionnaire (see Appendix B) is designed to measure the relative salience of the need areas. It is hoped that the further development of the ASIA questionnaire will lead to a better measure of need compatibility.

Summary

Four types of compatibility have been introduced. Originator compatibility (oK) is based essentially on the originate-receive diagonal of the diagram in Figure 6–1. Reciprocal compatibility (rK) is similar to oK but is based on major axes of that diagram. Interchange compatibility (xK) is based on the high interchange–low interchange diagonal of that diagram. Need compatibility (nK) is derived from a relation among need areas.

In the formulation of the formulas for these types of compatibility two details should be noted: (a) the subscript *ij* denoting individuals will customarily be understood to apply to each compatibility symbol, and will always be omitted except where the meaning is unclear; (b) since for each measure of compatibility a low score means high compatibility, the formulas actually give a direct measure of *in*compatibility. If for some application of the formulas it becomes desirable to have a high score mean high compatibility, the expression in each formula can simply be subtracted from the maximum score, 18.

To review the formulas for compatibility presented so far:

I. Reciprocal Compatibility

$$rK = |e_i - w_j| + |e_j - w_i|$$

II. Originator Compatibility

$$oK = (e_i - w_i) + (e_j - w_j)$$

III. Interchange Compatibility

$$xK = |(e_i + w_i) - (e_j + w_j)|$$

Compatibility Indices

Combining compatibility scores raises one additional problem. In general, several scores may be combined to obtain a composite measure. For example, all measures of compatibility in the affection area may be combined to obtain a general measure of *affection compatibility,* which will be symbolized, K^A:

$$K^A = f(rK^A, oK^A, xK^A).$$

The other type of combination produces a measure for each *type* of compatibility over all need areas. For example, *total reciprocal compatibility* (rK) over all areas:

$$rK = f(rK^I, rK^C, rK^A).$$

The next decision involves the method of combining values to obtain the summary measures. This decision requires a consideration of the relative importance of each measure, which, in turn involves a theoretical consideration.

For the measure of an *area compatibility* (K^I, K^C, K^A) the weight given to each *type of compatibility* (rK, oK, xK) will depend upon the relative importance of each type for the purpose under consideration. The only discrimination mentioned thus far is that rK and oK may be more important for dyadic compatibility, whereas xK may be more important for the compatibility of groups greater than two. In this case, if group compatibility were being measured, it would be reasonable to weight xK more heavily; for example, one weighting might be

$$K^I = rK^I + oK^I + 2xK^I.$$

However, the data thus far available do not provide sufficient information for such weighting. The area compatibilities therefore will be obtained by the simplest form of combination—simple addition with equal weighting. For the present, then, the following formulas will be used to compute area compatibilities:

$$K^I = rK^I + oK^I + xK^I,$$
$$K^C = rK^C + oK^C + xK^C,$$
$$K^A = rK^A + oK^A + xK^A.$$

For the measure of a type of compatibility, the weight given to each area of compatibility depends on the relative importance of each area for a specific purpose. In subsequent chapters this problem is explored more fully. For purposes of definition it is sufficient to say that, when inclusion behavior is occurring, compatibility in the inclusion area is most important; when control behavior occurs, compatibility in the control area is most important; and when affection behavior occurs, affection compatibility is the most important element of the total compatibility. Weights may then be assigned to each area compatibility to determine the most useful total measure.

Let θ_I, θ_C, θ_A equal a coefficient for each area compatibility. Then

$$rK = \theta_I rK^I + \theta_C rK^C + \theta_A rK^A.$$

When interaction is primarily in the affection area, as, for example, in the later stages of a well-integrated group (see Chapter 9), then $\theta_A > \theta_C$ and $\theta_A > \theta_I$. This property holds for each area. The above condition defines the properties of θ. Thus

$$rK = \theta_I rK^I + \theta_C rK^C + \theta_A rK^A,$$
$$oK = \theta_I oK^I + \theta_C oK^C + \theta_A oK^A,$$
$$xK = \theta_I xK^I + \theta_C xK^C + \theta_A xK^A.$$

Total compatibility (K) can be computed by combining either area compatibilities or compatibility types, and extending the logic presented above:

$$K = \theta_I K^I + \theta_C K^C + \theta_A K^A = rK + oK + xK.$$

Another approach to the problem of weighting involves the use of empirical regression equations, that is, to weight the various compatibility measures differently for different situations, depending on which weightings afford the highest prediction. This method may be used to supplement the rational approach mentioned above.

To summarize all types of compatibility and their relations to one another it is helpful to present them in the matrix form shown in Table 6–1.

TABLE 6–1. Relations between Compatibility Measures

		AREAS OF COMPATIBILITY			
		I	C	A	Row Sums
TYPES OF	r	$\theta_I r K^I$	$\theta_C r K^C$	$\theta_A r K^A$	rK
COMPATI-	o	$\theta_I o K^I$	$\theta_C o K^C$	$\theta_A o K^A$	oK
BILITY	x	$\theta_I x K^I$	$\theta_C x K^C$	$\theta_A x K^A$	xK
Column Sums		$\theta_I K^I$	$\theta_C K^C$	$\theta_A K^A$	K Total

The sum of rows defines rK, oK, and xK, while the sum of columns defines $\theta_I K^I$, $\theta_C K^C$, and $\theta_A K^A$. Both the sum of rows and the sum of columns add to K and constitute the definitions of K given above. The θ coefficients are included in the terms that include rK, oK, and xK, while they are multipliers for K^I, K^C, and K^A. Although the two definitions of K are mathematically equivalent, they have interesting psychological differences, one set dealing with compatibility for each interpersonal need area and the other dealing with different types of compatibility.

These remarks complete the definition of compatibility. From this point on, the term compatibility and the symbol K will have the meaning described above. This definition constitutes an explication of the term "compatibility" in the sense discussed earlier; the remaining terms in Postulate 3 will now be discussed.

Goal Achievement (g)

Goal achievement is the degree of optimal performance toward a goal. It is defined specifically in terms of what the group members want rather than what is imposed on them from outside. This distinction is important, since some studies (76) have indicated that a cohesive group will do a worse job if the members don't want to do what is imposed upon them. Defining group goal in this way avoids the problem of whether or not external motivation is a condition for good group performance. That is, if members of the group do not want to do their assigned task, compatibility will contribute to their efficiency in *not* doing it (for example, a compatible group should be more capable of mutiny). The problem of motivation for a group to do a job assigned by a boss can be dealt with by including the boss as a group member and assessing the compatibility of the group, and what they accept as their goal. Examples of group goals are productivity, cohesion, and satisfaction. Examples of goals more appropriate to dyads are liking, working with, and respecting. The Postulate of Compatibility states that the more compatible the group, the more it will approximate its goals. In the above examples, in other words, the members of the compatible group will be more productive, more cohesive, more satisfied, like one another more, work better together, and respect one another more than will those of the incompatible group. These are only a few examples; group goals may include any aim desired by the group.

Optimal Performance

Performance toward the achievement of a group goal is defined in terms of how closely the group approaches its own optimal performance, rather than how closely it approaches an absolute standard. The reason for this definition is evident in the following example: a highly compatible group of grammar school children could not be expected to *defeat* the most incompatible professional football team; however, they would perform better relative to their physical and mental limitations. Often there are practical difficulties determining what an optimal performance is for a given group. However, for purposes of testing the compatibility postulate, this difficulty can be circumvented by equating groups with respect to ability and varying compatibility. *Hence g is the degree to which a group approaches its own optimal performance toward its self-specified goal.*

PLAUSIBILITY

Compatibility refers to the successful operation of an interpersonal relation. The less compatible the relation, the more time must be spent in finding ways of dealing with the difficulties. Thus there is less energy available to devote to a task, and there is more internal dissatisfaction. Again it is important to mention that compatibility does not necessarily imply liking. It has mainly to do with ability to work together successfully.

Interpersonal difficulty is almost inevitably converted into task difficulty. When someone makes a suggestion early in a group meeting, it is not easy for someone else to say, "Your suggestion is all right, but I don't want your idea to be the one that gets accepted because I want to be the leader of this group." But it is quite acceptable for him to say, "Yes, that's not a bad idea, but I think it might be better if we did this." The merits of suggestions often become secondary to their use as instruments for attaining interpersonal ends. One familiar result of this is prolonged, apparently pointless discussions about trivia, such as procedural matters or length of coffee break. These topics are useful to the group, however, because they provide a vehicle for expressing interpersonal needs. They also function as "goblet issues"— issues for sizing up one another—which will be discussed in Chapter 9.

The general plausibility argument for the Postulate of Compatibility runs as follows. Consider, for example, a group consisting of some members who desire low affection interchange (underpersonal) and some who desire high affection interchange (overpersonal). The overpersonals are strongly oriented toward having close personal relations with the group members, while the underpersonals have a strong need to avoid relating in a close personal fashion. These needs can seldom be expressed directly; therefore they are usually expressed in terms of the task on which the group is working. For example, if the group is trying to solve a chess-type problem together, the overpersonals will tend to focus on the person who gives a suggestion and respond partly on that basis, while the underpersonals might tend to ignore pointedly the source of suggestion and respond entirely to its content; hence the overpersonals are more likely to notice the suggestion of a usually silent member than would the underpersonals.

This disagreement on how the decision-making process should proceed will be a constant source of friction and make cooperation difficult. The difficulty arises, *not* from disagreement among members on specific issues that confront the group, but rather from the problems arising in finding *a technique for resolving these disagreements.* Each decision on which there is less than initial unanimity will cause difficulty for the group. Another example may clarify this notion. The story of the relation between Van Gogh and Gauguin when they lived together is an excellent demonstration of affection interchange incompatibility (xK^A). Van Gogh was a man of high sensibilities and great needs for giving and receiving love—often stating that to him these were the only things which mattered. Gauguin, on the other hand, was the epitome of the controlled emotion, underpersonal, who, for example, carefully avoided a strong relation with one woman by enjoying a rapid turnover. These basic interpersonal propensities were expressed directly in the artistic productions of the two men, Van Gogh featuring the vivid, strong, emotional style, while Gauguin strove for controlled, minimally emotional productions. The near-homicidal outcome of their furious relation lends plausibility to the incompatibility of such a combination. Clearly, they had difficulty working together.

Interchange incompatibility in the control area (xK^C) commonly arises over the reaction to structure in the group. It is a common phenomenon (14), especially in unstructured groups, for a division to form early in the group's history between those who like "structure," that is, an established hierarchy with each member's role clearly stated and delineated (autocrats), and those who want the group "unstructured," that is, without power differences or pecking orders but with freedom for members to work out each problem as it arises (abdicrats). This difference pervades all decision making, just as did the affection interchange incompatibility in the Van Gogh example, since it refers to the whole process by which people will relate to one another regarding decision making, and not just to specific disagreements.

An example of inclusion interchange incompatibility (xK^I) is commonly found in the interdisciplinary research teams so prevalent today in industry, government, and universities. There is frequently a conflict between those who prefer to work in teams (oversocial) and those who prefer working alone (undersocial). Again this difference affects the decision-making procedure, since whenever a decision must be made, the members of one group have the tendency to work it out together, while those of the other group tend to retire by themselves to find a solution.

Thus in all three situations interchange incompatibility leads to difficulty in the procedure of decision making. When a decision arises, there is division regarding whether the decision should be made together or alone; by people in charge or by the decision of the group as a whole; and by considering the personal feelings involved or ignoring emotional factors. This type of incompatibility often leads to the feeling, "Oh, what's the use; we keep running into the same troubles time after time."

As a result of originator incompatibility, different types of difficulties arise in the group. Inclusion originator incompatibility (oK^I), as in all the originator incompatibilities, is of two types, competitive and apathetic. The competitive type arises when both people wish to associate only in relations they originate, and balk at anyone else trying to bring them together. This occurs when several people in a group want to remain together only at their own suggestion (such as, "Come on over to my house") but not at someone else's suggestion; the result is difficulty in getting together. The apathetic incompatibility occurs when both persons merely wait to be invited and neither invites. This is the type of relation that never gets started or is often described as "dull."

Control originator incompatibility (oK^C) is one of the more common types. The competitive mode occurs when several members struggle for leadership and none will accept the leadership of the other. This situation leads to power struggles that are usually easily observable. Sometimes, however, the struggle by some members is more covert and difficult to observe; nevertheless, the incompatibility is usually felt by the group members. The apathetic form of oK^C occurs when no one is willing to make suggestions and everyone wants to be told what to do. The result is that usually nothing is accomplished.

Affection originator incompatibility (oK^A) of the competitive type occurs when all members of an interpersonal relation want to give affection but not receive it. This ordinarily leads to the situation where all feel uncomfortable and frustrated. The apathetic type is a fairly common cause of divorce, namely, a relation in which both partners want to receive love but neither is willing to give it.

Hence in originator incompatibiltiy there is always difficulty in the assignment of initiating and receiving roles to various members. In the competitive type, incompatibility leads to the general feeling of struggle and conflict. Apathetic incompatibility leads more to a feeling of emptiness and boredom in the relation. Reciprocal incompatibility follows originator incompatibility so closely that it is not worth while to detail the various types.

The reader is reminded that these types represent logical and existent types but not necessarily equally frequent types. From past experience it is probable that the most frequent types are all three types of interchange incompatibility, apathetic inclusion, competitive control, and apathetic affection. Further, the exampes given are not always pure cases of the type of incompatibility they illustrate but serve simply to concretize the category.

It seems plausible that the types of incompatibilities listed above which are derived from theory include at least most of the types commonly experienced or experimentally uncovered. Winch (95), for example, found evidence for what is called here control originator incompatibility (oK^c). The maxims mentioned above, "Birds of a feather flock together," and "Opposites attract," can be explicated as the interchange and originator compatibilities. Need incompatibility ("He's not interested in the same things I am") has not yet been adequately researched; therefore the data presented in the next chapter will be relevant only to the other types of compatibility. However, in the last section of Chapter 7, "Future Research," the approach to a new measuring instrument for exploring need compatibility is discussed.

Since all these types of incompatibilities lead to difficulties with decision making, productivity is interfered with. Since incompatibility leads to frustration and nonfulfillment of needs, there will be less likelihood of successful personal relations.

In the following chapter the results of several large-scale experiments are presented. These experiments were designed to test the ideas presented in this chapter and summarized in the Postulate of Compatibility. They constitute the empirical evidence relevant to the evidential probability of the Postulate of Compatibility.

7

The Postulate of Compatibility:
Evidence

EVIDENCE

Theorem 3–1. **If the compatibility of one dyad, y_1, is greater than the compatibility of another dyad, y_2, then the members of y_1 are more likely to prefer each other for continued personal contact.**

Evidence for Theorem 3–1 comes from a study of a college fraternity. In addition to providing this evidence, the study will be helpful in demonstrating various techniques of data analysis that use the formulas in the preceding chapter, since it is the first empirical application of the compatibility formulas for oK, rK, and xK. Further, the richness of the types of analysis of the data suggested by the compatibility postulate will provide evidence for the third criterion of explication, fruitfulness of the definition of compatibility. The success of this study is partly dependent on the adequacy of the explicatum, "compatibility," and partly on the truth of Theorem 3–1; hence the fruitfulness criterion is subjected to test. The presentation of this study thus has the following functions:

1. Evidence for Theorem 3–1
2. Demonstration of techniques of data analysis using compatibility formulas
3. Demonstration of fruitfulness of the explication of "compatibility"
4. Demonstration of fertility of the entire theory

The original fraternity study was carried out, and the data made available to the author, by Alexander, Gonzales, Herminghaus, Marwell, and Wheeless. Their own findings appear in a term paper (3).

The Fraternity Study

PURPOSE

The objective of this study was to explore the relations between interpersonal orientations ("personality") and specific dyadic relations in a fraternity. In particular, it was undertaken to test the usefulness of the definitions of compatibility described above for the prediction of several sociometric relations among group members.

SUBJECTS

One complete fraternity from Massachusetts Institute of Technology numbering thirty-three members was used for this study. A fairly typical cross section of Eastern college fraternity men, it included freshmen, sophomores, juniors, and seniors.

PROCEDURE

All subjects were given FIRO–5B3 and a sociometric questionnaire. The actual administration of the test was carried out by a member of the fraternity "who held a position of trust and respect." (p. 8)

"The sociometric test consisted of questions designed to determine the true feelings of the members of the fraternity about each other. The questions covered a range of likes and dislikes of members in situations of close personal relations, and also the choice of leaders." (p. 8)

The two main relations inquired about were roommate and traveling companion. The remainder of the questions referred to fraternity offices. The FIRO–5B3 tests were scored for all men, and three types of compatibility (rK, oK, xK) were computed for each need area for each dyad. Every dyad therefore received nine compatibility scores, each ranging from 0 to 18. A distribution was made of the scores of every fraternity member with those of every other member for each type of compatibility, and the median located. Everyone above the median was considered compatible with that member on the particular type of compatibility being measured, and everyone below the median considered incompatible.

For example, assume the scale scores shown in Table 7–1 on e^I and w^I for eleven people, and assume we are computing oK^I [$=(e_i{}^I-w_i{}^I)+(e_j{}^I-w_j{}^I)$].

TABLE 7–1. Hypothetical Scores on e^I and w^I for Eleven Subjects

Subject	e^I	w^I	$e^I - w^I$
A	9	2	7
B	7	1	6
C	2	6	−4
D	0	4	−4
E	8	9	−1
F	1	8	−7
G	9	2	7
H	6	0	6
I	4	4	0
J	3	1	2
K	5	3	2

For subject A we computed oK^I with all other subjects and divided these scores at the median (Table 7–2).

TABLE 7–2. oK^I Scores for Subject A with Other Subjects Divided at Median

	Subject A									
	B	C	D	E	F	G	H	I	J	K
$oK_a \cdot^I =$	13	3	3	6	0	14	13	7	9	9
Compatibility $=$	−	+	+	+	+	−	−	+	−	−

Plus means above the median, or "compatible." A lower score indicates greater compatibility; hence for each member the other members are divided in half and considered "compatible" or "incompatible" for each measure, namely, oK^I, oK^C, oK^A, rK^I, rK^C, rK^A, xK^I, xK^C, xK^A. In addition, various combinations are made from these basic measures.

With this data, sociometric choices may be explored to determine the compatibility of the chooser and chosen. For example, if A selected D he selected a compatible person. The proportion of those actually selecting a "compatible" person may be compared with the chance probability of selecting a compatible person, namely, one-half. This type of analysis may be carried out for each type of compatibility.

RESULTS

Roommate. The following question was asked on the sociometric questionnaire: "Thinking of all the members of your fraternity, which three men would you pick to room with next semester (in order)?"

The results shown in Table 7–3 were obtained by computing the percentage of people choosing a compatible member as first choice for roommate, as described above (chance is approximately 50 per cent).

Roommate is frequently a relation of high interchange in all need areas. In Chapter 9 the development of interpersonal relations is postulated as going through the ordered sequence: inclusion, control, and affection. Longer and closer relations become primarily affectional, while shorter relations re-

TABLE 7–3. Per Cent Choosing "Compatible" Person as Roommate

TYPE OF COMPATIBILITY		PER CENT COMPATIBLE	SIGNIFICANCE
Originator	oK^I	77	$p<.01$
	oK^C	68	.05
	oK^A	81	.01
Reciprocal	rK^I	58	–
	rK^C	63	–
	rK^A	72	.05
Interchange	xK^I	58	–
	xK^C	52	–
	xK^A	65	.10
By Need Areas	K^I	63	–
	K^C	69	.05
	K^A	75	.01
Total Compatibility	K	75	.01

Significant Relations: oK^I, oK^C, oK^A, rK^A, K^C, K^A, K

veal more concentration on inclusion and control. From this point of view the results are especially encouraging. Not only do they indicate a large number of significant relations between several types of compatibility and roommate choice (seven of thirteen significant at .05 or better), but the stress on the affectional area (*all* affection measures are significant) is consistent with the closeness of the relation of roommate.

Another type of analysis was made which was in a sense even more illuminating and psychologically meaningful. Since roommate is such a close relation, it seems reasonable to expect a person to choose someone with whom he is compatible in all three areas (one cannot choose a separate person for separate areas). Hence the choice of a roommate may be predicted by a process of analysis and synthesis. First each need area is analyzed to determine compatibility in the area. Each dyad is rated compatible (+) or incompatible (−). Then the three area compatibilities are combined to make a pattern compatibility for each dyad. These patterns are of eight types. Listed in the order inclusion, control, affection, these types are: + + +, + + −, + − +, + − −, − + +, − + −, − − +, − − −. The + + + indicates compatibility in all three areas, − − + indicates compatibility only in the affection area, and so on. This pattern represents the total interpersonal relation between two people.

If there is no relation between compatibility and roommate choice, chance selection would place approximately one eighth of all roommate choices in each pattern, including + + +. If our analysis and synthesis of each interpersonal relation has merit, there should be significantly more than one eighth in the + + + pattern. That is, there should be a tendency to select for roommates students with whom compatibility exists in all three areas. The results for each type of compatibility are given in Table 7–4. The expected values are also given, since the patterns were not always equally frequent in the population, owing in part to difficulties in getting an exact median because of tied scores.

TABLE 7–4. Number of Roommates Chosen Who Were Totally Compatible

TYPE OF COMPATIBILITY	CHANCE EXPECTANCY FOR $+ + +$ PATTERN *Per Cent*	OBSERVED *Per Cent*	SIGNIFICANCE
rK	13.0 (4.1 cases)	31.3 (10 cases)	$p < .001$
oK	19.0 (5.9 cases)	47.0 (15 cases)	.001
xK	13.6 (4.3 cases)	25.0 (8 cases)	.001

For oK and rK about two and a half times as many $+ + +$ people were chosen as chance would indicate, whereas for xK slightly less than twice as many; all are very significant results. This type of analysis is most encouraging because it indicates that the total compatibility relation between any dyad can be described in such a way that it represents meaningfully actual choice behavior.

One external factor actually was working against this result. Since the members of the fraternity ranged from freshman to senior, the pattern of acquaintance was highly variable. Of all the $+ + +$ dyads, 34 per cent were between members two or more classes apart; hence it may be inferred that only about two thirds of the $+ + +$ dyads were well acquainted. This inference is supported by the fact that only 10 per cent of all roommate choices were between dyads two or more classes apart. This factor makes the results even stronger. Optimal conditions for this type of prediction would be in a dormitory situation where everyone began unacquainted and had ample opportunity to meet everyone else.

Traveling Companion. The following question was asked on the sociometric questionnaire: "Thinking of all the members of your fraternity, which three men would you pick to travel with to the West by car (in order)?" Travel *West* (from MIT) was used to indicate a trip of about two weeks' duration.

With the same procedure as used for roommates, the percentages shown in Table 7–5 were obtained for people choosing a compatible member as first choice for traveling companion. Once more, chance is approximately 50 per cent.

Again the number of significant relations is well above chance (four of thirteen). The fact that all the significant relations are in the control area is most interesting in light of the development hypothesis discussed later and referred to above. Traveling companion is a strictly limited relation that terminates in a few days. As such, the development hypothesis indicates that control compatibility should predominate. Ordinarily there will not be as much affection interchange as in a roommate relation. In contrast to roommate choice, where all areas were important, especially affection, only the control area seems relevant for the traveling companion.

TABLE 7–5. **Per Cent Choosing Compatibles as Traveling Companion**

TYPE OF COMPATIBILITY		PER CENT COMPATIBLE	SIGNIFICANCE
Originator	oK^I	61	–
	oK^C	71	$p<.05$
	oK^A	71	–
Reciprocal	rK^I	42	–
	rK^C	74	.01
	rK^A	59	–
Interchange	xK^I	45	–
	xK^C	52	–
	xK^A	52	–
Area	K^I	44	–
	K^C	75	.01
	K^A	63	–
Total Compatibility	K	69	.05

Significant Relations: oK^C, rK^C, K^C, K.

The consistently better results from oK and rK again suggest that xK may not be as appropriate for dyads as for larger groups.

The results of the compatibility pattern analysis for selection of traveling companion are shown in Table 7–6.

TABLE 7–6. **Number of Traveling Companions Chosen with Various Compatibility Patterns**

TYPE OF COMPATIBILITY	CHANCE EXPECTANCY FOR $+++$ PATTERN	OBSERVED	SIGNIFI-CANCE
	Per Cent	*Per Cent*	
rK	13.0 (4.1 cases)	28.1 (9 cases)	$p<.001$
oK	19.0 (5.9 cases)	34.4 (11 cases)	.001
xK	13.6 (4.3 cases)	12.5 (4 cases)	—

Again the number of $+++$ chosen for rK and oK for traveling companion is significantly greater than chance. Further noting the popularity of other patterns, we find that the next most highly chosen patterns are $-++$ and $++-$, both compatible in the control area.

It appears, then, that the control area is the important one for a relation like traveling companion.

Other Choices. In the sociometric questionnaire, fraternity members were asked to select members for various offices in the fraternity. The qualifications for these offices are ambiguous, and the relation of the chosen to the chooser is not always clear or consistent from member to member; for instance, some may work more closely with the house manager than do others. For these reasons the results, although on the whole positive, are more difficult to interpret. They shall be presented to demonstrate the consistency of predictability of various types of choices from compatibility measures, and to offer data for further speculation regarding the areas of application of the various types of measures of compatibility. See Table 7–7.

TABLE 7-7. Per Cent of Compatible Persons Chosen for Various
Fraternity Offices

TYPE OF COMPATIBILITY	OFFICE			
	House Manager	Chancellor	Pledge Trainer	Bursar
oK^I	88**	73*	58	80**
oK^C	85**	54	54	48
oK^A	58	81*	62	96**
rK^I	85**	69*	65	64
rK^C	73**	46	42	48
rK^A	65**	69	65	60
xK^I	62	66	50	56
xK^C	50	42	38	76**
xK^A	46	70*	54	52
K^I	77**	73*	54	64
K^C	69*	46	39	48
K^A	50	69	65	60
K	77**	73*	54	63
Significant Relations	oK^I, rK^I, K^I oK^C, rK^C, K^C K, rK^A	oK^I, rK^I, K^I oK^A, xK^A K		oK^I xK^C, oK^A

* = $p < .05$
** = $p < .01$

The first result of interest is the high number of significant relations
(sixteen of fifty-two at .05 level or better). Secondly, in contrast to *roommate,*
where the emphasis was on affection compatibility, and to *traveling companion,* where the emphasis was on control compatibility, for *chancellor* and
house manager the emphasis is on inclusion compatibility. When the fraternity members were asked on the questionnaire to describe the desirable
traits for the house manager, they mentioned the following most frequently:
"reliable," "hard worker," "a leader," "tactful," 'mechanically efficient."
The requirement of leadership ("getting people to do what you want them
to do") could account for the control compatibility in the selection of house
manager. For chancellor the trait mentioned by some members that was not
used to describe house manager was "friendship." This characteristic may
account for the necessity for affection compatibility with chancellor that did
not appear for house manager.

However, the strikingly common characteristic of chancellor and house
manager is the strong tendency for inclusion compatibility to be important.
This fact suggests a generalization very much in keeping with the group development hypothesis. For relations in which contact is sporadic and to be
determined by approximately mutual agreement (such as fraternity officers
to member), inclusion compatibility is most essential for successful interaction. For relations that of necessity involve interaction but are of relatively
short duration (such as traveling companion), control compatibility is the
most important requirement. For relations involving close contact over a
long period of time (such as roommate), affection compatibility is the most
essential requirement for harmonious coexistence.

STABILITY

Since this study is presented to demonstrate the technique for assessing compatibility, as well as to provide evidence for Theorem 3–1, it is appropriate to discuss some properties of the measures of compatibility, rK, oK, xK, K. In particular, the stability (test-retest reliability) is a very important property of these measures, since compatibility is presumed to be a deep-seated and relatively invariant characteristic of an interpersonal relation.

With the test-retest data described in Chapter 4 it is possible to determine the stability of the several measures of compatibility used in the fraternity study. The stability will be reported in two ways. First, correlations between the compatibility scores of dyads received on the test, and the retest from a sample of 127 (57 for the affection scales) are presented. (This is the same sample used in the stability test for FIRO–B, Chapter 4.) Then the percentage of people who remain in the same category from the test to the retest is reported for various groupings of scale scores. The groupings include (1) retaining each raw compatibility score, (2) dividing the scores at the quartiles to form four compatibility scores, (3) dividing the subjects into equal thirds, (4) dichotomizing the population. By presenting stability data in this form it is possible to see the balance between increasing the number of discriminable points in assessing compatibility and reducing the stability of the measure. (See Table 7–8.)

TABLE 7–8. Stability (Test-Retest) of Compatibility Scores

MEASURE	CORRELATION		PER CENT REMAINING IN SAME CATEGORY			
	Full Scale (product-moment r)	Two Categories (tetrachoric r)	Full Scale	Four Categories (Quartiles)	Three Categories (Tertiles)	Two Categories (Median)
rK^I	.57	.58	14	42	51	70
rK^C	.51	.51	15	39	49	67
rK^A	.67	.72	15	48	57	74
Mean $\overline{rK}$	$\overline{.58}$	$\overline{.60}$	$\overline{15}$	$\overline{43}$	$\overline{52}$	$\overline{70}$
oK^I	.65	.75	17	45	49	77
oK^C	.55	.55	21	46	52	69
oK^A	.53	.59	37	51	51	70
Mean $\overline{oK}$	$\overline{.58}$	$\overline{.63}$	$\overline{25}$	$\overline{47}$	$\overline{51}$	$\overline{72}$
xK^I	.81	.84	17	57	66	86
xK^C	.72	.75	20	55	58	77
xK^A	.81	.82	23	56	74	81
Mean $\overline{xK}$	$\overline{.78}$	$\overline{.80}$	$\overline{20}$	$\overline{56}$	$\overline{66}$	$\overline{81}$

About 70 per cent of the respondents for rK and oK and about 80 per cent for xK remain in the same half of the distribution through both administrations of the questionnaire. An examination of the trend indicates that dichotomizing leads to sufficiently better stability than does division into finer categories, that the use of dichotomized scores seems appropriate.

These results provide justification for dividing compatibility scores at the median in the fraternity study.

This completes the description of the fraternity study testing the Postulate of Compatibility as specifically applied to preferences among dyads. The next studies are relevant to the postulate as applied to productivity measures for groups, in particular, five-man groups.

> **Theorem 3–2.** **If the compatibility of one group, h, is greater than the compatibility of another group, m, then the productivity goal achievement of h will exceed that of m.**

The term "productivity" will be defined specifically with respect to a task. For most problems an objective measure is obtainable of the degree to which the goal is achieved. For nonobjective problems pooled ratings of judges may be used.

The first experiment performed by the author that is relevant to Theorem 3–2 was performed in Washington in 1952 and has been reported at length in an article entitled, "What Makes Groups Productive?" (77) The reader is referred to this article for details. The Harvard experiment reported below is in part a replication of the Washington experiment; thus results from the Washington experiment will be presented when appropriate for comparison with the replicated result.

Both experiments were made before the present form of the theory was evolved. Therefore some of the present concepts must be inferred from the measures and techniques used in the experiments. Connections between old and new concepts will be pointed out when appropriate. As is true with the evolution of FIRO–B, although the concepts change, the basic ideas underlying these experiments and the present theory are sufficiently similar to warrant considering the experiments as directly relevant to the theory.

The Harvard Compatibility Experiment

PURPOSES

The purposes of this experiment were (1) to replicate several parts of the Washington experiment which involved constructing compatible and incompatible five-man groups based on FIRO–Q, and predicting that the compatibles would be more productive; (2) to administer several other personality measures to supplement the FIRO and give some insight into other aspects of group behavior; and (3) to include measures of recalled parental behavior and defense mechanisms to explore the relations of these measures to group behavior.

DESIGN AND PROCEDURE

Invitations were sent to every tenth freshman at Harvard (selected from an alphabetical list) to participate in an experiment to be conducted over a six-week period. When about one hundred accepted, they were called together and given the FIRO–1 and a few other questionnaires. On the basis of the results of the FIRO–1 and a consideration of the students' mathematics and verbal scores on the Scholastic Achievement Test, twelve groups were formed. Four groups followed the patterns described previously (75), Compatible Pattern O; four followed the Incompatible Pattern, and four followed a new pattern, a compatible group based on the fact that all members were underpersonal. This last will be called Compatible Pattern U. Triads of groups (one from each compatibility type) were matched on intelligence as well as possible within the limitations of composition requirements (Table 7–9).

TABLE 7–9. Composition Patterns for Three Types of Groups

VARIABLES (FIRO-1 NAMES)	COMPATIBLE GROUP MEMBERS (TYPE O)				
	FP_o	MS_o	M_o	M_o	M_o
Personalness (Affection)	H	H	H	H	H
Dependence (Control)	L,M	M,H	L,M	L,M	L,M
Assertiveness (Inclusion)	H	L,M	L,M	L,M	L,M
Intelligence	H	H	L,M	L,M	L,M

	COMPATIBLE GROUP MEMBERS (TYPE U)				
	FP_u	MS_u	M_u	M_u	M_u
Personalness	L	L	L	L	L
Dependence	L,M	M,H	M,H	M,H	M,H
Assertiveness	H	L,M	L,M	L,M	L,M
Intelligence	H	H	L,M	L,M	L,M

	INCOMPATIBLE GROUP MEMBERS				
	FP_o	MS_o	FP_u	MS_u	M_n
Personalness	H	H	L	L	M
Dependence	L,M	L,M	H	H	M
Assertiveness	H	L,M	H	L,M	L
Intelligence	H	L,M	H	L,M	L,M

Overpersonal Subgroup   Underpersonal Subgroup

Antagonistic Subgroups

Key:
FP = focal person
MS = main supporting member
M = member

o = overpersonal
u = underpersonal
n = neutral

H = roughly, highest quartile
M = roughly, second or third quartile
L = roughly, lowest quartile

The fundamental basis for compatibility in this experiment—as well as in the Washington experiment—would in the present theoretical formulation be best approximated by affection interchange compatibility (xK^4). All compatible group members for pattern O were overpersonal; all members of Compatible Pattern U were underpersonal; some members of the incompatible groups were overpersonal and some underpersonal. The other need areas were not systematically controlled, except that the two key figures in the compatible groups, the focal person (*FP*) and the main supporting member (*MS*), were designed to have high control originator compatibility (oK^c). The rationale behind the composition pattern beyond the interpersonal orientations (the *FP* and the *MS*) has been discussed in the previous publication and will be briefly summarized at this point.

It was found in the Washington experiment that a stable group structure for a five-man group seems to require not one, but two, key figures. These have been called the Focal Person (*FP*) and the Main Supporting Member (*MS*). The role of the focal person is to initiate the personal atmosphere (high affection interchange) of the group, and the *MS* to support the *FP* and, with him, to form the core of the group. For the incompatible groups two pairs of *FP–MS*'s are put in the same group. These pairs differ in that one pair wishes an atmosphere with much personalness, whereas the other desires little personalness—hence the affection interchange incompatibility.

It should be emphasized that the designation of focal person is a predictive act of the experimenter when he composes the groups on the basis of their FIRO scores, without the knowledge of the group members. As far as the group is concerned, there are five members at initially equal status levels, and the experimenter treats them that way at all times. Results of the success of selecting a focal person who actually functions "focally" in the group are given in Table 7–18.

Each of these twelve groups were brought to the group laboratory of the Harvard Social Relations Department and run through fourteen meetings over a period of six weeks. There were four one-hour meetings a day at 4:00, 5:00, 7:30, and 8:30 P.M., Monday through Friday; and at 10:00 and 11:00 A.M. and at 1:00 and 2:00 P.M., Saturday. Each group met twice a week at the same time (except Saturday), three days apart (such as Monday at 5:00 P.M. and Thursday at 5:00 P.M).

Each group was given exactly the same sequence of tasks (shown in Table 7–10).

All discussion tasks and group problems are presented in Appendix B.

Productivity differences between groups were measured by comparison of the objective productivity scores received on each task. The intercept contests in the eleventh to fourteenth meetings were games played between two teams of different compatibility types such that each team played approximately the same number of contests against groups of differing compatibility types.

TABLE 7–10. Schedule of Activities of Groups in the Harvard Experiment

MEETING	TASK
1	Indoctrination: discussion (Name): discussion (Prison)
2	Building task (Toy); discussion (Cheat)
3	Intercept task
4	Intercept task; discussion (Child)
5	Free behavior, no task, standings announced, each group told "all groups are close, you are among lower ones"
6	Discussion (Groups); concept task
7	Building tasks (2)
8	Intercept tasks; discussion (Traffic)
9	Group projective; concept task
10	Building task; intercept task
11–14	Intercept contests (pairs of groups)

The discussion tasks were administered in a standard fashion. The experimenter read aloud a short (three-paragraph) description of a situation involving a difficult decision (typically based on authority vs. friendship, or something similarly related to the interpersonal areas). Each subject then wrote down what he would do in that situation and the reasons for his decision. The group was later allowed from fifteen to thirty minutes to discuss the problem and come to a "group decision," a purposely ambiguous phrase not specifying unanimity, majority, or any other procedure for decision making. Then the group was asked to appoint one of its members to be the spokesman and present the group's decision. The experimenter returned on the group's signal and, before hearing the group's decision, first had the subjects write their own individual postdiscussion decision. This assignment fulfilled the conditions of a standard attitude change study (see Chapter 4).

A typical meeting proceeded as follows. The members of the group arrived about five minutes before the hour and went directly to the laboratory room (they had all been given a tour of the observation room at the first meeting, so they were fully aware of the observers). The recording apparatus (Gray Audograph) was turned on in the observation room. The experimenter watched through a one-way mirror for several minutes, allowing the group time for free discussion. The members were under the impression that they were simply waiting for the session to begin. Generally about five minutes was allowed unless there was some especially important interaction occurring.

The experimenter then entered the experimental room, greeted the group, and presented the day's activity. He attempted to be distantly friendly with all groups, trying not to encourage or discourage any single group. After he was assured that the instructions were understood, the experimenter left the room, to return only when summoned at the end of an activity. The experimenter attempted to be with the group only when necessary, allowing maximal opportunity for unfettered group interaction. After the group's activity was finished, he returned to the room and completed the hour's work. Usually he then left, allowing a few more minutes for free behavior; later he returned and dismissed the group.

All experimental tasks were new to the subjects. There was no indication that any subject had special knowledge that would assist him in the solution of the tasks. The previous acquaintance of the subjects with one another varied; on the whole, the members of any one of the five-man groups were typically unacquainted. No group ever met *as a group* prior to the experiment.

Virtually no restraints were placed on the groups regarding seating arrangements or communication. With regard to leadership, the experimenter never designated a particular member as any type of leader. In some tasks the experimenter named certain *roles* (for example, coordinator, recorder) which had to be filled by men chosen by the group itself. The group could always oust the man they chose from any role at any time. (The term "oustable" shall be used for this type of role.)

Motivation to perform optimally was engendered in the subjects by (1) a talk to all subjects on the importance of the experiment to various industrial, governmental, military, and research activities; (2) a statement at the outset of the experiment that the experimenters wanted only participants who would appear promptly at *every* meeting and participate fully; (3) a reward of $25 to the "best" group, and several $10 prizes for the "best" individual performances, (4) payment of $1 per hour of meeting for each subject.

There was one further condition that is relevant to the conduct of this experiment and others like it. A special problem arose with regard to attendance at meetings. The design required sixty subjects (twelve groups of five men) to attend, on time, fourteen tightly scheduled meetings each, covering a period of six weeks. Since group composition was the key variable, it was not feasible to replace men after the groups had been formed. If any member dropped out, his whole group would have to be eliminated, because otherwise the design would be upset. To meet this problem it was decided to take the chance of losing all our volunteers at the outset, in the hope that if they stayed under the drastic conditions then imposed, they could be relied upon. The subjects were told that they would be paid only at the end of the experiment—that if they missed any *one* meeting *they would not be paid anything,* no matter how many meetings they had already attended. (This threat was, of course, not carried out). This condition resulted in the situation that attendance at each meeting made attendance at the following meeting more imperative. It emphasized to the subjects the great importance of attendance, which was strongly stressed and forthrightly explained on several occasions. Prior to the beginning of the experiment all the subjects were told the conditions, and given a chance to leave if they wished.

This technique, fortunately, was highly successful. After the first week, during which four or five meetings were rescheduled, there were only about five meetings that had to be rescheduled because one member forgot to appear. Since there were 141 meetings altogether, this record was most gratifying. In other words, of 705 instances where a man could have forgotten to attend, he actually forgot only about 10 times, less than 2 per cent. It seems safe to say that this type of long-run experiment, depending on repeated appearances of the same subjects, is quite feasible.

TASKS

Game (Intercept). This task of Game (Intercept) is described in Appendix B. Briefly, it is a modified chess-type game which requires that the entire group come to a decision within thirty seconds. One man was chosen oustable coordinator by the group and had complete authority and responsibility for making the decisions.

Concept. This is the task used by Bruner (20) for individual concept formation studies. It was adapted to the group situation and administered similarly to the intercept task, except that (1) there were *two* oustable coordinators with equal authority, and (2) there was a penalty for total time rather than for a time limit for individual moves. This served to introduce a new type of decision, that between taking a chance by acting quickly and not taking a chance but being more cautious and deliberate.

Toy. The group was assigned the task of building a specified structure as fast as possible. The materials used are sold commercially under the name "Toy." The task was a division-of-labor type requiring the coordination of several different jobs.

QUESTIONNAIRES

Throughout the course of the experiment several questionnaires were administered. Following is the list of questionnaires and their abbreviations:

1. Slater, *Parental Role Preference Questionnaire* (PRP)
2. Blum, *Blacky Projective Test* (B)
3. Blum, *Defense Preference Inquiry* (DPI)
4. Schutz, *Fundamental Interpersonal Relations Orientation* (FIRO–1)
5. *California F–scale* (Authoritarianism) (A)
6. Edwards, *Personal Preference Schedule* (PPS)
7. La Forge and Suczek, *Interpersonal Checklist* (IPC)
8. Guilford, *R* (*Rhathymia*) *and C* (*Cyclothymia*) *Scales*
9. Bales and Couch, *Value Profile* (VP)

These questionnaires were administered intermittently over the entire fourteen meetings so that the required work would be spread over a reasonable period.

OBSERVATION

Each meeting was observed by from two to five observers, all graduate students in the Department of Social Relations. No observer knew which groups were composed according to which compatibility pattern. The primary observational data were a series of ratings made once or twice a meeting. When there were two activities in one meeting, for example, a discussion and an objective task, two ratings were made at that meeting; otherwise only one rating was made. The ratings were for a variety of roles commonly noted in group meetings, such as discussion guider, influencer, and promoter of personal feelings (see Appendix B). The observer was first asked to decide whether or not any members of the group clearly fulfilled the description of the role, and then he was asked to rank all five group members with respect to this role. The weighted sum of all rankings for all meetings was computed for each role for each group member. These ratings were standardized and used as the behavioral data. An on-going category system was used to record the behavior only for a few meetings which involved special projects.

SOCIOMETRICS

In order to obtain the most comparable data the subjects were given a rating sheet almost identical to that used by the observers. These were filled out at both the fifth and tenth meetings. In addition, the subjects filled out regular sociometric questions regarding "like," "work with," and "influences."

RESULTS

Productivity. Since all the tasks were of different types, it was difficult to combine scores to obtain an over-all productivity measure. It was therefore decided to rank all twelve groups on each task and use the sums of these ranks for the total productivity score. This procedure minimized the effect of scoring differences between tasks.

There were four objective tasks: Toy, Concept, Game, and Game Contest. Where there was more than one concurrence of the same task (as in Toy and Concept), the ranks were averaged to give a final rank for that task. Thus the final rank was based on one rank for each task. (See Table 7–11.)

With the use of the Mann-Whitney U-test the difference in ranks between the combined compatibles and the incompatibles is significant beyond the .02 level. Hence, to that degree, Theorem 3–2 is confirmed.

There is virtually no difference in productivity between the overpersonal compatibles (OP–K's) and the underpersonal compatibles (UP–K's). The UP–K's have one final rank less, while the OP–K's have two and one-half total ranks less. Neither difference is significant. The ideal result of the

TABLE 7–11. Ranks on Productivity for All Groups on All Tasks

Overpersonal Compatible Groups	Toy	Concept	Game	Contest	Final Total	Final Rank
No. 1	3	8	7	10	28	9
2	1	1	11	1	14	1
3	7.5	4	2	4	17.5	2
4	10	10	1	6.5	27.5	8
				Total	87	20

Underpersonal Compatible Groups					Final Total	Final Rank
No. 5	6	6	4	2	18	3
6	2	7	10	3	22	4
7	10	5	5	6.5	26.5	7
8	7.5	2.5	2	11	23	5
				Total	89.5	19

Incompatible Groups					Final Total	Final Rank
No. 9	10	11.5	8	6.5	36	11
10	12	11.5	9	9	41.5	12
11	4.5	9	6	6.5	26	6
12	4.5	2.5	12	12	31	10
				Total	134.5	39

final ranking would have placed the incompatibles ($\bar{K}$'s) in ranks 9, 10, 11, and 12, and shown the first eight ranks distributed among the compatible groups. Actually, this outcome occurred with the exception of $\bar{K}$ group 11 and $OP-K$ Group 1, who ideally should have interchanged ranks 6 and 9.

The result that points to the aspect of the experiment requiring more investigation is the inconsistency of the ranks for each group. The variation in the ranks makes it statistically tenuous (with the use of Kendall's "W") to assign a stable productivity rank to any group with any confidence. This conclusion may mean (1) the number of tests of productivity was inadequate to stabilize performance, (2) the tasks required different abilities of the groups, and thus they performed differentially, or (3) groups are always erratic in their performance whatever the reason, and several measures are always necessary to obtain a meaningful estimate of productivity.

These productivity results confirm those presented in the Washington experiment, where $OP-K$ groups were found to be significantly more productive than incompatibles. The Harvard experiment therefore may be considered a successful replication of the Washington experiment with regard to Theorem 3–2.

The Logic Problem Experiment

A second experiment bearing directly on Theorem 3–2 was performed on eight five-man problem-solving groups (73). After these groups of naval personnel had completed an experiment on problem solving that lasted for four meetings, they were given FIRO–1. From the results of this test alone, plus intelligence measures, and with no knowledge of the results on the problem-solving task, the groups were rated on compatibility. Dr. Richard Rudner kindly made the subjects available to us for testing, and also gave us the productivity ratings the groups received on their tasks.

The tasks were logical problems put in the format of coding problems. Members of each group were given several problems, and their responses objectively graded. The compatibility ratings were made by techniques that antedated the present objective methods, but they were based on the same fundamental theoretical ideas as those of the Harvard experiment. Only four degrees of compatibility were discernible. The results of the correlation between the rank order of the eight groups on productivity measure and the rank order of the groups on compatibility are shown in Table 7–12.

TABLE 7–12. Comparison of Productivity and Compatibility for Rudner's Groups

Group	Productivity Rank	Compatibility Rank	
A	1	1.5	
B	8	7	
C	4	3.5	
D	3	5	rho=.51
E	6	7	not significant
F	7	1.5	
G	5	7	
H	2	3.5	

For such a small number of groups this correlation is not statistically significant, although in the right direction. Upon examination of the results, a curious thing appeared. Every group is predicted correctly to within two ranks except group F, which is 5½ ranks discrepant. Inquiry revealed that the man in that group who we had predicted would be the focal person appeared at all four meetings—drunk! If this fact is considered an adequate excuse for eliminating group F (strictly speaking, it is not, because degree of sobriety was not systematically checked throughout all groups), then the rank order looks remarkably better (Table 7–13).

TABLE 7–13. Comparison of Productivity and Compatibility on Rudner's Groups (Eliminating Group F)

Group	Productivity Rank	Compatibility Rank	
A	1	1	
B	7	6	
C	4	2.5	
D	3	4	rho=.91
E	6	6	$p < .01$
G	5	6	
H	2	2.5	

The remarkably high correlation that followed the elimination of Group F adds encouragement for the truth of Theorem 3–2.

Theorem 3–3. **If the compatibility of one group, *h*, is greater than the compatibility of another group, *m*, then *h* will be more cohesive than *m*.**

The Cohesion–Compatibility Experiment

This theorem states the relation between "compatibility" and a well-known small group concept, "cohesiveness." To the extent that cohesiveness measures general satisfaction with the group activities and a member's place in those activities, it should be related to compatibility. A study was carried out by Gross (42) to test this theorem directly.

PURPOSE

To test the relation between compatibility and cohesiveness.

SUBJECT

For the construction of the cohesiveness scale, fifty-five Harvard freshmen were used. For the experimental study, forty-five of these freshmen were used. All subjects were first selected randomly from the freshman roster, and then volunteers were selected from this list. The selection was made by Professor R. F. Bales for a project of his in which these subjects were participating. The subjects were formed into five-man groups performing a series of experimental tasks and discussions. Professor Bales kindly made these subjects available to us for testing after they had met three times.

PROCEDURE

Since the concept of cohesiveness is so difficult to define and measure, Gross collected nine criteria of cohesiveness that had been used in various studies, combined them into one questionnaire, and administered it to these eleven five-man groups after their three meetings. The Guttman scaling procedure showed that seven of these items formed a unidimensional cumulative scale (Table 7–14).

Each group member was scored on this eight-point (seven-item) scale, and the group was given a score equal to the sum of the individual members' scores on cohesiveness. The nine groups (for which complete data were available) were then ranked from 1 to 9 on cohesiveness.

In addition, FIRO–4 was administered because, unfortunately, FIRO–B was not yet available. From FIRO–4 the only available compatibility measures were control interchange (xK^c), control originator (oK^c), and affection interchange (xK^A). With the aid of the compatibility formulas presented in Chapter 6, compatibility scores for all dyads were combined to give a group compatibility score. Groups were then ranked according to this criterion.

TABLE 7–14. Cohesiveness Scale: Cumulative Scale Items
("Accept" answer categories in italics)

1. How many of your group members fit what you feel to be the idea of a good member?

   a. *All of them.*
   b. *Most of them.*
   c. Some of them.
   d. Few of them.
   e. None of them.

2. To what degree do you feel that you are included by the group in the group's activities?

   a. *I am included in all the group's activities.*
   b. *I am included in almost all the group's activities.*
   c. I am included in some of the activities, but not in some others.
   d. I don't feel that the group includes me in very many of its activities.
   e. I don't feel that the group includes me in any of its activities.

3. How attractive do you find the activities in which you participate as a member of your group?

   a. *Like all of them very much.*
   b. *Like almost all of them.*
   c. Like some of them, but not others.
   d. Like very few of them.
   e. Like none of them.

4. If most of the members of your group decided to dissolve the group by leaving, would you like an opportunity to dissuade them?

   a. *Would like very much to persuade them to stay.*
   b. *Would like to persuade them to stay.*
   c. Would make no difference to me if they stayed or left.
   d. Would not like to try to persuade them to stay.
   e. Would definitely not like to try to persuade them to stay.

5. If you were asked to participate in another project like this one, would you like to be with the same people who are in your present group?

   a. *Would want very much to be with the same people.*
   b. *Would rather be with the same people than with most others.*
   c. Makes no difference to me.
   d. Would rather be with another group more than present group.
   e. Would want very much to be with another group.

6. How well do you like the group you are in?

   a. *Like it very much.*
   b. *Like it pretty well.*
   c. It's all right.
   d. Don't like it too much.
   e. Dislike it very much.

7. How often do you think your group should meet?

   a. *Much more often than at present.*
   b. *More often than at present.*
   c. No more often than present.
   d. Less often than at present.
   e. Much less often than at present.

RESULTS

Rank-order correlations were computed among all four types of compatibility and cohesiveness, with the results shown in Table 7–15.

TABLE 7–15. Rank-Order Correlations between Various Measures of Compatibility and Cohesiveness

TYPE OF COMPATIBILITY

Control Interchange (xK^C)	.05	
Control Originator (oK^C)	.44	$p_{.05} = .66$
Affection Interchange (xK^A)	.40	$N = 9$
Total Compatibility (K)	.81	

Since a significant correlation at the .05 level is .66, only the correlation between total compatibility and cohesiveness is statistically significant. However, the large size and consistent predicted direction of the two other correlations are encouraging.

Thus, with an impressive correlation of .81, Theorem 3–3 is confirmed. It is interesting that the best predictor of cohesion is total compatibility. This suggests that group members are disturbed by problems in all three interpersonal areas; therefore the best technique for determining their over-all satisfaction with the group (that is, cohesiveness) is to combine all types of compatibility (K). The rather high correlation with the affection factor (xK^A) is not surprising, since the successful Washington and Harvard experiments were based primarily on xK^A. However, the size of the correlation with control originator compatibility (oK^C) is unexpected. The implications of this result for a theory combining the Postulate of Compatibility with the Postulate of Group Development (Theorem 4–3) will be discussed in the next chapter.

The Street Corner Group Study

The next study is nonexperimental. It is relevant to Theorem 3–3 if one assumes that remaining together voluntarily over a period of three to six years, as did the Tigers, is a measure of cohesiveness. This was the assumption regarding the Tigers, a street corner gang, who did remain together.

The charge is often made that laboratory groups are not "real" groups. They are artificial, contrived, have no history, offer no involvement, are not embedded in a larger social system, and so forth. However, if the basic factors in predicting many interesting aspects of group behavior have to do with interpersonal needs, then, since these needs are present in all persons at all times, there should be great similarities among behaviors exhibited in any group. That is to say, any group is "real" that involves interaction between people.

One way of testing this idea is to investigate a natural group with the same measuring instruments that were used with the experimental groups in the Washington and Harvard experiments, and to see if the same predictions hold. Owing to a fortunate circumstance, it was possible to do this. A student at Harvard, Arnold Abelow, did his honors thesis (1) on this topic.

By selling ice cream on a summer job Abelow was able to become a participant-observer in a street corner gang in one of the underprivileged areas of Boston. He gained such general acceptance from the group that it was a simple matter for him to obtain their agreement to take the FIRO–2, the POP, and an extended sociometric questionnaire. Hence data available on a natural group is comparable to data available on a set of several experimental groups. Theorem 3–3 requires that the natural group be established as compatible, and then it must be shown that the group structure, specifically in terms of FIRO scores, be similar to compatible group structures. Satisfaction of this condition will aid in testing whether or not the Postulate of Compatibility is applicable to natural groups as well as to experimental groups.

Perhaps the best way to establish that the Tigers were compatible is to point out that membership was voluntary, and that the Tigers had been together for six years. The present membership represents the end result of a screening process in which the basis of screening was the ability of the new member to "get along with" the present members. In the words of Abelow (1):

"... The Tigers ranged in age from Mutt, Aleno, O'Malley, who were fifteen, to Porky, Harold, and Lennon, who were twenty. The median age of the group was seventeen. All the Tigers attended high school except Porky, Harold, and Lennon, who had already graduated and Cukes and Danny who had left school to work. The SES level of the Tigers extended from upper-lower to lower-middle. The group was Catholic except for Mutt, who was Protestant. Cukes, Aleno, Tiny, Mario, and Al were Italian, Danny was Greek, and the rest were Irish. The Tigers took pride in their appearance, either wearing khaki trousers or slacks, but never neckties or sport coats. The Tigers were typical of other groups in Falcon Heights in that they spent much of their free time loitering and 'hanging.'

"Some Tigers had been in the 'Lit' Tigers, which was a subdivision of an older group. Most of the older Tigers had stopped 'hanging' or, like Stony, Slim, Mike, George, Mick, and Pat, were in the Army. Mario, Porky, Al, Lindy, and Towers, however, were former members of the 'big' Falcons. Others like Samson, Harold, and Don had made contact with the group through school and had started 'hanging' with the Tigers two years after their inception. On the other hand, Joe O'Connor had transferred his allegiance to the Tigers from 'another gang down the projects.' Thus, to use Jenning's term, the Tigers were

a 'psychegroup' in that there was a spontaneous, 'free' association."
(pp. 1, 2)

The reader is referred to the original report for further information about the compatibility of the group.

The patterns of compatibility of our experimental groups were of two types—the overpersonal and the underpersonal. A priori, there is no compelling reason to feel that the Tigers would be one type or the other, although one might feel that since they are a social group it is more likely that they would be overpersonal. However, Theorem 3–3 would say that they would be either one or the other, but not follow the incompatible pattern.

The actual results of the Tigers on FIRO–2 can be seen more clearly if we compare the results with those given by a random sample of Harvard students on FIRO–2 (Table 7–16).

TABLE 7–16. Responses on Personalness Scale (FIRO–2); "Tigers" and Harvard Students

	PERSONALNESS		
	+	−	
Tigers	15	3	$\chi^2 = 3.84$
Harvard	122	66	$p < .05$

With regard to the three members of the Tigers who were underpersonal, there are some interesting additional data. All three had in some way become alienated from the group. This determination had been made prior to the testing; it was not discovered simply as a result of the aberrant responses of those three members. Abelow writes (after the testing):

"There is one thing in common about these three individuals. These three Tigers were not frequent participators with the group. Take Danny's case, for instance. Although I had seen him at Nick's and at dances, I had never thought he belonged to the Tigers. I was most surprised to see him present at the Neighborhood House. Thus, as mentioned previously, I asked Cukes whether Danny associated with the group. Although Cukes said, 'He's still with us,' a case can be made to show why Danny appeared at the test session, even though I had never seen him with the Tigers at Nick's or at dances.

"Although the FIRO scores indicate Danny was free from anxiety in independence and integration [old names for Control and Inclusion] need areas, the degree to which Danny needed affection differed considerably from the need of the group as a whole. As an underpersonal type, Danny 'maintained emotional distance between himself and others by avoiding them.' Since the Tigers were not satisfying Danny's own particular need of affection, he had either withdrawn from the group or had curtailed his participation to the extent that I had never seen him with the Tigers. It is interesting to note that on the sociometric questions, 'who is the least valuable member of the group,' Danny received the most choices. Apparently the tests themselves and Dr. Schutz's visit to Falcon Heights were all allurements which Danny could not afford to pass up.

"Like Danny, Don did not participate with the group frequently, because, as Dick said on December 30, 1955, 'He always sees his girl and never even checks in at the corner.' Since Don could be classified as underpersonal, the same explanation which we gave for Danny's behavior toward the group is also applicable in Don's case. Don's own basic need of affection was not being satisfied by the group. His incompatibility with the group would thus lead to his curtailment of interaction with the Tigers, and he would seek a new set of interpersonal relations which would reward him. Seeing a girl might have been a subtle, yet appropriate way for Don not to 'check in at the corner.' In contrast to Don, who 'always sees his girl,' Mario 'was married to Frances,' as the Tigers would say, but was primarily with her at dances [and spent much time with the Tigers].

"We have already discussed at some length the case of Harold. In addition to the possible explanations offered for Harold's owl ['jerk'] type behavior—that he might have been socially mobile and that his age might have had a direct effect on how he felt about himself—we can also point out that Harold's own, distinctive need for affection was not equilibrated with the need of the group as a whole. Being underpersonal, Harold could maintain emotional distance from the group by infrequent participation, by not giving the group a useful resource, and by going off by himself. If the Tigers, as a whole, were overpersonal and thus made wanting to be liked a master value of the group, then they would exercise aggression toward Harold because he showed them he did not like them when he did not invite anyone to go with him when he went by himself, or when he 'owled off' in his automobile. It is interesting to note that Billy Lennon, who was liked when he did not try to inculcate the group with middle-class values, was overpersonal, which means that he was compatible with the group in the need for affection." (p. 121–123)

Harold had already been given a special chapter as the "owl," or scapegoat, of the group prior to the testing session, Hence the affection dimension illuminates many of the interesting interpersonal relations in the group.

Thus the Tigers exhibit a high degree of affection interchange compatibility (xK^A). The three members who do not feel comfortable exchanging affection at such a high rate have become alienated from the group. It is interesting to note that neither the control nor inclusion (participation) measures on FIRO–2 revealed any significant differences between the Tigers and the Harvard sample. This study may be considered another piece of evidence for the major importance of compatibility in the affection area for harmony in long-established and close relations.

The next series of theorems specifies the Postulate of Compatibility by focusing on individual relations within the five-man group. The group composition patterns presented above lend themselves to testing within-group choices. Most of the results reported occurred as part of the Harvard experiment.

Theorem 3–4. **For each subgroup in an incompatible group each member should prefer to work with the other member of his subgroup more than with either member of the antagonistic subgroup or with the neutral member.**

The measure used to test this hypothesis is the ranking given by each member to every other member on "work well with." In the Washington experiment in nine of ten instances the hypothesis was confirmed by this measure. However, in the Harvard experiment only four of sixteen choices of "man most desired to work with" were the choice of the other subgroup member. This is exactly chance; hence *Theorem 3–4 is not confirmed.*

The Training Group Study

A study (13) unrelated to the Washington experiment was performed to test the general idea behind Theorem 3–4, namely, that high inter-change compatibility in the affection and control areas (xK^A, xK^C) leads to "working well with" behavior based on two FIRO–2 dimensions, affection and control. At the third and ninth meetings of six Bethel training groups a sociometric question was asked, "With whom do you get along best?" Choices were compared with FIRO–2 scores of the members. The responses to FIRO–2 approximate the xK^A and xK^C measures. (See Table 7–17.) Hence Theorem 3–4 suggests that respondents with similar FIRO–2 scores should choose each other.

TABLE 7–17. Choices on "Get Along Well With" by FIRO Types

	CHOSEN 3rd Meeting				CHOSEN 9th Meeting		
CHOOSER	AB	AU		CHOOSER	AB	AU	
AB	48	17	$\chi^2 = 12.38$	AB	60	12	$\chi^2 = 13.38$
AU	14	14	$p < .01$	AU	14	12	$p < .001$
	3rd Meeting				9th Meeting		
	OP	UP			OP	UP	
OP	22	11	$\chi^2 = 7.98$	OP	18	4	$\chi^2 = 6.17$
UP	17	14	$p < .01$	UP	10	14	$p < .02$
OP = overpersonal; UP = underpersonal; AB = abdicrat; AU = autocrat.							

The statistical tests made by Bennis and Peabody were not made against a chance model but against a "Monte Carlo" model based on the actual composition of the group (it was borne in mind that no person would choose himself) rather than on the matrix for all groups combined. Thus the model took into account the number of possible choices, rules against self-choice, and the composition of each group on the basis of individual FIRO–2 scores. Therefore, on the basis of the indications shown by this data, *Theorem 3–4 is confirmed for dyads in the relation of "getting along well."*

Theorem 3–5.   In the incompatible groups, members of the overpersonal subgroups will have a greater tendency to like each other well than will the members of the underpersonal subgroups.

The measure used for this hypothesis is rank on the sociometric question, "Whom do you like best in this group?" In the Washington experiment the average ranking of overpersonal subgroup members for each other was 1.0, while that of underpersonal subgroup members for each other was 2.2, a highly significant difference. However, in the present experiment this result was not replicated; as a matter of fact, there was even a slight reversal. The underpersonal subgroup members ranked each other a mean of 2.5, while the overpersonal subgroup members had a mean of 2.9. Hence, *Theorem 3–5 is not confirmed.*

Theorem 3–6.   In the incompatible groups overpersonal subgroup members will tend to rank the man they like best higher on competence than an objective estimate would justify. The underpersonal subgroup members will not have this tendency.

The "objective estimate" used in the Washington experiment was an intelligence test, and the ratings used were "like" and "competence." For the present experiment the objective estimate of competence is the observers' pooled ranking of the members on "best ideas." The ratings by the subjects were "like" and "best ideas." In the Washington experiment the overpersonal subgroup ranked its best-liked members an average of 1.0 rank higher on "competence" than an objective estimate would warrant, while the underpersonal subgroup members averaged only 0.58 of a rank higher. In this experiment the overpersonals averaged 0.94 of a rank higher, but the underpersonals averaged 1.0 rank higher. Hence the halo effect seemed to be a general one not restricted to attitudes toward personalness. *Theorem 3–6 is not confirmed.*

Theorem 3–7.   In the compatible groups those predicted to be focal persons and those predicted to be main supporting members should rank each other very high on the relation "work well with."

The measure used to test this hypothesis is rank on "work well with." In the Washington experiment all six of the overpersonal focal persons and overpersonal main supporting members chose each other first on "work well with." In the Harvard experiment for the overpersonal compatible groups—the same type that was used in the Washington experiment—five of eight selected rank 1, while the other three chose rank 3. The selection of rank 1 five times in eight could have occurred by chance in this situation, with a probability less than .03.

With the underpersonal compatible groups there were only three selections of rank 1, three of rank 3, and two of rank 4, a nonconfirmatory result. Hence *Theorem 3–7 is confirmed for overpersonal compatible groups, but not for underpersonal compatible groups.*

Theorem 3–8. **In all groups focal persons will be chosen as group leaders by the group members.**

The report of the Washington experiment discusses several successful results pertinent to the prediction of leadership, using the concept of the focal person. For a variety of reasons it was not possible to replicate those results in the Harvard experiment, but the earlier results are of such interest that they will be summarized here anyway. The results bear on the question of leadership and leadership selection. With the development of the more refined and objective measuring techniques reported in Chapters 4 and 6 it should be possible to continue to explore this area.

The focal person (designated privately by the experimenter on the basis or patterns of FIRO scores) was, in fact, elected to a leadership role in the Washington experiment with what seemed like uncommon frequency. If election to the positions of coordinator and evaluator in the intercept and plotting problems is accepted as a measure of leadership, some *post hoc* predictions were borne out by the results shown in Table 7–18.

TABLE 7–18. *Post Hoc* **Prediction of Leadership from Focal Person Designations**

GROUP	PREDICTION (*POST HOC*)	OCCURRENCE	PREDICTION	CHANCE
E	*K* would be leader.	*K* was leader.	1/1	1/5
F	*M* would be leader, ousted by *E*.	*M* ousted by *E* in tenth meeting.	2/2	1/20
G	*D* would be leader.	*D* was leader.	1/1	1/5
H	*S* would be leader, ousted by *G*.	*S* ousted by *G* in ninth meeting.	2/2	1/20
J	*B* would be leader.	*B* was leader ousted by *M*.	0/1	1/5
K	*T* would be leader, ousted by *C*.	*T* was leader.	1/2	1/20
L	No strong leadership.	Low status member given role. Role relegated to minor importance.	1/1	1/2
M	No leadership.	Leader role consciously rotated through all members.	1/1	1/2

These predictions were not made prior to the experiment but were constructed *post hoc* in the following way:

1. A compatible pattern O focal person was "predicted" to be the leader.
2. For incompatible groups a situation was predicted where the FP_o would be selected originally and eventually would be ousted by the FP_u.
3. For compatible pattern W (pattern with no focal person) leadership was predicted to be weak, and it was predicted that the result would be a degrading of the leadership role.
4. For incompatible pattern R (same as the above incompatible pattern but with no FP's) a situation of no leadership was predicted, and it was predicted that the result would be a rotation of the leadership role.

According to a crude estimate of the accuracy of prediction, it appears that these *post hoc* predictions were correct nine of eleven times, or .82. Chance, making a few assumptions, would correctly predict eight of seventy-nine, or .10.

It was unfortunate that circumstances did not permit a replication of this result in the Harvard experiment. Instead, a composite measure of observers' ratings was made that comprised measures of "guiding group discussion," "influencing decisions," "attaining status and prominence," and "amount of participation." This index may be considered a measure of *centrality* of a member. It was felt that in general—though not necessarily in every instance—the focal persons should rate higher on this measure than would other types of members. This belief was easily tested by converting the scores of all sixty members on the centrality measure into standard scores. McCall T–scores (mean = 50, standard deviation = 10) seemed to be the simplest. For the eight overpersonal focal persons the mean centrality measure is 56. For the underpersonal focal person the mean score is 51. Combined, the mean score is 54. Thus it appears that overpersonal FP's are high on this centrality measure, but the underpersonal focal persons are not. This result may be interpreted as consistent with the above finding that a focal person—chosen on the basis of personality—has distinct "focal" characteristics when observed in a group, provided he is an overpersonal focal person. For underpersonal focal persons the picture is not yet clear.

FUTURE RESEARCH

Aside from the necessity for a broadening and deepening of the lines of experimentation described in this chapter, there is one type of compatibility that requires development almost from scratch. Need compatibility (nK) was defined in terms of the relative importance of each need area for a given individual. A method is required for assessing which areas of interpersonal needs are most salient for a given individual, in the sense that interaction in that area is most desired or most avoided. Several problems arise around the term "salient." If we recall the terminology regarding needs and anxieties (Chapter 2), the most salient need area would be the one in which the individual has highest anxiety.

If the parental interchange in one need area was completely satisfactory and left no anxiety, while parental interchange in another area was unsatisfactory and left the child with a residue of anxiety in that area, it seems that the second is more salient. However, if the reaction to the anxiety is withdrawal from interchange in that area, the area acquires a negative salience in that the actor strives to avoid it. For example, if the control problems operated satisfactorily and the individual was capable of both giving and taking orders, but the affection area was unsatisfactory in that not enough affection was received or allowed to be expressed, then affection is the more salient area. He can operate without anxiety in the control area while there is an unresolved issue in the affection area. Two major types of response to the affection difficulty have been discussed, a denial of the need to be liked and a lessening of emotional interchange between self and others (underpersonal), and an increase of emotional interchange to the point where each new relation offers a renewed opportunity to obtain the affection never received earlier (overpersonal). The second response is similar to the one described by Freud as the repetition compulsion. If the second response were used, then the affection area would certainly be the one the actor sought first in an interpersonal relation. If the first response is utilized, this area becomes the one pointedly avoided.

It appears, then, that in order to approach the problem of the relative salience of the three interpersonal areas a measure of relative strength of interpersonal anxieties is first required. Before an approach to such a measure can be presented, it is necessary to discuss the concept of anxiety in more detail.

The concept of anxiety is widely used in the clinical and psychiatric literature. Our concern is to deal with the concept as applied to interpersonal situations. Most clinical accounts of anxiety deal with "primary anxiety" and with "anticipatory anxiety." Fenichel (34), for example, says,

"The pain of the unavoidable early traumatic states, still undifferentiated and therefore not yet identical with later definite affects, is the common root of different later affects, certainly also of anxiety. The sensations of this 'primary anxiety' can be looked upon partly as the way in which tension makes itself felt and partly as the perception of involuntary vegetative emergency discharges. ... (p. 42)

"With anticipatory imagination and the resultant planning of suitable later action, the idea of danger comes into being. The judging ego declares that a situation that is not yet traumatic might become so. This judgment obviously sets up conditions that are similar to those created by the traumatic situation itself, but much less intense. This, too, is experienced as anxiety. ..." (p. 43)

Anxiety may be looked upon as the conscious or unconscious (verbally unaware) anticipation of psychic pain. More specifically, anxiety may be said to involve the anticipation of nonsatisfaction of a need, or even the consequent reinforcement of a negative self-perception (such as, "I am stupid").

Focusing on the interpersonal situation, the present theoretical development suggests that there are six basic sources of anxiety, three based on deprivation: (1) the anticipation of being ignored, or being insignificant; (2) the anticipation of not being influential, or not being competent; (3) the anticipation of not being loved or being lovable; and three based on excess, (4) the anticipation of being enmeshed, or being denied privacy, (5) the anticipation of having to take on too much responsibility, to be obligated, and (6) the anticipation of having more affection than can be handled, to be smothered.

This analysis suggests a parallel classification for the concept of "hostility." There are six types of hostility arising from the six sources mentioned above. These distinctions between types of anxiety and types of hostlity have important practical implications. For example, if a school child's hostility stems from fear of being ignored, the teacher may handle it by focusing some attention on the child. If, however, it rises from anticipation of being required to take responsibility which he is incapable of handling, such a response by the teacher would probably raise his anxiety and increase his hostility. He must be handled by assurances of assistance, and a minimizing of demands.

One implication of this type of classification is that it focuses attention on three specific areas in which to look for the source of anxiety. It seems quite likely that there are several different behavioral consequences depending on the source of the anxiety. It is expected that an individual may be free from anxiety in one or two of the areas even if he is highly anxious in the remaining areas.

Another implication of such a classification comes in the form of a suggestion for a measuring instrument. If all interpersonal anxieties can be classified into the three areas, an exhaustive list of anxieties can be made and used as a basis for measurement. One such list led to an instrument developed by Nancy Waxler in collaboration with the author. This instrument is called ASIA, for "areas of salient interpersonal anxiety."

Each item on ASIA begins by describing a hypothetical person. For every need area a situation is described with the following elements: (a) a person is described as characteristically behaving toward one end of the expressed dimension or the other, (b) the person is also described as being somehow dissatisfied with his behavior and wishing he could act more toward the middle of the expressed dimension, (c) the respondent is asked to guess why he thinks the hero does not change his behavior.

In this way the *expressed* axis is used to construct all possible types of anxiety within this theoretical framework, where anxiety is defined as the discrepancy between where a person behaves and where he would like to behave. Since he may be on either side of an ideal position on each of the three expressed dimensions, there are six possible situational sources of anxiety. They are diagrammatically shown in Figure 7–1.

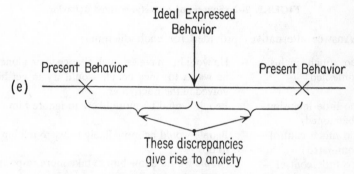

FIGURE 7–1. Sources of Anxiety: Expressed Behavior

A sample situation for too little affection (ASIA is in Appendix B):

When *C* is with people he is usually rather cool and reserved. He does not get very close to people and doesn't confide to them his feelings and worries.

However, sometimes he feels that he might enjoy his relationships with people more if he were not so cool and reserved.

Why would you guess he does not behave differently?

C is afraid that if he were close and personal. ...

The construction of the answer categories for these items utilizes the *wanted* dimension. The assumption is made that one set of reasons one doesn't change in one area concerns the more unwanted consequence that would occur in the same or another need area. For example, for *C* above one alternate answer is, "People would be more likely to try to tell him what to do"; in other words, people would deviate from the ideal position he wants them to have on the wanted control dimension. Again, there are two directions of deviation from the idea on each of the three wanted axes, hence six reasons for not changing undesirable behavior. These are shown diagrammatically in Figure 7–2.

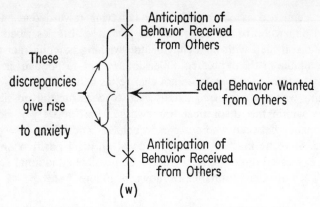

FIGURE 7–2. Sources of Anxiety: Wanted Behavior

Answer alternatives provided for each dilemma:

1. (too much inclusion—enmeshed)	He wouldn't have as much chance to be alone when he wants to since people would try to get him involved in their activities.
2. (too little inclusion—abandoned)	People would be more likely to ignore him.
3. (too much control—dominated)	People would be more likely to try to tell him what to do.
4. (too little control—undirected)	People would allow him to take more responsibility than he can handle.
5. (too much affection—smothered)	Certain individuals would try to become more intimate and personal with him than he would like.
6. (too little affection—unloved)	Certain individuals would be likely to be less friendly toward him.

Similarly, hypothetical problems are constructed for all six situations and the respondent asked to rank the same alternatives in order of appropriateness. If we assume that the respondents project their own feelings into these problems, a score may be obtained for the relative concern each anxiety area has for an individual.

Hence from the ASIA questionnaire the following information is obtainable:

1. The reaction of others most anxiety-producing to the respondent
2. The types of behavior the respondent expresses that make him most anxious
3. The specific responses of others to particular situations that make the respondent most anxious

The next step after ascertaining the pattern of salience is to discern how the individual copes with his anxiety. This step leads to an investigation of defense (coping) mechanisms. Discovery of these will then afford us the two ingredients needed for predicting the relative likelihood of an actor desiring to interact in each of the three interpersonal need areas, the salience of the area, and the mechanism used for coping with the area anxiety. Unfortunately, work has not yet progressed to the point where these properties are measurable. The general plan is to give alternatives representing various coping mechanisms for each problem, thereby connecting the defense with a specific anxiety. The method of presenting alternatives in this way was suggested by the work of Blum and Cutler (19). Once this measure is obtained, research may proceed on need compatibility and further investigations of the relations between need areas.

8

The Postulate of Compatibility:
Situational Factors

FUTURE RESEARCH (Continued)

Up to this point little attention has been given to certain important sociological concepts relevant to the compatibility postulate. Such terms as "role," "norm," "sanction," and "situation" should be explicable in terms of the present theoretical framework. The criticism has been made that these terms are not defined with sufficient precision. It is possible to define them in terms of specific numerical expressions by using the concepts and measuring instruments introduced in the ICA framework. Unfortunately, since there is at present only one empirical study relevant to these concepts, the entire discussion must be placed under "Future Research."

There is no question that environmental factors have an effect on the interpersonal phenomena under discussion so far. The problem raised by these factors is twofold:

1. What is the extent of the influence of these factors on interpersonal phenomena?
2. How can these factors be conceptualized most usefully to determine their importance?

The first problem is an empirical one, for which there are few data available. The second is a theoretical issue which will be considered in light of the present theoretical framework.

What is required is a schema for the classification of different types of roles, situation, norms, and sanctions. From the standpoint of interpersonal behavior this classification should be such that the interpersonal behavior of people varies, depending on the category (type) of situation, role, and the like in which they find themselves. In other words, it is of no value to define two different roles if all the interpersonal behavior exhibited by people is identical in both roles. This behavior is not a function of the role as defined and therefore there is no predictive advantage in taking account of roles.

For this reason the desirable classification schema defines classes in such a way that interpersonal behavior varies in significant ways with the class. From what has gone before, it follows that interpersonal behavior will be affected by situational factors to the extent that those factors impinge on the expression of the interpersonal behavior. In other words, the important characteristic of situational factors is the extent to which they require, encourage, or reward certain types of interpersonal behavior, and prohibit, discourage, or punish other types of interpersonal behavior. If this characteristic of a role, norm, sanction, or social situation may be ascertained, it may serve as a useful basis for classification. For example, if one role requires the role occupant to control others, while another role requires him to be controlled, it is a good guess that an individual's behavior in the two roles will be importantly different.

The Social Situation

A social situation refers in general to the circumstances in which interaction takes place. Any task of a group is an integral part of the external situation. The term "situation" will always mean "social situation."

Since Figure 6–1 will be referred to extensively in this chapter, it is repeated here.

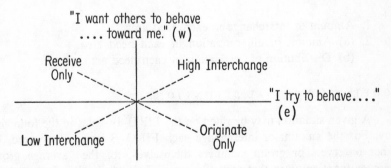

FIGURE 6–1. General Schema for Interpersonal Behavior Measured by FIRO–B

To describe a situation it is appropriate to describe the behavior of the group members with respect to the diagonals, interchange and origination. These, rather than the major axes, are chosen for describing the situation because diagonals are oriented more toward interaction than individual behavior. To determine a point on the diagonal requires knowledge of two persons' real or desired behavior, while a point on the major axes may be determined by reference to only one person's behavior.

Hence, a group situation is defined by

1. The amount of interchange in each need area which characterizes the situation (high interchange to low interchange).
2. The amount of differentiation of originating and receiving behavior in each need area which characterizes the situation (high origination differentiation to low origination differentiation).

The differentiation criterion requires further explanation. When applied to a dyad, this originate-receive diagonal is used to determine the complementarity of the two people on this dimension. With regard to larger groups, a fruitful use of the diagonal is for discriminating between a situation in which everyone falls at one extreme or the other (high differentiation), and a situation in which everyone is near the center of the dimension (low differentiation.) Examples of various situations having high and low differentiation will be given below for each need area.

Although differentiation is an important characteristic of a situation from the standpoint of its effect upon interpersonal behavior, one further property must be added. For a high-differentiation situation it is important to know how many individuals are high originators and how many are high receivers. For example, in the control area it may make a considerable difference in the interpersonal behavior if there is one person controlling all the rest (high control originators), or if there are several (for instance, a "central committee") controlling the rest.

A complete description of a situation, then, is given by its characteristic:

1. Amount of interchange in each need area.
2. (a) Amount of differentiation in each need area.
   (b) Distribution of origination in each need area.

SCORING OF SOCIAL SITUATIONS

A given situation may be rated on the FIRO–B scales in the following way. For the amount of interchange each FIRO–B item is answered, by either observers or group members themselves, for the "average group member functioning in that task situation." This phrase is substituted for the word "I" in each FIRO–B item and the six scores obtained. Examples of FIRO–B items used for classifying task situations are

1. The average group member functioning in this task situation tries to have close relations with the others.
2. The average group member functioning in this task situation lets other people control his actions.

The score for a situation is computed:

Inclusion interchange $(x^I) = e^I + w^I$
Control interchange $(x^C) = e^C + w^C$
Affection interchange $(x^A) = e^A + w^A$

To determine the differentiation score for a task situation the persons interacting must first be grouped according to differential behavior. For example, in an infantry squad on maneuvers, there might be two groups who behave differently, the sergeant and the remainder of the squad. The members of the squad need not be differentiated, since in the situation, maneuvers, their behavior is essentially the same. The phrase, "the average member of each subgroup in the situation ..." is substituted for the word "I" in FIRO-B items and scores obtained. Differentiation scores are obtained by adding the (e-w) for the various subgroups and averaging the difference. For example, on expressed control (e^C) the sergeant may score 9 and the squad 2, whereas on wanted control (w^C) the sergeant may score 3 and the squad 7. The control differentiation score (o^C) is

$$o^C = (e^C_{sgt} - w^C_{sgt}) + (e^C_{squad} - w^C_{squad}) = (9-3) + (2-7) = +1$$

(Low score indicates high differentiation.)

By inspection, the number of subgroups at the high and low ends of the origination axis could be determined. Hence, in this fashion any situation may be specified by the adapted FIRO–B with respect to interchange, differentiation, and differentiation distribution. This characterization will be useful for comparing situations as well as comparing individuals and groups with the situation in which they behave.

This classification will now be discussed for each need area, with examples of various types of situations.

INCLUSION

A situation in the area of inclusion is defined by

1. Inclusion interchange—the amount of interchange of interaction and contact among group members characteristic of the situation.
2. Inclusion differentiation—the amount of differentiation among members with regard to originating and receiving inclusion characteristic of the situation.

For the sake of exposition a dichotomous classification will be used for illustrating various types of situations. A situation is said to have high or low interchange and high or low differentiation. The terms "high" and "low" are approximated by the terms "required in the situation" and "prohibited in the situation."

The communication experiments of the Bavelas type (10) illustrate a situation that virtually prohibits "togetherness" and allows only a minimum amount of contact (written notes) between members. A second example in which interaction is virtually prohibited is the Crutchfield adaptation of the Asch conformity experiment (30). In this situation the subjects do not communicate with other subjects except by means of lights indicating the responses of other subjects—and these lights are usually not veridical. The atmosphere of the experiment is one in which close association is not permitted.

On the other hand, the discussion groups typical of many small group experiments or the plotting problems described in Appendix B are characterized by high inclusion interchange in that they require close interaction and contact.

In the plotting problem, for example, the nature of the situation is such that a high degree of contact and inclusion of other members is required by the task, since they all have a role in contributing to a successful outcome of the group task.

Situations vary along the inclusion differentiation dimension from high differentiation to low differentiation. High differentiation means that each member of the group has a distinct unambiguous role with respect to the origination of inclusion behavior. An example of this type of situation is fraternity rush-week ritual. Here the old fraternity members can include or exclude, but not be excluded (high inclusion origination), while the candidates can be included or excluded but cannot exclude (low inclusion origination) anyone. Hence the old members are the inclusion initiators only, while the rushees are the inclusion receivers only.

The social interaction situation involving restrictive covenants in real-estate dealings demonstrates high inclusion differentiation together with low inclusion interchange. The owners who exclude the minority group are the originators of interaction only, and the minority group members are inclusion receivers only.

The usual discussion task situation exemplifies the low inclusion differentiation situation. The requirements of the situation allow each member to originate and receive inclusion equally. (However, since the rules of the situation do not *require* an equal amount of origination and receiving, the discussion task is not the extreme of low inclusion differentiation.) A second example of low inclusion differentiation is the totally connected network in the Bavelas-type communication experiments (25). In this situation all members may communicate and be communicated with equally.

If the variables are dichotomized, Table 8–1 presents the four types of task situations in the inclusion area, with examples of each.

TABLE 8–1. Classification of Task Situations in the Inclusion Area

	HIGH INTERCHANGE	LOW INTERCHANGE
HIGH DIFFERENTIATION	Fraternity rushing	Restrictive covenants
LOW DIFFERENTIATION	Plotting problem	Bavelas circle

CONTROL

A situation in the control area is defined by

1. Control interchange—The amount of interchange among group members with regard to control and influence characteristic of the situation.
2. Control differentiation—The amount of differentiation among members regarding origination and reception of control and influence characteristic of the situation.

Situations vary along the interchange dimension from high control differentiation to low control differentiation. The dimension refers to the degree to which the situation calls for members mutually to influence and/or control one another. High interchange is well exemplified by a military structure where almost every man both controls, and is controlled by, other men. Any formal organization also has this characteristic, since position in the organization usually carries with it power over others as well as the requirement to take orders. A leadership structure also falls into this category.

When a hierarchy is imposed on a group by an experimenter, some member or members are required to control and some members to be controlled. In the famous experiments of Lewin, Lippitt, and White (59) the differences in "atmosphere" (which is almost equivalent to our term "amount of interchange") almost exactly correspond to high, middle, and low values of control interchange; the authoritarian atmosphere requires control, the democratic atmosphere neither requires nor prohibits control, and the laissez-faire atmosphere virtually prohibits control behavior.

High control differentiation refers to a situation in which some members are controllers and are not controlled, while other members are controlled and do not control. The simple authoritarian structure of one leader (originator only) and many followers (receivers only) is a good example of high control differentiation. Low control differentiation means a situation in which each member, regardless of the amount of control exercised in the situation (control interchange) controls to the same extent that he is controlled. Both the democratic and laissez-faire structures exemplify task situations of low control differentiation which differ in control interchange. Both require of each member about equal amounts of control and controlled behavior, while the interchange of control is less in the laissez-faire situation.

Finally, many traditional therapy situations provide an example of a low control interchange relation in that neither person exercises much power over the other. However, there is high control differentiation in that when control is exercised, as in termination of an interview, or determination of fee, it is usual that the therapist is the controller and the patient the controlled.

Again, by dichotomizing control interchange and control differentiation the results shown in Table 8–2 were obtained.

TABLE 8–2. Classification of Task Situations in the Control Area

	HIGH INTERCHANGE	LOW INTERCHANGE
HIGH DIFFERENTIATION	Autocratic structure	Therapy situation
LOW DIFFERENTIATION	Military structure	Laissez-faire structure

AFFECTION

A situation in the affection area is defined by

1. Affection interchange—The amount of interchange among members with regard to affection characteristic of the situation.
2. Affection differentiation—The amount of differentiation among members regarding initiation and reception of affection characteristic of the situation.

High affection interchange describes a situation in which many close, personal feelings are exchanged and close relations exist. Examples of high affection interchange include the marital situation, the family, dating relations, and some fraternal organizations. In these situations close affectional ties are virtually required. Low affection interchange task situations, those in which virtually no affection is exhibited, include board meetings, military wartime strategy conferences, and so forth. Here the expression of close personal feelings is usually considered inappropriate.

High affection differentiation occurs when each member is either clearly in the role of originator of affection and not receiver, or receiver of affection and not originator. Examples of high affection differentiation are mother and infant before he is capable of true affection; the unrequited love affair; and the adulation of a movie star in which only one gives affection and only one receives it. Low affection differentiation, where all members originate and receive equally, is exemplified by the ideal marriage, and the ideal family. Results of dichotomizing to enumerate types of situation in the affection area, with examples, are shown in Table 8–3.

TABLE 8–3. Classification of Task Situations in the Affection Area

	HIGH INTERCHANGE	LOW INTERCHANGE
HIGH DIFFERENTIATION	Parent-infant relation	Hero adulation
LOW DIFFERENTIATION	Marital relation	Committee meeting

Certain variables commonly used in experiments in group behavior create situations in which one or another value in one or more need areas is encouraged. For example, in terms of interchange, large groups as opposed to small groups probably tend to discourage interchange inclusion, make control interchange necessary for efficient operation, and discourage affection interchange, since there is less opportunity for close relations to develop. The same characteristics usually attend variables such as communication nets, which allow few connections. Other experimental setups could be similarly classified. Likewise, putting subjects under increased time pressure usually increases inclusion interchange, control interchange, and control differentiation, and probably has two effects on affection interchange: increased time pressure reduces the opportunity for close relations to develop but forces intense feelings, such as hostility, into the open.

SUMMARY

1. Unquestionably situational, or external, factors affect interpersonal behavior.

2. The effect of these factors—such as time pressure, size of group, communication pattern, leadership structure—on interpersonal behavior may be understood and predicted by assessing their effect on the opportunity for satisfying the three interpersonal needs.

3. Situations may be incorporated into the ICA framework by describing their interpersonal aspects.

4. The classification of situations was made such that groups interacting in any situation of a given class behave in essentially the same way, and such that this behavior is different from their behavior in a different class of task situations.

5. It is implied that properties of task situations other than those used in this classification scheme are relatively ineffective for predicting interpersonal phenomena. For example, if a "mechanical" task falls into the same interpersonal category as an "intellectual" task, the behavior of a group on each task should not be importantly different.

To test the fruitfulness of this explication of the term "task situation" an experiment done as a part of the Washington experiment is relevant. Since it was performed before the present theoretical framework was evolved, liberty shall be taken to express it in the present terminology.

Theorem 3–9. The effect of compatibility on productivity (the C–P effect) increases as the task situation requires more interchange in the three need areas.

The plausibility of this theorem is dependent on the underlying basis for the classification of task situations. One of the most common techniques for avoiding interpersonal difficulties is to withdraw from contact or to rely on standard conversation, small talk, and the rules of etiquette. (See Chapter 9 for a more extended discussion.) If people are in an interactional situation in which they are free to escape, cover over, or avoid differences, their compatibility need not affect their productivity appreciably. However, if they are placed in a situation in which they are forced to make decisions mutually and forced to reveal their feelings, then compatibility will have a considerable effect on their dealings together. That love affairs carried on through letters often fade suddenly when the lovers are rejoined exemplifies this phenomenon for affection interchange compatibility. The mother of quarrelsome children, who solves the problem by separating them, is reducing their inclusion interchange and thus decreasing the strains on their limited compatibility. Similarly, when a military unit goes on liberty its effectiveness may be greatly enhanced by the decrease in control interchange.

In general, the more people are required to cooperate and interchange contact, power, and love, the more important is the effect of compatibility on their performance together.

As a part of the Washington experiment Theorem 3–9 was tested directly. Three types of problems were given the subjects: coding, intercept, and plotting (see Appendix B). For each type of problem, several tasks were given, each task requiring successively more interchange in all three areas. All groups performed all problems, and the order of presentation was counterbalanced between compatible and incompatible groups; that is, there were several sequences, but each was followed by one compatible and one incompatible group.

1. *Coding problem.* Two coding tasks were given, the second more difficult than the first. Neither problem required a great deal of interchange in that one person could solve the task almost as well as the whole group.

2. *Intercept problem.* Several intercept tasks were given; these were designed (by increasing the difficulty and shortening the time for making decisions) to increase the required interchange. This problem forced interchange in that all men had to make the same decision concurrently. Differentiation increased also, in that it became more and more necessary to have one man make the final decision and the others merely aid him. The factor of social pressure was added when, after all individual tasks were completed, groups competed against each other.

3. *Plotting problem.* Three plotting tasks were given which increased the required interchange by decreasing the time allowed for completing each task. This limitation forced group members to rely on one another more heavily in this division of labor problem. (In this sense, the plotting problem necessitated more interchange than the intercept problem, since it was possible for men in the intercept tasks to withdraw without requiring another member to replace him immediately for a specific part of the job.) In the plotting tasks group members varied in how much work they had to do; therefore the increased time pressure necessitated that for optimal goal achievement the relatively idle needed to help the relatively busy.

From these considerations it was hypothesized that the coding problem, requiring the least interchange, would show the least effect of compatibility on productivity (C–P effect). At the time of the experiment it was not known whether the C–P effect would appear more in the intercept or the plotting problem, but current considerations would note that the plotting problem, requiring more interchange, should give rise to the greater C–P effect.

An analysis of variance was computed for the results across tasks for each type of problem, and across compatibility types.

The results showed no differences whatever between the compatible and incompatible groups on the coding problem. On the plotting problem there was a significant difference between compatibles and incompatibles throughout all tasks (F–test significant at $p < .03$). The intercept problem showed no over-all difference between compatibility types, but a very significant interaction term ($p < .01$), indicating that the compatibles outperformed the incompatibles on the difficult problems only. The difference in performance among intercept tasks was considerable ($p. < .001$).

These results may be interpreted in the following way: The coding tasks did not require enough interchange to elicit the C–P effect; this condition was also true of the simple intercept problems, but when required interchange increased, the C–P effect became significant; even the simplest plotting problem required enough interchange to elicit the C–P effect. This interpretation is corroborated by the following factors:

1. Increasing required interchange for the intercept problem had the effect of maintaining the decided superiority of the compatible groups over the incompatible. In the Washington experiment seven of eight direct contests between compatible and incompatible groups were won by the compatibles, and in the Harvard experiment contests between these two types of groups showed the compatibles winners in five of six contests. Twelve victories of fourteen contests, using the binomial expansion, could have occurred by chance less than .01. Thus, with the addition of social pressure, the superiority of the compatibles continued.

2. Subjects' informal comments about the difficulty of the plotting problem were frequent, and there was general dislike for the plotting problem (on a five-point scale the mean rank on liking the intercept problem was 2.08; the code problem, 2.26; and the plotting problem, 2.76). This result is presented graphically in Figure 8–1 (77).*

This study suggests that the aim of the classification of task situations has been met. Situations with differing interchange values do lead to importantly different interpersonal phenomena, namely, variation in the C–P effect.

For the future it is advantageous to discuss the compatibility of an individual, or a group, and a task situation. Since a situation may be defined in terms of interchange and differentiation, all the formulas introduced in Chapter 6 may be applied to a dyad consisting of an individual, or group, and a situation where both are defined in terms of FIRO–B scores.

* The figure is reprinted from W. C. Schutz, "What Makes Groups Productive?" *Human Relations*, 8, 1955, 429–465.

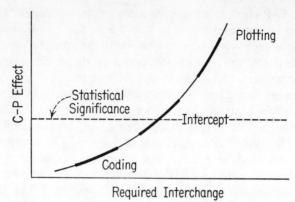

FIGURE 8-1. Interpretation of Productivity Results in Terms of Required Interchange and C-P Effect

Role

Attempts to define "role" in the ICA framework point out relations between various aspects of this concept, and the concepts "norm" and "sanction." The aim of giving an interpersonal definition to "role" is explication in the sense discussed previously. For a statement of the explicandum, the concept as it is usually used, a quote from Parsons (67) is helpful:

> "The role is that organized sector of an actor's orientation which constitutes and defines his participation in an interactive process. It involves a set of complementary expectations concerning his own actions and those of others with whom he interacts. Both the actor and those with whom he interacts possess these expectations." (p. 23)

Another approach to the concept of role is provided by Sarbin (75), who has elaborated what he calls "role theory":

> "A *role* is a patterned sequence of learned *actions* or deeds performed by a person in an interaction situation." (p. 225)

These approaches appear to highlight different aspects of the role concept.

An explication of the concept of role may be accomplished with the use of three variables:

1a. The behavior which the group (minus the role in question) expresses (e_h)
1b. The behavior which the group wants someone to express (w_h)
2a. The behavior expressed by the role player (e_r)
2b. The behavior which the role player wants from the group (w_r)
3. The perception of the situation by the role player (rol) or by observers (obs)

Table 8–4 shows how these variables may be arranged.

TABLE 8–4. Schema for Defining "Role," "Norm," and "Sanction"

	ROLE PLAYER'S PERCEPTION	OBSERVER'S PERCEPTION
BEHAVIOR OF GROUP (Alter)	e_h (rol) w_h (rol)	e_h (obs) w_h (obs)
BEHAVIOR OF ROLE PLAYER (Ego)	e_r (rol) w_r (rol)	e_r (obs) w_r (obs)

The Parsonian terms "alter" and "ego" correspond as indicated in the diagram. Inspection of the cells indicates several interesting properties of this matrix. Cells "e_h (rol)" and "w_h (rol)" correspond to what is often called *role expectation*. "Role expectation" may be defined as the role player's perceptions of what behavior the other group members want him to express in the role, and what behavior he perceives they express toward him.

Cells "e_h (obs)" and "w_h (obs)" correspond to *role definition*. "Role definition" is thus defined as the objective (observer's) view of what behavior the group members want from the role player and what behavior they express toward him. Role expectation and role definition seem to cover much of what is included in Parson's statement.

Sarbin's conception of role is better covered by cells "e_r (obs)" and "w_r (obs)," which, taken together, may be called *enacted role*. "Enacted role" is thus defined as the observer's perception of how the role player behaves toward the group and how he wants them to behave toward him.

This leaves cells "e_r (rol)" and "w_r (rol)," which apparently are not commonly discussed in the literature. The name *perceived role performance* seems applicable to those cells. This term is thus defined as the role player's perception of his expressed behavior toward the group and what behavior he wants from them.

MEASUREMENT OF ROLE

To obtain e_h and w_h for defining "role," the FIRO–B items are amended by substituting "group members" for the subject of the sentence "I," and "the role player" for the object of the sentence, usually "people." Some examples of FIRO–B items adapted to the definition of various aspects of role are

1. Group members try to be with the role player.
2. Group members let the role player decide what to do.
3. Group members try to have close relations with the role player.

To obtain e_r and w_r for purposes of defining "role," the substitutions are reversed, "group members" being substituted for "people," and "role player" being substituted for "I." Some examples of FIRO–B items for measuring e_r and w_r are

1. The role player lets the group members strongly influence his actions.
2. The role player tries to include group members in his plans.
3. The role player tries to get close and personal with the group members.

The adapted FIRO–B is then filled out by the role player (rol) or by observers (obs). The result is six scale scores (e^I, w^I, e^C, w^C, e^A, w^A) for both the role player and the group; from the standpoint of the group and of the observers, a total of twenty-four scale scores. These scores may then be combined, as indicated in Table 8–4, to obtain numerical representations of role expectation, role definition, perceived role performance, and enacted role.

EXAMPLES OF ROLES

To illustrate various types of roles as defined in this system, examples fitting all possible types (dichotomized) of *role definitions* will now be presented. As indicated earlier, a role is defined by

1. The characteristic behavior of other people in the situation toward the individual playing the role in each interpersonal need area (e_h^I, e_h^C, e_h^A).
2. The behavior the other people in the situation characteristically want from the person playing the role in each need area: (w_h^I, w_h^C, w_h^A).

INCLUSION

A role in the inclusion area is defined by

1. The amount of interaction with other people which the role player characteristically originates toward other members.
2. The amount of interaction the others characteristically originate toward him.

In the Bavelas "star" communication pattern (10) the central member is required to originate association (communication) with every other member. Only in that way will he be able to solve his problem. He may not expect communication (in some arrangements) from others through their own origination. They may even be prohibited from initiating communication by the rules laid down.

A peripheral member of the "star" pattern is prohibited from originating communication, but he must receive communication. A member in a small discussion group is required both to originate interaction and to be included in the group. A criminal is prohibited from associating with a group and to a slightly lesser extent from being associated with, by the group members. The owner of a small food store or a military recruiter has a similar inclusion role in that he is virtually prohibited from originating contact with potential customers, but it is virtually certain that he will receive contact and associations. As a final example, a new traveling salesman is required to originate interaction but may expect virtually no one to originate contact toward him. (See Table 8–5.)

TABLE 8–5. Classification of Roles in the Inclusion Area

	HIGH EXPRESSED	LOW EXPRESSED
HIGH RECEIVED	Central-star	Recruiter
LOW RECEIVED	Traveling salesman	Criminal

CONTROL

The control area includes the roles usually discussed under the heading of leadership. An authoritarian leadership role requires the role player to control others and virtually prevents others from controlling him. The person in a follower role in an authoritarian structure must be controlled but is prohibited from controlling. The military officer is required both to be controlled by his superiors and to control his subordinates. The role of a member of a Quaker meeting exemplifies low control interchange; that is, he neither controls nor is controlled.

A role in the control area is defined by

1. The amount of control an individual characteristically exerts over others.
2. The amount of control others characteristically exert over him.

(See Table 8–6.)

TABLE 8–6. Classification of Roles in Control Area

	HIGH EXPRESSED	LOW EXPRESSED
HIGH RECEIVED	Military officer	Follower
LOW RECEIVED	Autocrat	Quaker

AFFECTION

A role in the affection area is defined by

1. The amount of affection a role player characteristically expresses toward other group members.
2. The amount of affection he characteristically receives in this role.

More informal, close groups such as the family furnish examples for this area. The role of the wife or husband usually requires expressing affection and receiving affection from the spouse. At the other extreme, the marine drill instructor is virtually prohibited from expressing affection, and his role rarely elicits affection from others. One asymmetric role is exemplified by the parent-infant relation in that the parent originates but does not receive affection, while the infant receives but does not originate affection.

Table 8–7 gives a summary of the preceding discussion.

TABLE 8–7. Description of Roles in Affection Area

	HIGH EXPRESSED	LOW EXPRESSED
HIGH RECEIVED	Spouse	Infant
LOW RECEIVED	Parent of infant	Drill instructor

Norm

The concept of *norm* is readily explicable in the present framework. If "average group member" is substituted for "role player," cell "w_h (obs)" closely approximates the usual meaning of norm. Then "norm" is defined as the behavior the group wants from the average group member.

MEASUREMENT OF NORMS

The only items needed for defining "norm" are the w scales, half of FIRO–B, with the substitutions of "the group" for "I," and "average group member" for "people." Examples of FIRO–B items adapted to the definition of "norm" are

1. The group lets the average group member decide what to do.
2. The group expects the average group member to invite the other members to things.
3. The group likes the average group member to act cool and distant toward the other members.

The norm of a group is then defined as a set of three numbers; these are scale scores computed from the adapted FIRO–B for w^I, w^C and w^A.

Sanction

The term "sanction" introduces a new element in the schema. Parsons (68, p. 15) states, "The contingent reactions of an alter to ego's actions may be called sanctions." The time dimension is introduced, since sanction refers to the reaction of the group (alter) to a behavior of a particular group member (ego) or role player. In the present framework this is the e_h (obs) in response to an enacted role e_r (obs), w_r (obs). "Sanction" is then defined as the behavior of the group toward an individual member, in response to that individual's expressed and wanted behavior toward the group.

MEASUREMENT OF SANCTION

The adaptation of FIRO–B for purposes of defining "sanction" involves an additional element. "The group" or "group members" is substituted for "I," and "members who ..." is substituted for "people." The phrase "members who ..." is completed by describing the expressed and wanted behavior of a group member in his enacted role ,which is defined by the six scale scores e^I, w^I, e^C, w^C, e^A, w^A. This limits the present definition of sanctions to those applied to interpersonal behavior. Examples of FIRO–B items adapted for use in defining "sanction" are

1. The group tries to be with members who are (underpersonal).
2. The group's personal relations with members who are (autocratic) are cool and distant.
3. The group lets (overpersonal) members control their actions.

The sanction is defined as six scale scores derived from the adapted FIRO–B, with respect to specific members' interpersonal behavior.

Summary

The above definitions are summarized in Table 8–8:

TABLE 8–8. Explication of "Role," "Norm," and "Sanction"

		PERCEPTION OF ROLE PLAYER	PERCEPTION OF OBSERVER	
BEHAVIOR OF GROUP	e_h w_h	Role expectation	Role definition ←	Norm (for role player=average group member)
BEHAVIOR OF ROLE PLAYER	e_r w_r	Perceived role performance	Enacted ← role ←	Sanction=response e_h to previous e_r and w_r

All these concepts are measurable adaptations of FIRO–B which use a technique analogous to that used for defining "task situation."

This completes the explication of the terms "role expectation," "role definition," "enacted role," "perceived role performance," "norm," "sanction," and "situation." These terms were all given explicit numerical definitions in terms of the ICA framework, and of adaptations of the FIRO–B scales. This process provides exactness and simplicity for the definitions. A third criterion for the adequate explicatum, similarity to the explicandum, was met by quoting fairly well-accepted sociological definitions for these terms. Whether or not these explications will satisfy the final criterion for an adequate explication, fruitfulness, remains to be seen. Fruitfulness can be determined only by using these definitions as a basis for empirical investigations. If they prove fruitful, the definitions have the added virtue of being part of a more extensive theoretical framework and thus mutually supportive with that framework.

9

The Postulate of Group
Development

Postulate 4. *The Postulate of Group Development.* **The formation and development of two or more people into an interpersonal relation (that is, a group) always follows the same sequence.**

> *Principle of Group Integration.* **For the time period starting with the group's beginning until three intervals before the group's termination the predominant area of interaction begins with inclusion, is followed by control, and finally by affection. This cycle may recur.**
> *Principle of Group Resolution.* **The last three intervals prior to a group's anticipated termination follow the opposite sequence in that the predominant area of interpersonal behavior is first affection, then control, and finally inclusion.**

This postulate[1] states that every interpersonal relation follows the same course of development and resolution. The time intervals mentioned in the statement of the postulate are successive, exhaustive intervals which change when, and only when, the predominant area of interaction (I, C, or A) changes. Thus rating of interaction may be accomplished through the use of the FIRO Content Questionnaire described at the end of this chapter. The recurrent property of these cycles means that after a group has gone

[1]Much of the material in this chapter is strongly influenced by Bennis and Shepard (14) and draws from later discussions with, and a memorandum of, Bennis (12). For the clinical descriptions I have drawn heavily from discussions with E. V. Semrad and the Group Research Project of the Massachusetts Mental Health Center supported by Public Health Training Grant 2M6378.

through the phases of inclusion, control, and affection it may begin another such cycle prior to its separation period. Hence the Postulate of Group Development says that the sequence of interaction for any interpersonal relation or group is

$$I C A I C A \ldots A C I.$$

PLAUSIBILITY

For establishing the meaning and plausibility of the Postulate of Group Development it will be convenient to use examples from certain group process training groups. These are groups run by Elvin V. Semrad of the Massachusetts Mental Health Center for the purpose of teaching the participants the principles of "group process." Semrad conducts them by allowing the participants to interact as a group and by supporting them in making observations about their own behavior (78). They characteristically run weekly for thirty to forty-five weeks and are made up of young social workers, psychologist, and psychiatrists. They will be referred to as "Semrad groups."

Recently the author was interviewing a member of a thirty-meeting Semrad group to get an idea of her feeling about the experience. In response to the question, "How would you describe what happened in this group?" she replied, "Well, first you're concerned about the problem of where you fit in the group; then you're wondering about what you'll accomplish. Finally, after a while you learn that people mean something. Your primary concern becomes how people feel about you and about each other." This constitutes a splendid statement of the Principle of Group Integration.

Inclusion Phase

The inclusion phase begins with the formation of the group. When people are confronted with one another they first find the place where they fit. This involves being in or out of the group, establishing one's self as a specific individual, and seeing if one is going to be paid attention to and not be left behind or ignored. This anxiety area gives rise to individual-centered behavior, such as overtalking, extreme withdrawal, exhibitionism, recitation of biographies, and other previous experience. At the same time the basic problem of commitment to the group is present. Each member is implicitly deciding to what degree he shall become a member of the group—how much investment he will withdraw from his other commitments and invest in this new relation. He is asking, "How much of myself will I devote to this group? How important will I be in this setting? Will they know who I am and what I can do, or will I be indistinguishable from many others?"—the problem of identity. He is, in effect, primarily deciding on his preferred amount of inclusion interchange, and his preferred amount of inclusion initiation with the other members—just how much actual contact, interaction, and communication he wishes to have.

Hence the main concerns of the formative process are "boundary problems," problems that have to do with entering into the boundaries of a group, and belonging to that group. Boundary problems are problems of inclusion.

Characteristic of groups in this phase is the occurrence of what Semrad has called "goblet issues." The term is taken from an analogy to a cocktail party where people sometimes pick up their cocktail glass, or goblet, and figuratively use it to peer through to size up the other people at the party. Goblet issues are those which, in themselves, are of minor importance to the group members but which function as vehicles for getting to know people, especially in relation to the self. Often a goblet issue is made of the first decision confronting a group. In groups run by Semrad for the purpose of teaching group dynamics (78) he characteristically provides them with a decision to make at the outset, by stating that other groups in the past had usually taken minutes of every meeting, and asking whether or not they would like to. In some groups discussions leading to a decision about this issue continue for fifteen meetings, and then often without a conclusion. But there has been a great deal of learning in the group in that the members all have a fairly clear picture of one another. Each member knows who responds favorably to him, who sees things the way he does, how much he knows compared to the others, and how the group leader responds to him; and he has a fair idea of what type of role he can expect to play in the group.

The goblet issue is by no means confined to Semrad groups and cocktail parties. The frustrating experience of having groups discuss endlessly topics of little real interest to anyone is very common. Each group finds its own goblet issues within the framework of its aim. "The weather" is fairly universal; "rules of procedure" is common in formal groups; "do you know so-and-so?" often characterizes new acquaintances from the same location; relating incidents or telling stories has a goblet element for business gatherings; and "where are you from?" often serves for military settings. Mark Twain apparently overlooked the fact that nobody really *wants* to "do anything about the weather"; people merely want to use it as a topic for sizing up others. Such discussions are inevitable; contrary to outward appearances, they do serve an important function, and groups not permitted this type of testing out will search for some other method of obtaining the same information, perhaps using as a vehicle a decision of more importance to the group.

Control Phase

After the problems of inclusion have been sufficiently resolved, control problems become prominent. Once members are fairly well established as being together in a group, the issue of decision-making procedures arises, which involve problems of sharing responsibility and its necessary concomitant, distribution of power and control. Characteristic behavior at this stage includes a leadership struggle, competition, discussion of orientation to the task, structuring, rules of procedure, methods of decision making, and sharing responsibility for the group's work. The primary anxieties at this phase revolve around having too much or too little responsibility, and too much or too little influence. Each member is trying to establish himself in the group so that he will have the most comfortable amount of interchange and the most comfortable degree of initiation with the other members with regard to control, influence, and responsibility.

Affection Phase

Finally, following a satisfactory resolution of these problems of control, problems of affection become focal. The individuals have come together to form a group, they have differentiated themselves with respect to responsibility and power, and now they must become emotionally integrated. At this stage it is characteristic to see such behavior as expression of positive feelings, direct personal hostility, jealousies, pairing behavior, and, in general, heightened emotional feeling between pairs of people. The primary anxieties in this stage have to do with not being liked or not being close enough to people, and with too much intimacy. Each member is striving to obtain for himself in the group his most comfortable amount of affectional interchange and most comfortable position regarding initiating and receiving affection. Each is deciding, like Schopenhauer's, via Freud (36), porcupines, how to get close enough to receive warmth yet far enough away to avoid the pain of sharp quills. Thus we have the picture of the group members attempting successively to achieve an optimal amount of interchange and an optimal degree of initiating and receiving, with respect to the group, regarding interaction, responsibility or influence, and love or emotional closeness.

Discussion

These are not distinct phases. The group development postulate asserts that these problem areas are *emphasized* at certain points in a group's growth. All three problem areas are always present but not always of equal salience. Similarly, some persons do not always go along with the central issue for the group. For certain individuals a particular problem area will be so personally potent that it will transcend the current group issue. For any person, his area of concern will be the resultant of his individual problem areas and those of the group's current phase. Perhaps a somewhat closer approximation to the developmental phenomena is given by the "tire changing" model. When a person changes a tire and replaces the wheel, he first sets the wheel in place and secures it by sequentially tightening each bolt, but just enough to keep the wheel in place and make the next step possible.

Then the bolts are tightened farther, usually in the same sequence, until the wheel is firmly in place. And, finally, each bolt is gone over separately to secure it fast. In a way similar to the bolts, the need areas are worked on until they are handled satisfactorily enough to continue with the work at hand. Later on they are returned to and worked over to a more satisfactory degree. If one bolt was not tightened well on the first sequence, on the next cycle it must receive more attention, and so on.

Since all groups have members with interpersonal needs that must be satisfied by the other members, this analysis should hold for any interpersonal relation. Every time people form themselves into groups, including two-person groups, the same three interpersonal problem areas are dealt with in the same order. In certain social situations external forces may be imposed to alter the manner of handling the problem areas, but they still must be dealt with. For example, in the military organization the uniform is certainly an aid to a feeling of belonging or inclusion. The stripes or bars on the arm or shoulder contribute to a clarification of the problems of responsibility and power distribution. And fraternization rules and customs have an influence on the expression of affection. However, these external factors by no means solve the interpersonal problems. The uniformed soldier may still feel that he is being ignored as an individual or that he is not being treated as an important person. The sergeant may feel that he should have more influence than his inexperienced lieutenant. And the friendly captain may feel sharply the conflict between the rules of personal separation for officers and enlisted personnel, and his desire to get to know one of his corporals personally, especially if she is a WAC.

A qualification of the postulate occurs because not all group gatherings meet long enough to develop through all stages. This fact is of great importance in research on small groups since it indicates the great difficulty of generalizing from groups that meet for a few meetings—perhaps working only on inclusion and possibly control problems—to more long-term or permanent groups. This factor is also of great importance when combined with the concept of compatibility. Since the definition of "compatibility" asserts three basic types of compatibility, corresponding to these three areas (K^I, K^C, K^A), the particular phase through which the group is going is pertinent to predicting how well the relation will function.

A final observation about the sequence of group development relates to the discussion of mental illness in Chapter 2. If there is any validity to the assertion that the pathological consequences of difficulties in the three need areas are, respectively, psychosis, psychopathy, and neurosis, then irrational behavior at each stage of group development should be qualitatively different. At the beginning quasi-psychotic behavior should not be unexpected, next psychopathic behavior, and, finally, in the affection phase, neurotic behavior. Some examples will clarify this notion.

Recently in one Semrad group the behavior of one member at the outset of the group appeared dissociated. He would wander into the discussion with some associations of his own, apparently almost oblivious of the conversation. Occasionally he would make references to private matters no one else knew about. He would often talk so softly no one could possibly hear him. As the group progressed, this behavior declined, and his contributions became much more oriented to the proceeding discussion. He was even moved to observe, in a later meeting, how he seemed to hear everyone much better now than he used to. This might be described as quasi-psychotic behavior, in that it was apparently dissociated from the here-and-now. It started at the initial meetings of the group and gradually declined.

In another Semrad group, during the middle phase, which could reasonably be called the control phase, there was a great deal of talk about the group's "delinquency." Prolonged discussion revolved around the topic of the members' doing what they were not supposed to do, for instance, writing papers, ignoring the leader's wishes, and in general having fun when they should be working. This type of problem occurs frequently as the struggle between work and gratification. Such "delinquency," as the members labeled their actions, may be considered quasi-psychopathic behavior.

Frequently when groups are dealing with the affection area, the problem of separation arises. One frequent technique for handling separation illustrates well the quasi-neurotic behavior during the affection stage. One member will be somewhat uncomfortable in the face of the impending rupture of the friendships he has formed; thus he will deliberately antagonize the other members until he is rejected from the group. This, of course, is precisely what he does not want, and is a quasi-neurotic solution for his discomfort.

It will be interesting to pursue this notion for the development of groups and also for the resolution phase as stated in the Postulate of Resolution. Groups or relations that are imminently terminating or markedly reducing their interaction exhibit fairly characteristic behaviors. Absences and latenesses increase, there is more daydreaming, people forget to bring materials to the group, discussion of death and illness is frequent, the importance and goodness of the group is minimized, general involvement decreases, and often there is a recall of earlier experience. It seems that members have a desire to discuss the events within the group that were not completely worked through at the time they occurred; in this way they hope that their relations will be successfully resolved. Often, when one member feels that his reaction in an earlier meeting was misunderstood, he will recall the instance and explain what he really had meant to say, so that no one will be angry with him. Or perhaps a member wants to tell another what an important comment that member made in an earlier meeting and how much better it made him feel. And on and on it goes, with all unresolved incidents being reworked. After this process of résumé the group members seem more capable of accepting their separation and resolving their relations.

In the process of resolution there seems to be a particular sequence in which these problems are dealt with. The personal positive and negative feelings are dealt with first, as in the examples in the above paragraph. Next, discussion focuses on the leader and on the reasons for compliance or rebellion to his wishes. Later come discussions about the possibilities of continuing the group and about how committed each member really was; finally, about the fact that they are all going into different groups and will no longer be members of the present one. This sequence reverses the formation sequence by first decathecting (withdrawing investment from) the affectional ties, then the control problems, and finally the inclusion phenomena.

Another important variable in understanding the withdrawal of investment from the group is individual differences. Depending upon both their major need areas and the preferred methods of coping with anxiety, individuals respond very differently to impending separation. A common technique is the gradual withdrawal of investment characterized by increased absence, lateness, low participation, and so forth. A second common method is to disparage and demean the group, as if to say, "You see, I won't miss such an unimportant group." Another less common technique is to shift the responsibility for separation onto the other group members by becoming antagonistic and forcing them to reject him from the group. A fourth technique for handling separation is so basic that it becomes a character trait. The person using this technique refrains from becoming invested in people from the beginning of their meetings, since the pain of separation is so great.

Thus there are different coping techniques for handling separation anxiety. There are also individual differences with respect to need areas. One individual may be concerned primarily with affection, and orient his behavior in the final stages of the group entirely to working through his positive and negative feelings toward each of the members individually, rather than working on problems concerning the group as a whole. Again, the behavior of group members during the closing stages of an interpersonal relation is a function of the needs of the individual members and the stage of the group's development.

Individual Development

It is interesting to speculate on the generality of this sequence. There is scattered evidence to indicate that the interpersonal development throughout an individual's lifetime occurs in three major cycles of group or interpersonal development (see Figure 9–1). This first major cycle involves integration and resolution with parental figures, where the child must learn to deal with those older and more experienced than he. The resolution of this relation involves working from the relation of child to parent, to the relation of adult to parent. This resolution usually begins in adolescence and coincides with the beginning of the second major cycle, the integration and resolution of relations with peers. The resolution of this relation coincides with the integration phase of the third major cycle, relations to child figures, those who are younger, less experienced, and more dependent than the self. Resolving the relation with the children is often followed by a resolution of one's whole life. In a manner similar to the group decathexis mentioned earlier, people relive their lives, memory by memory, with the result that they resolve all their relations and convert them into pleasant memories.

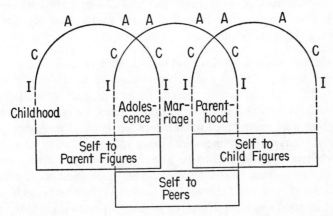

FIGURE 9–1. Summary of Interpersonal Cycles in Individual Development

CHILDHOOD

This three-cycle hypothesis seems reasonable for childhood for the reasons mentioned earlier. The three phases of inclusion, control, and affection parallel the oral, anal, and phallic stages, respectively, differing only in that they emphasize the predominant interpersonal relation rather than the important erogenous zone. The only point of serious contention concerns the placing of inclusion rather than affection at the first stage.

A great deal of the literature stresses the importance of love in the initial stages of the child's development; indeed, in the early drafts of this book the affection area was placed first. However, owing to a suggestion from Semrad, inclusion seemed to fit more logically as the first stage. For the infant the initial stages of development are almost completely narcissistic, being occupied with supplying the needs of the self and avoiding a diffuse anxiety probably best described as fear of abandonment. The affectional relation requires a rather mature individual, one capable of investing something of himself in another person, a feat not possible for a child before perhaps four or five years of age. In addition, the oedipal problem which arises in the phallic stage is certainly centered on the affectional area.

The present theoretical approach suggests that during the first year the infant has a need, not especially for love, but principally for inclusion. Perhaps the two are often confused, since for the first year love ordinarily includes attention and inclusion. However, the crucial relation is one of inclusion. In some studies the inference has been made that love is withdrawn from the child because the parent physically leaves. However, it may be that the lack of attention is the predominant factor. A crucial experiment still remains to be made on this difference.

The classical experiment in this area was made by Spitz (84, 85). A few quotes from Munroe's (66) summary* of the Spitz experiment will demonstrate that the results found could just as well—perhaps better—be explained as resulting from the lack of inclusion rather than affection. Spitz himself used the term "mothering."

"Spitz followed the development of 34 infants in their own homes, but he has not reported on these observations; he used them, instead, as control for two contrasting institutional groups, each with a population of 90 to 100 babies. In one institution, called the Nursery, unmarried mothers were encouraged to care for their babies themselves, or with 'fairly' adequate substitutes—i.e., other young women in the institution —when the mother had to be away. The over-all ratio of care was about two babies to one 'mother.' The other institution, called the Foundlinghome, had facilities for physical hygiene and nourishment at least as good as in the 'Nursery,' in fact, better as regards the professional medical standards. Here there was no positive cruelty toward the babies, but the nursing staff was so limited that each nurse cared for about ten babies. The two institutions were selected for study because the groups involved were essentially similar in ethnic and economic background and the infants apparently about equal in endowment at the age of four months. (In the 'Foundlinghome' regime, the mothers usually suckled the babies for a few months but then renounced their motherhood completely.)

"Considered as a group, the Nursery babies made normal progress as determined by the (1) general impression of activity and emotional responsiveness, (2) maintenance of the developmental quotient (DQ) and on regularly administered psychological tests, and (3) physical examination and health record. There were no deaths and no serious epidemics, even though only commonsense precautions were taken against infection.

"The fate of the Foundlinghome babies was tragic on all these counts: (a) The general impression was one of apathy and deathly silence. (b) The mean DQ of the group dropped progressively with age to a group mean of 45 (low-grade moron). This statistical finding is made more vivid by the statement that among 21 children aged 2 1/2 to 4 1/2 years (there were 91 in the total group), only five could walk unassisted, eight could not even stand alone, only one had a vocabulary of a dozen words, six could not talk at all, and eleven had only two

*Reprinted from *Schools of Psychoanalytic Thought,* by Ruth L. Munroe, by permission of The Dryden Press, Inc. Copyright, 1955, by The Dryden Press.

words. (c) The health record shows that, despite elaborate medical precautions ('No person whose clothes and hands were not sterilized could approach the babies'), 34 of these 91 babies died. All but one of the older group was seriously underweight, despite a carefully supervised and varied diet.

"From these contrasting data, Spitz draws the conclusion that 'mothering' is essential to the infant far beyond the mere provenance of physical care. He supports his intergroup observations with instances of variation within the Nursery group. When the mother left for a period of several months, the child very often developed a condition which Spitz calls 'anticlitic depression,' similar in kind to the condition of the babies found in the Foundlinghome. The condition was dramatically reversible on the mother's return, although it is not certain how long a delay can be tolerated before the extreme and apparently irreversible condition observed in Foundlinghome infants sets in."

Thus the main variable seemed to be the amount of attention the children received (two babies to one "mother" vs. ten babies to one nurse). The description of the children as "apathetic" is congruent with the idea that lack of interaction diminishes motivation to live (see Chapter 2).

In a follow-up study by Goldfarb (41) the results are similarly interpretable. The degree and kind of psychological difficulties were found to be dramatically correlated with duration of stay in the institution, age at entrance, foster-home placement, and the like, and *amount of parental interest*. Again, there is no necessity for assuming love as the relevant factor. The terms used by Spitz and Goldfarb, "mothering" and "parental interest," may both be interpreted as more nearly inclusion than affection.

ADOLESCENCE AND YOUNG ADULTHOOD

The stage of adolescence may be formulated in terms of the group development postulate. The adolescent is caught in the midst of two powerful processes; he is separating from the close relation he had with his parents when he was a younger child and trying to work through his new relation to a successful resolution, and he is becoming integrated with his peer group. With regard to his parents, he must work through each interpersonal area to the point where he does not have such dependent feelings but is capable of being more of an autonomous individual. The final resolution of the affectional problems with the parents must be worked through so that the adolescent can feel real affection for his parents as parental figures and not as love objects or sexual rivals. The socially inappropriate sexual impulses and resultant guilt feelings toward the mother have to be accepted and replaced with an appropriate heterosexual relation between adult and mother. The control area often leads to direct conflict about taking responsibility and striking out for oneself. A new balance must be established in which the adolescent takes on more responsibility and has more decision-making prerogatives. Finally, the actual physical separation—the inclusion problem—is dealt with. It seems that the separation from parents can be accomplished successfully only if the affection and control areas have been satisfactorily worked through. The parents and the adolescent must have a secure feeling about the degree of closeness mutually felt; otherwise physical separation will become symbolic of affectional conflicts, above and beyond the realistically based desires for increased or decreased contact. Similarly, control problems regarding mutual influence and control can cause no end of difficulty unless successfully resolved. The final area of the relation finds resolution when mutual agreement is reached regarding the optimal amount of inclusion or interaction that will exist between the parent and adolescent.

While these tremendously powerful relations are being worked through, the adolescent is striving to integrate himself with his peer group. It is this group with whom he will be primarily oriented throughout the next years of his life especially, and from whom he will receive most of his gratification. The cycle of interpersonal integration begins again, just as it did in infancy, except that this time the individual is integrating with his peers rather than with his parents. First, the inclusion problem looms large. The tremendous adolescent emphasis on joining, on being a member of the gang, on being like the others, on getting into one of the numerous clubs, on "belonging," characterizes this area. The conflict between inclusion with peers and parents is exemplified by the parents' lament, "It seems as though you'd rather be with your friends than stay home with us." Control problems usually come out in the guise of leadership, "big man on campus," and the frequent adolescent tests of skill and manliness such as hot-rod racing and gang fights. The affectional ties again develop, finally, as the adolescent begins to pay attention to the opposite sex and dating, and as the establishment of close personal relations takes the center of the developmental stage.

If this analysis approximates the adolescent's interpersonal situation, there is little wonder that this period is one of strife and turmoil, even under the most favorable circumstances. The combination of resolution with the parents and integration with peers, involving all three areas occuring in reverse order, means that the adolescent's behavior and feelings in these areas are under constant cross pressures.

PARENTHOOD

The coming of children ushers in the third major type of interpersonal relation. The parent must resolve his relations with peers, because of demands for spending less time with them and more time with his children. He usually must give up spending many evenings with the boys, dating, going to dances, even going out often at night, and instead must devote part of this time to integrating himself with his children. The first problem is making the decision to give up peers for children and deciding just how much time will be devoted to them. The question of the importance of the child to the parent is an early issue.

Next, discipline becomes the issue; finally, the parent develops a genuine affection feeling for the individual person emerging from the infant. These phases are the other side of the child development coin.

The sequence of resolution of peer relations at this stage is not yet clear enough to be described, nor is there much relevant empirical work on the problem of the impact of children on peer relations. Perhaps more research will be forthcoming.

Theorem 4–1. **(1) If a group is high on inclusion compatibility (K^I) but low on K^C and K^A, the group members will be most compatible during the initial stages of their relation.**

(2)   If a group is high on K^C, but low on K^I and K^A, group members will be most compatible during the middle stages of their relation.

(3)   If a group is high on K^A, but low on K^I and K^C, group members will be most compatible during the last stages of their relation prior to the separation sequence.

From the Postulate of Group Development and the Postulate of Compatibility this theorem may be derived informally. Since the definition of compatibility includes the idea that the need area in which the group is interacting is the determinant of whatever area of compatibility is most important, the group development postulate allows it to be said that inclusion compatibility is the most important ingredient of total compatibility for the first phase of the development of an interpersonal relation, control compatibility for the second phase, and affection compatibility for the third phase.

In many ways this theorem embodies the most exciting consequence of the theory to date. Since there are three separate areas in which compatibility is measured, it is necessary to find some way of determining which measures to use for a particular application of the compatibility formulas. The postulate that groups progress through definite stages during which certain problem areas are primary suggests a technique for such a determination.

If the group is involved in inclusion problems, it seems reasonable that the compatibility existing between members with regard to inclusion should be the primary determinant of the group's behavior. Similarly, if control problems and power struggles are the issue, then compatibility regarding control should be the main governor of the group's activity. For the longer-term groups which reach the affection phase, how well people fit together with regard to affection should be central. It is important to note that these appropriate compatibilities are only *primary,* not all-determining, because (a), following the "tire-changing" analogy, all three problems are being worked on in varying degrees, so that rarely will a phase be purely in one area; (b) there is a cumulative effect, as in infant development, such that the unresolved parts of problems arising in earlier phases persist residually during subsequent phases; and (c) certain individuals are preoccupied with one area almost regardless of the phase of the group.

The last point indicates the importance of need compatibility (nK). Certain persons may be so centrally concerned with a given area that the natural course of the group leaves them relatively unaffected. Their chief source of difficulty in the group is that interchanges between group members do not occur often enough in their salient interpersonal area. This, a different source of difficulty from those described earlier, indicates again the importance of need area compatibility (see Chapter 6).

The implications of Theorem 4–1 for compatibility are very great. If, for example, the compatibility of an *ad hoc* committee which meets once is to be predicted, the predictive emphasis should be on inclusion and control compatibility. However, an industrial work group or research team whose members characteristically work together over a long period of time should be evaluated primarily on the basis of affection compatibility.

The evidence for this theorem is highly inferential but promising. It comes primarily from three studies already reported. In the Washington and Harvard studies the principal basis for composing the groups was the affection interchange compatibility (xK^4). The study by Gross, investigating cohesion and compatibility, found a relation between cohesion and both affection and control compatibility. One primary difference between the sets of experimental subjects used in these studies is that the first groups (Washington-Harvard) met for ten and fourteen meetings, whereas those used by Gross had met only three times. If it is assumed that the Washington-Harvard groups had a greater chance of reaching the affectional phase, then the results would be consistent with theory. The control compatibility loomed large for a group with only three meetings, while the affection compatibility alone was adequate to make significant predictions for ten and fourteen meeting groups.

Obviously, there are many loopholes in this argument; that is, there was no measure made of control compatibility in the Washington and Harvard experiments. Some of the difficulties will be discussed and solutions proposed in the following section.

The evidence from the fraternity study (Chapter 7) presents a novel type of confirmation of Theorem 4–1. It will be recalled that inclusion compatibility was most important for choosing fraternity officers, especially chancellor and house manager, while control compatibility was salient for traveling companion, and affection compatibility was most necessary for roommate harmony. The relations with elected officers have the quality of relations between members at the beginning meetings of groups. The pattern of contact and association has not yet been established. The amount of interaction is up to the two people involved. If a fraternity member likes to be included in activities, it is well that his chancellor or house manager likes to participate in activities. On the other hand, if he likes to be left alone, it is desirable to have an officer who does not associate with others much, that is, leaves them alone.

This property doesn't hold for traveling companion or roommate. Here the relation implies close contact. There is no longer any doubt of association. The main issue is the nature of the relation. In the early stages—the two weeks with the traveling companion—the control patterns dominated the relation. There really isn't enough time for affectional ties to become preeminent. Roommate, on the other hand, is a very high interchange relation. Discussion of personal fears, anxieties, and feelings are common among roommates. If there is not agreement on the behavior in this area, difficulties must ensue. These discussions, which are in the affection area, do not ordinarily occur on a trip.

Thus the fraternity study provides evidence for the development postulate by demonstrating that relations of different degrees of interchange highlight different areas of compatibility, in accordance with the developmental sequence presented.

FUTURE RESEARCH

To do more research on Theorem 4–1 it is necessary to develop better measures. Since specific types of incompatibility are postulated for different need areas, it would be desirable to be able to make more specific the types of incompatibility present in a group at a given time. In that way the sequence of problems and problem areas may be charted.

The basis for the construction of such a measure is once more found in the expressed-wanted diagram (see Chapter 6) for each need area. Since the types of incompatibility are described in terms of these diagrams, items may be framed to explore all of these possible types. The two descriptions of incompatibility obtained by using the axes and using the diagonals also suggest two possible types of questions. With the use of the diagonals, items describing the group situation as a whole may be formed. If the major axes are followed, items may be formed describing specific role behavior. For each dimension, dissatisfaction may arise because the situation is too far to either extreme of the center of the dimension. A check list to be used by the subjects, and also by observers, is the FIRO Satisfaction Questionnaire (FSQ), reproduced as Table 9–1. The items are randomized in the instrument but grouped here to illustrate the connection of the items to the dimensions.

With such a rating sheet, now being compiled, it would be possible to discover specific dissatisfactions by specific members at particular times in the group's development. This information would help to determine a criterion measure with which the compatibility and development theorem may be tested. From the measures of compatibility, specific sources of dissatisfaction may be predicted and compared with results of the FSQ.

TABLE 9–1. FIRO Satisfaction Questionnaire

Following are some common types of dissatisfaction
people have in groups. First check (√) all those that
apply to your group or yourself and put a minus (—)
next to all those that definitely don't apply. Mark all
statements.

After you have done that, rank the four statements that
most apply to your group 1 to 4, and the four that apply
least, 9 to 12. Do the same for statements applying to
yourself.

Classi-fication*		SITUATION
x^I+	1.	This group wants to do everything together too much.
x^I-	2.	This group doesn't want to do things together enough.
o^I+	3.	There is always somebody trying to get us to do everything together.
o^I-	4.	People in this group have to get a special invitation before they'll do anything together.
x^C+	5.	This group makes too many rules to follow; there's not enough spontaneity.
x^C-	6.	This group doesn't have enough structure; we should make rules, put someone in charge, and give everyone some responsibility.
o^C+	7.	There is always somebody in this group trying to take charge of things.
o^C-	8.	No one in this group is willing to take charge of things.
x^A+	9.	This group spends too much time on personal relationships and personal feelings.
x^A-	10.	There isn't enough attention paid in this group to personal relationships.
o^A+	11.	There is always someone in this group trying to get the discussion around to personal relationships and personal feelings.
o^A-	12.	Nobody in this group is willing to start talking about how we feel toward each other.

INDIVIDUALS

e^I+	1.	I don't have enough contact with people in this group in what I do.
e^I-	2.	I'd rather work by myself than in a group.
w^I+	3.	People don't always include me in what they are doing in this group.
w^I-	4.	People don't leave me alone enough in this group.
e^C+	5.	I don't have enough influence in this group.
e^C-	6.	I have too much responsibility in this group.
w^C+	7.	People in this group are always trying to tell me what to do.
w^C-	8.	Nobody in this group has ever told me what I'm supposed to do.
e^A+	9.	I don't have enough opportunity to get to know someone in this group well.
e^A-	10.	I don't like to be expected to tell everyone about myself like I am in this group.
w^A+	11.	People in this group don't try to get to know me as well as I'd like them to.
w^A-	12.	People in this group are always trying to get personal.

*Classification Key:

x = Interchange	e = Behavior of self
o = Originator	w = Wanted behavior
$+$ = Too much	I = Inclusion behavior
$-$ = Not enough	C = Control behavior
	A = Affection behavior

One difficulty with using this prediction is that too many inferences must be made about the developmental stage of the group simply from the length of time the members have met. In order to meet that difficulty another instrument is now being developed.

The reasoning behind the instrument is this. Data related to the primary interpersonal concerns of the group may be derived by asking both group members and observers to describe the covert problem areas for the group and the motives of the group members. If a check list is made exhausting the various problems based on I, C, and A it is possible to obtain information on the salience of each area during any given time period. By plotting the change in salient areas over time, theorems derived from Postulate 4 may be tested. Following is a questionnaire now being used in a study of group development. The individual items are listed in the order I, C, A. Some of the topics were suggested in a memorandum by Shapiro (80) that listed a large number of subjects discussed by several Semrad groups. (See Table 9–2.)

TABLE 9–2. FIRO Content Questionnaire

In the column below, check those topics which you feel group members were really thinking about at this meeting. Then rank them from 1 to 4, Number 1 being the most thought-about topic.

———— 1. How important is the group to the leader?
———— 2. How much does the leader respect the capabilities of the group?
———— 3. How much does the leader like the group members?
———— 4. How important is the group to each member?
———— 5. How much do the group members learn from the group?
———— 6. How much do the group members like the group?
———— 7. Some members are more important in the group than others.
———— 8. Some members are respected more than others by the group.
———— 9. Some members are liked more than others by the group.
———— 10. How important is the leader to the group?
———— 11. How much does the group respect the leader's competence as a leader?
———— 12. How much do the group members like the leader?
———— 13. The group is more important to some members than to others.
———— 14. Some people feel the group is more useful for learning than others.
———— 15. Some people like the group more than others.
———— 16. Some members are more important to the leader than others.
———— 17. Some members are more respected by the leader than others.
———— 18. Some members are liked more by the leader than are others.
———— 19. The leader is more important to some people than others.
———— 20. Some people think the leader is more competent than do others.
———— 21. The leader is liked more by some people than by others.
———— 22. Other: _____

In the column below, check those things you feel group members were really trying to do during this meeting. Then rank them from 1 to 4, Number 1 being the thing they were trying most to do.

—————— 1. The members are trying to make the leader feel the group is more important than he now feels it is.

—————— 2. The members are trying to show the leader how competent the group is.

—————— 3. The members are trying to make the leader like the group.

—————— 4. Some members are trying to be the center of attention and gain recognition from the leader.

—————— 5. Some members are competing with the leader for power and influence.

—————— 6. Some members are trying to be liked by the leader.

—————— 7. Some members are trying to get the others to feel the group is more important than the others do now.

—————— 8. Some members are trying to get the others to feel the group is more valuable for learning than the others do now.

—————— 9. Some members are trying to get the others to like the group more than the others do now.

—————— 10. Some members are trying to be the center of attention and gain recognition from the group.

—————— 11. Some members are trying to gain power and influence over the other group members.

—————— 12. Some members are trying to be liked by the group members.

—————— 13. Some members are trying to get the others to feel the leader is more important than the others do now.

—————— 14. Some members are trying to get the others to feel the leader is more valuable for learning than the others do now.

—————— 15. Some members are trying to get the others to like the leader more than the others do now.

—————— 16. Other: _____

For other types of groups it will be necessary to prepare different content lists appropriate to the type of group. In each instance, however, the classification of specific topics should follow directly from the definition of the three need areas. Hence research is continuing toward specifying more closely the developmental phase in which the group is operating, and the state of compatibility of the group and its members. Success in such a project would allow for prediction of the course of a relation between two or more persons from knowing their FIRO–B scores only.

The following is a typical example of such a description:

If the pattern of compatibility for A and B is $+ - +$, then A and B will be highly compatible during the initial inclusion stage of their relation; however, in the control stage that follows they will have strong competitive incompatibility. Following a tentative though unstable resolution of this difficulty, they will get along much better as the affectional state appears. If they are roommates, this might mean they will hit it off well on first meeting, have a difficult time adjusting to each other, then find that they can confide in each other and discuss their innermost anxieties, but still have disagreements over sharing responsibility and prerogatives in their rooming situation.

One final study concludes the discussion of group development. This application of the theory is sharply different from other applications that have been discussed. It relates to interpersonal behavior on the gross and complex level of society. From the postulates presented there is little justification for asserting that societies follow the same developmental phases as interpersonal relations in a small group. However, a study made by Sister Marie Augusta (81) produced data significant enough to warrant the particular interest of sociologists and historians.

Sister Marie proposed that historical periods, beginning with the Teutonic invasions of the second century, could be classified in terms of dominant interpersonal relations, as evolving from inclusion, through control and affection, and then reversing, affection, through control and inclusion. (See Figure 9–2.)

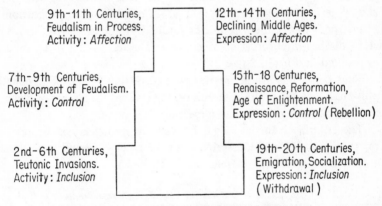

9th–11th Centuries, Feudalism in Process. Activity: *Affection*

12th–14th Centuries, Declining Middle Ages. Expression: *Affection*

7th–9th Centuries, Development of Feudalism. Activity: *Control*

15th–18 Centuries, Renaissance, Reformation, Age of Enlightenment. Expression: *Control* (Rebellion)

2nd–6th Centuries, Teutonic Invasions. Activity: *Inclusion*

19th–20th Centuries, Emigration, Socialization. Expression: *Inclusion* (Withdrawal)

FIGURE 9–2. A Theory of Evolution of Societies

To test these notions, Sister Marie, aided by Drinkwater's *Outline of Literature* (32) and several "great books" lists, evolved a list of 176 great books by including titles mentioned on all lists. It was assumed that these books reflected their times with some accuracy. Since the focus was on interpersonal relations, she constructed a lengthy description, with the aid of the author, of the three interpersonal need areas and asked judges to classify each book with respect to which need area was emphasized. There were nine judges knowledgeable in world literature and familiar with a large proportion of the books. They, of course, judged only the books with which they were familiar. No judge had any idea of the hypothesis being tested.

Because of the number of books available from various historical periods it was possible to test only the declining period, or group resolution, from the twelfth century on. Each book was classified into the need area assigned to it by the plurality of judges (Table 9–3).

TABLE 9–3. Predominant Interpersonal Need Area of Great Books by Historical Era

		INTERPERSONAL NEED AREA		
		Inclusion	Control	Affection
HISTORICAL PERIOD	Medieval	2	1	6
	Renaissance to nineteenth century	14	23	13
	Nineteenth and twentieth centuries	41	15	13

The prediction states that the books should fall on the major diagonal; that is, medieval books should stress affection, Renaissance books should stress control, and modern books should stress inclusion. A comparison of the proportion of choices for the category predicted to be largest for the medieval era, and the proportion expected by chance, showed that, with the use of the binomial test, the probability of obtaining the obtained proportion was $< .03$. The binomial test was employed because of the small cell frequency. A similar comparison of proportions for the Renaissance era, with the use of the "t" test, showed a $t = 2.11$ ($p < .02$). Comparisons of proportions for the nineteenth to twentieth centuries resulted in a $t = 4.50$ ($p < .01$). Comparison of the proportions obtained and expected in the three predicted cells resulted in a $t = 3.58$ ($p < .001$).

Thus the results are impressive, and surprising. What the implications of this study are for future research on the present theory is not clear, but the idea is intriguing, and it has some empirical support.

The criteria given the judges for classifying novels will be presented here, since they aid in the description of the types of phenomena classified into each interpersonal need area. (See Table 9–4.)

TABLE 9–4. Criteria for Classifying Great Books

CRITERIA FOR JUDGING INCLUSION

An awareness of a desire to belong.

Active effort for recognition, fame, reputation, success.

Much physical activity to gain entrance to the in-group, to be recognized, acclaimed, accepted.

Service—to prove one is worthy,
        to show that one is a member,
        to become an accepted member of the group.

Concern with the outcast, minority group, the rejected.

All themes of fighting for self-preservation, survival of the group.

Interest in integration, union, oneness.

Interest in people though not in any particular person.

Intense interest in man's efforts to eke out a livelihood for himself, his efforts to conquer nature and possess the land.

His conquering of the native, the forest, the elements and whatever opposes his cutting out for himself a home, a country, a place where he and his "own" can settle down and belong.

The inclusion expression is most deeply concerned with man's survival needs; concern over belonging is so dominant that warm interpersonal relations are so fleeting and superficial that true love is quite unknown and the inclusion expression is even mistaken for love.

Narcissism is so complete an absorption in the needs and interests of the self that one is quite unaware of others.

Deep concern about loneliness, the cruelty of the world to its children.

Sees man as an outcast, fugitive.

The great aloneness of man is stressed. His not belonging is the central theme.

Withdrawal from interaction with the group because one does not feel he belongs to the group, feels he is not wanted, no one cares.

Or he scorns the group because of its superficiality and does not want to belong.

Interest in a specific other not through a real mutual love but rather because that other can help the self belong here.

CRITERIA FOR JUDGING CONTROL

This theme centers around interest in the acquisition of power or control over others—the need to command, to be obeyed, to be served or to be commanded, to obey or to serve.

This control may be of armies, nations, business organizations, social movements, one's family, one's loved ones ... as long as the concern is with power and control it fits here.

The concern may be with being controlled, being protected by another who is powerful, desire to be released from responsibility, to be directed by others. Concern with independence, of conquering, of subjugating others not for fame, or security, but for the experience of being master, sovereign, controller, director, guider, lord, king, etc.

All concern with rebellion, refusal to serve, satiric rejection of the status quo, call to revolution, iconoclasm.

Rebellion against tradition in thought or action, against entrenched power of any form.

All throwing off of the yoke of subjugation, release from external repression, inhibitions.

Any expression of a need to be capable of directing, holding, or fulfilling responsibility.

Concern with submission, discipline, authority, dominance, conformity.

Concern over the dictates of conscience, moral directives.

Struggle for power—to master others.

CRITERIA FOR JUDGING AFFECTION

This theme is concerned with dyadic relations—i.e., of the self with a significant other.

Although many pieces of literature may have a love interest, works are classified in this category only if the dominant theme and dynamic flows from and is deeply concerned with warm, emotionally experienced interpersonal relations of a reciprocal nature.

Complete self-dedication to the interest of another person, or group or God Himself.

A quest for union with God, a loved one, a friend.

Altruism—love of mankind expressed in more than mere service.

Self-dedication based on joy in the beloved— (Mere servitude, no matter how intense is the inclusion theme, i.e., the need to belong, be accepted and recognized as one of the group—this goes in Category one).

Delight in the experience of the company of another. Warm, personal, joyous family relations, friendship relations, romantic love relations.

Concern about one's relations with particular persons rather than with people in general.

Love interest in the known other.

Deep concern over being rejected by a specific other because that other is so dear to the self.

A feeling that one is loved, is lovable and loved; or concern that one is not loved or is not lovable.

Belief that people are lovable and loved. Belief that people in general really do love each other, can love and feel grieved when not loved.

Strong negative feelings toward specific others who have thwarted one's efforts to establish warm personal relations.

All feelings of friendliness, tenderness and warmth.

This experience of affection is often accompanied by the desire to help people, to sacrifice one's personal interests. It is more selfless than selfish, seeks no fame or power but has one goal—the possession of the beloved.

The theme may center on one's concern that he cannot form warm personal relations, or that one is inclined to be overpersonal in his relations with those to whom he is attracted.

Joy and delight in being one with others; recognition of the deep and valued worth of others; laughter, joy, charity, sympathy are the characteristic atmospheres of this experience.

10

Toward a Formal Theory of
Interpersonal Behavior

In the preceding pages a theory was presented. As each element was introduced it was dutifully labeled and discussed. At this time a closer look will be taken at the theory as a theory. All the theoretical elements are assembled, commented on, and evaluated. References are made throughout to the chapters where fuller discussions of particular points may be found.

What is to follow constitutes a formal theory of interpersonal behavior in the sense discussed in Chapter 1. That is, it is an approximation to a formal theory within the limitations of our present embryonic knowledge of human behavior. There are several purposes served by presenting this theory in this quasi-formal fashion. Some of these purposes follow (see Chapter 1).

1. *To achieve conceptual clarity.* The necessity to state ideas explicitly leads to the identification of contradictions, omissions, repetitions, and confusions. Formalization fosters clear statements, explicit definitions, and clear logical sequences.

2. *To detect hidden assumptions.* Formalization requires that all steps leading to the statement of a theorem be made explicit. If the chain of reasoning is incomplete, a hidden assumption may be revealed.

3. *To gain from indirect verification.* If the relations between theorems are made explicit, then the verification of one theorem may indirectly verify the other, since they are parts of a logically interconnected system.

4. *To specify the range of conceptual relevance.* Formalization makes clear which aspects of a theory are affected by particular data. It makes explicit which theorems follow from which postulates and therefore which theorems and postulates are affected by a particular experimental result.

5. *To identify equivalent theories and theorems.* If theorems are explicitly stated in two theories, it is possible to see in what respects they are similar and in what respects different.

6. *To achieve deductive fertility.* By the verifying of a small number of postulates, many theorems are verified. Deductions from the postulates may lead to many unexpected results. Although deductive fertility is probably the primary aim of a formal theory, it is not yet realizable in the present theory, a fact that is unfortunate but hardly unexpected for a theory about behavior at the present state of knowledge. However, as stated in the introduction, the approach to theory building taken here explicitly aims at approximating a formal theory as closely as possible, in order to achieve whatever deductive fertility is available.

The method of presentation of this theory is relatively informal. The primitive terms are introduced and briefly described. The defined terms and the postulates (except the first) are all stated in relatively precise mathematical or logical terms. Theorems following from the postulates are stated only in words, with no attempt made to symbolize them. Throughout the presentation, explanatory comments are included to aid in the understanding of the theory.

RANGE OF THE THEORY

The phenomena which the theory is intended to cover are encompassed by the term "interpersonal," discussed in Chapter 2. Briefly, behavior of people in which participants take account of one another is called interpersonal behavior. More specifically, interpersonal behavior encompasses three types of relations: (a) *prior:* relations between previous experience and present interpersonal behavior (Chapter 5), (b) *present:* relations between elements of the interpersonal situation (Chapters 6–9), (c) *consequent:* relations between elements of the interpersonal situation and other behavior and attitudes (Chapter 4).

PRIMITIVE TERMS

These are the terms that are formally undefined within the theory, and from which all defined terms and postulates are formed. There are no logical requirements for the introduction of primitive terms, since they are undefined. However, the present system is an interpreted one; that is, the logical terms are given empirical meaning. Therefore the primitive terms must be made sufficiently clear to the reader.

An assumption underlying the selection of these terms as primitives, and of the definitions of the defined terms to follow, will now be made explicit. The assumption is that it is fruitful, with respect to the predictive and explanatory aim of this theory, to select *these specific* terms as primitive and to introduce *these particular* definitions for the defined terms. This assumption is important, because it specifies a possible source of inadequacy in the theory. If the theory does not predict well, it may be not only because of incorrect theorems and postulates but also because of a poor choice of definitions or of primitives.

The process of interpreting the primitive terms is called providing semantic rules. The primitive terms and their meanings follow:

1. *Interpersonal need.* A requirement for a person to establish a satisfactory relation between himself and other people. "Relation" refers to the amount of interchange between himself and others, and the degree to which he originates and receives behavior.

2. *Inclusion behavior (I).* Behavior directed toward the satisfaction of the interpersonal need for inclusion, the need to maintain and establish a satisfactory relation with people with respect to association. This term is used synonymously with *behavior in the area of inclusion.* For individuals two aspects of inclusion behavior (e^I and w^I; see below) are measured by FIRO–B (Chapters 2 and 4).

3. *Control behavior (C).* Behavior directed toward the satisfaction of the interpersonal need for control, the need to maintain and establish a satisfactory relation with people with respect to control and power. This term is used synonymously with *behavior in the area of control.* For individuals two aspects of control behavior (e^C and w^C; see below) are measured by FIRO–B (Chapters 2 and 4).

4. *Affection behavior (A).* Behavior directed toward the satisfaction of the interpersonal need for affection, the need to maintain and establish a satisfactory relation with people with respect to affection and love. This term is used synonymously with *behavior in the area of affection.* For individuals, two aspects of affection behavior (e^A and w^A; see below) are measured by FIRO–B (Chapters 2 and 4).

For group interaction, behavior during any time interval may be described as behavior predominantly in one of the three interpersonal need areas; that is, either I, C, or A behavior. This behavior is measured by the FIRO Content Questionnaire (Chapter 9). Relations may also be described as occurring predominantly in a particular area depending on the most characteristic type of behavior required by the relation. For example, "sweetheart" may be considered predominantly an affectional relation; "officer, enlisted man," predominantly control; and "fraternity man, pledge," predominantly inclusion (Chapter 7).

5. *Expressed behavior (e).* Actions taken by a person (Chapter 2).
6. *Wanted behavior (w).* Behaviors from other people that a person feels will satisfy an interpersonal need (Chapter 2).

7. *Feared behavior* (*f*). Behavior from other people that a person feels will not satisfy or would increase an interpersonal need (Chapter 2).

8. *Goal achievement* (*g*). Degree to which optimal performance toward a goal is achieved. The goal must be acknowledged by the group or individual as one they wish to achieve. "Optimal performance" means, under the best possible circumstances, the maximal performance of which the group or individual is capable. Some examples of group goals are productivity (measured by specific criteria appropriate to the task), cohesion (measured by the Cohesion questionnaire), and mutual liking (measured by responses to various types of sociometric questions). (Chapter 7.)

These primitive terms are introduced for the purpose of forming the defined terms and postulates introduced in the next sections. In addition to the terms listed above, the theory assumes the language of logic, mathematics, and grammatical expressions. These languages include such terms as "individual," "toward," "time," "statistical significance," and "correlation," and logical signs, especially "ε," which means "is a member of"; for example, "$b\varepsilon A$" is read, "b is a member of class A." If any term is used which has not been defined, it is to be understood in its usual meaning.

DEFINED TERMS

These are terms useful for formulating postulates and theorems, which are defined by using only the primitive terms and the logical languages assumed. Although they are all adequately defined by mathematical expressions, a brief description of each is provided.

DEF. 1. *Compatibility* (*K*). Compatibility is a property of a relation between two or more persons, between an individual and a role, or between an individual and a task situation, that leads to mutual satisfaction of interpersonal needs, and harmonious coexistence (Chapter 6).

(*a*) $K = rK + oK + xK,$

where rK = reciprocal compatibility,
oK = originator compatibility,
xK = interchange compatibility.

An alternate formulation is somewhat more useful for demonstrating the relation of compatibility to the Postulate of Group Development.

(*b*) $K = \theta_I K^I + \theta_C K^C + \theta_A K^A,$

where K^I, K^C, K^A = compatibility in the areas of inclusion, control, and affection,
$\theta_I, \theta_C, \theta_A$ = coefficients which vary with the area in which the group is interacting in the following way·

$$(e_h I): \theta_I > \theta_C \text{ and } \theta_I > \theta_A,$$
$$(e_h C): \theta_C > \theta_A \text{ and } \theta_C > \theta_I,$$
$$(e_h A): \theta_A > \theta_I \text{ and } \theta_A > \theta_C,$$

where $e^h = $ the behavior of the group h.

This specification of θ embodies the idea that each area (I, C, A) of compatibility is most pertinent when the group is interacting in the corresponding need area. The values of θ cannot yet be determined beyond the inequality stated above. Very likely another set of coefficients should be assigned to rK, oK, and xK, perhaps to reflect differences in situational factors (Chapter 8). However, for now these coefficients are assumed to be equal to one.

DEF. 1a. *Area Compatibility* (K^I, K^C, K^A). Compatibility in an interpersonal need area (Chapter 6).

$$K^I = rK^I + oK^I + xK^I,$$
$$K^C = rK^C + oK^C + xK^C,$$
$$K^A = rK^A + oK^A + xK^A,$$

where rK = reciprocal compatibility,
oK = originator compatibility,
xK = interchange compatibility.

DEF. 1b. *Reciprocal Compatibility* (rK) Compatibility based on reciprocal need satisfaction; primarily applicable to dyads (Chapter 6).

(a) $rK \;= \theta_I rK^I + \theta_C rK^C + \theta_A rK^A,$
(b) $rK^I = |e_i{}^I - w_j{}^I| + |e_j{}^I - w_i{}^I|,$
(c) $rK^C = |e_i{}^C - w_j{}^C| + |e_j{}^C - w_i{}^C|,$
(d) $rK^A = |e_i{}^A - w_j{}^A| + |e_j{}^A - w_i{}^A|,$

where rK^I, rK^C, rK^A = reciprocal compatibility in the areas of inclusion, control, affection.

$e_i{}^I, e_i{}^C, e_i{}^A$ = behavior of individual i in the areas of inclusion, control, affection (subscripts indicating individuals on rK symbol are always assumed).

$w_j{}^I, w_j{}^C, w_j{}^A$ = behavior individual j wants from other in the areas of inclusion, control and affection.

DEF. 1c. *Originator Compatibility* (oK). Compatibility based on differences in tendencies to originate or initiate behavior. Primarily applicable to dyads (Chapter 6).

(a) $oK \;= \theta_I oK^I + \theta_C oK^C + \theta_A oK^A,$
(b) $oK^I = (e_i{}^I - w_i{}^I) + (e_j{}^I - w_j{}^I),$
(c) $oK^C = (e_i{}^C - w_i{}^C) + (e_j{}^C - w_j{}^C),$
(d) $oK^A = (e_i{}^A - w_i{}^A) + (e_j{}^A - w_j{}^A),$

where oK^I, oK^C, oK^A = originator compatibility in the areas of inclusion, control, and affection.

DEF. 1d. *Interchange Compatibility* (xK). Compatibility based on desired amount of interchange between self and others. Primarily applicable to groups (Chapter 7).

(a) $xK = \theta_I xK^I + \theta_C xK^C + \theta_A xK^A$,
(b) $xK^I = |(e_i^I + w_i^I) - (e_j^I + w_j^I)|$,
(c) $xK^C = |(e_i^C + w_i^C) - (e_j^C + w_j^C)|$,
(d) $xK^A = |(e_i^A + w_i^A) - (e_j^A + w_j^A)|$,

where xK^I, xK^C, xK^A = interchange compatibility in the areas of inclusion, control, and affection.

A summary of the definitions of compatibility may clarify the relations between the various aspects of compatibility (Table 6–1).

TABLE 6–1. Relations between Compatibility Measures

		AREAS OF COMPATIBILITY			
		I	C	A	Row Sums
TYPES OF	r	$\theta_I rK^I$	$\theta_C rK^C$	$\theta_A rK^A$	rK
COMPATI-	o	$\theta_I oK^I$	$\theta_C oK^C$	$\theta_A oK^A$	oK
BILITY	x	$\theta_I xK^I$	$\theta_C xK^C$	$\theta_A xK^A$	xK
Column Sums		$\theta_I K^I$	$\theta_C K^C$	$\theta_A K^A$	K Total

Hence the sums of rows define rK, oK, and xK, while the sums of columns define $\theta_I K^I$, $\theta_C K^C$, $\theta_A K^A$. Both the sum of all rows and the sum of all columns add to K, and constitute the two definitions of K given above. The θ coefficients are included in the terms that include rK, oK, and xK, while they are the multipliers for K^I, K^C, and K^A. Although the two definitions are mathematically equivalent they have interesting psychological differences: one deals with compatibility within need areas, and the other deals with types of compatibility.

DEF. 2. *Role Definition.* The behavior which the other group members express toward the role player, and the behavior they want from him.

Role Definition = e_h(obs), w_h(obs),
where h = other group members,
obs = from the standpoint of outside observers.

DEF. 3. *Role Expectation.* The role player's perception of the behavior which the other group members express toward him, and his perception of the behavior which they want from him.

Role Expectation = e_h(rol), w_h(rol),
where rol = from the standpoint of the role player.

DEF. 4. *Enacted Role.* The behavior the role player expresses toward other group members, and the behavior he wants them to express toward him.

Enacted Role $= e_r(\text{obs}), w_r(\text{obs})$,
where $r =$ role player.

DEF. 5. *Perceived Role Performance.* The role player's perception of his own expressed behavior toward other group members, and his perception of the behavior he wants from the group.

Perceived Role Performance $= e_r(\text{rol}), w_r(\text{rol})$

DEF. 6. *Norm.* The behavior the members of a group (that is, the group) want from any person who is a member of that group.

Norm $= w_{h.a}(\text{obs})$,
where $w_{h.a} =$ behavior h wants from any group member a.

DEF. 7. *Sanction.* The behavior expressed by group members (that is, the group) toward an expressed or wanted behavior of a particular group member.

Sanction $= e_h(\text{obs})$, in response to $e_r(\text{obs})$ or $w_r(\text{obs})$.

The five definitions above are summarized in Table 8–8.

TABLE 8–8. Explication of "Role," "Norm," and "Sanction"

		PERCEPTION OF ROLE PLAYER	PERCEPTION OF OBSERVER	
BEHAVIOR OF GROUP	e_h w_h	Role expectation	Role definition	← Norm (for role player=average group member)
BEHAVIOR OF ROLE PLAYER	e_r w_r	Perceived role performance	Enacted role	← Sanction = response e_h to ← previous e_r, w_r

All values used for defining the above terms are derived from FIRO–B scales adapted to this purpose. Each definition consists of a set of numbers, representing scores on the appropriate FIRO–B scales (Chapter 8). Definition 2 through definition 7 are not required for the statement of the postulates. However, they are important concepts used in the study of interpersonal relations that are expected to be useful for formulating new postulates for the system. It is helpful, too, to demonstrate the approach to conceptualizing situational factors from the standpoint of interpersonal behavior. All seven of the above definitions provide semantic rules for the use of certain terms in the logical system. Logically, it is sufficient merely to define them in terms of the basic terms. Empirically, however, it is important to provide meaning for these terms beyond formulas. These definitions form a part of the explication process. Thus it is assumed that these terms successfully render old concepts into new. Carnap gives four criteria for an adequate explicatum: (1) similarity to the explicandum, (2) exactness, (3) fruitfulness, (4) simplicity. The third criterion, fruitfulness, must be judged in part by the adequacy of the theorems in which the explicatum is used, and the new theorems to which it leads.

POSTULATES

These are the propositions expressing what are taken to be the most fundamental ideas embodied in the theory. In the ideal instance, all theorems in the system are derivable from these postulates. In the present instance, they represent the best estimate of the most basic ideas in the theory presented.

> **Postulate 1.   *The Postulate of Interpersonal Needs.***
> **(a)   Every individual has three interpersonal needs: inclusion, control, and affection.**
> **(b)   Inclusion, control, and affection constitute a sufficient set of areas of interpersonal behavior for the prediction and explanation of interpersonal phenomena.**

This statement means that there are some important areas of interpersonal behavior for which failure to consider any of the interpersonal need areas leads to a poor correlation between prediction and outcome, and the addition of any further variables will yield at best a small increment in predictive power (Chapter 2). This postulate is stated with sufficient clarity that further specificity is unnecessary.

> **Theorem 1–1.   If a representative battery of measures of interpersonal behavior is factor-analyzed, the resulting factors will reasonably fall into the three need areas, inclusion, control, and affection.**

"Reasonably fall" may be made more specific by including measures of the three areas in the battery, and by predicting that each area measure will be heavily loaded on one factor, and that no interpersonal factor will not include a highly loaded I, C, or A Scale.

> **Postulate 2.   *The Postulate of Relational Continuity.* An individual's expressed interpersonal behavior will be similar to the behavior he experienced in his earliest interpersonal relations, usually with his parents, in the following way:**
>
> > *Principle of Constancy.* **When he perceives his adult position in an interpersonal situation to be similar to his own position in his parent-child relation, his adult behavior posi-**

tively covaries with his childhood behavior toward his parents (or significant others).

Principle of Identification. **When he perceives his adult position in an interpersonal situation to be similar to his parent's position in his parent-child relation, his adult behavior positively covaries with the behavior of his parents (or significant others) toward him when he was a child.**

This postulate may be made more precise by repeating Figure 5–1 here.

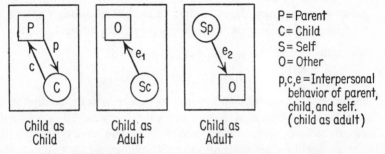

P = Parent
C = Child
S = Self
O = Other
p, c, e = Interpersonal behavior of parent, child, and self. (child as adult)

Child as Child   Child as Adult   Child as Adult

FIGURE 5–1. Schema for Postulate of Relational Continuity

The first diagram schematizes the relation of the parent and child. In the second diagram the child-become-adult occupies a role similar to the one he had as a child (Sc). In the third diagram he occupies a role similar to the one his parent occupied toward him (Sp). The Postulate of Relational Continuity specifies the relations between e_1, e_2, p, and c. To demonstrate the postulate, all possibilities for e_1 and e_2 (the term e will be used to designate both e_1 and e_2) are enumerated:

1. e covaries positively with c.
2. e covaries negatively with c.
3. e does not covary with c.
4. e covaries positively with p.
5. e covaries negatively with p.
6. e does not covary with p.

The term "covaries" means "varies concomitantly in a statistically significant sense." It is to be interpreted as a statistical concept measured by the appropriate statistical measure, for example, product-moment correlation, chi-square, rank-order correlation. The Principle of Constancy asserts that for e_1, possibility (1) is true; that is, e_1 covaries positively with c. The Principle of Identification asserts the truth of (4) for e_2; that is, e_2 covaries positively with p. It should be noted that the Principle of Constancy implies that (2) and (3) are false but is noncommittal about (4), (5), and (6). Similarly, the Principle of Identification implies that (5) and (6) are false, and is noncommittal about (1), (2), and (3). Thus the Postulate of Relational Continuity is formulated as follows:

1. Principle of Constancy

$$P(e_1, c) > s$$

2. Principle of Identification

$$P(e_2, p) > s,$$

where P = an appropriate measure of covariance,
   s = the level required for statistical significance.

Postulate 3.   *The Postulate of Compatibilty*. If the compatibility of one group, h, is greater than that of another group, m, then the goal achievement of h will exceed that of m.

In mathematical terms this postulate is simply stated:

$$\text{If } K_h > K_m, \text{ then } g_h > g_m.$$

The definition of compatibility introduced earlier is fully utilized in this postulate. Since the definition of K includes the coefficents, θ, the Postulate of Compatibility incorporates the notion that different areas of compatibility are more pertinent during different kinds of interaction; for example, if the group is interacting in the affection area, or if the interpersonal relation is primarily affectional, as "sweetheart," then K^A is the most important ingredient of K in determining the compatibility of the group.

Also utilized in the statement of the postulate is the definition of "goal achievement." This term was defined as the degree to which the group approaches its optimal performance on a goal it desires to achieve. The theorems specify various aspects of the postulate.

Theorem 3–1.   If the compatibility of one dyad, y_1, is greater than the compatibility of another dyad, y_2, then the members of y_1 are more likely to prefer each other for continued personal interchange.

Theorem 3–2.   If the compatibility of one group, h, is greater than the compatibility of another group, m, then the productivity goal achievement of h will exceed that of m.

Theorem 3–3.   If the compatibility of one group, h, is greater than the compatibility of another group, m, then h will be more cohesive than m.

Theorems 3–4, 3–5, and 3–6 were not confirmed in further testing; therefore they are not included here. These theorems are discussed in Chapter 7.

Theorem 3–7.   In the compatible groups, those predicted to be focal persons and those predicted to be main supporting members should rank one another very high on the relation "work well with."

Theorem 3–8. In all the groups focal persons will be chosen as group leaders by the group members.

Theorem 3–9. The effect of compatibility on productivity (the C–P effect) increases as the task situation requires more interchange in the three need areas.

Postulate 4. *The Postulate of Group Development.* The formation and development of two or more people into an interpersonal relation (that is, a group) always proceed in the same sequence, as follows:

> *Principle of Group Integration.* For the time period starting with the group's beginning until three intervals before the group's termination the predominant area of interpersonal behavior begins with inclusion, is followed by control, and finally by affection. This cycle may recur.
>
> *Principle of Group Resolution.* The last three intervals prior to a group's anticipated termination follow the opposite sequence in that the predominant area of interpersonal behavior is first affection, then control, and finally inclusion.

The postulate may be specified more precisely.

> *The Principle of Group Integration*
>
> when $t_1 < t_i < t_n-2$,
>
> $e_h(t_i)\varepsilon I$, for $i = 3m + 1$,
>
> $e_h(t_i)\varepsilon C$, for $i = 3m + 2$,
>
> $e_h(t_i)\varepsilon A$, for $i = 3m + 3$,
>
> where $m =$ any integer,
>
> $t_1, t_2, \dots t_n =$ time intervals of an interpersonal relation.

They are successive, exhaustive intervals which change when, and only when, the predominant area of interpersonal behavior (I, C, A) changes, measured by FIRO Content Questionnaire (Chapter 9).

$h =$ any group or interpersonal relation, including a small training group, an infant and parent, and the like.

> *The Principle of Group Resolution*
>
> when $t_i > t_n-1$,
>
> $e_h(t_i) A$, for $i = n-2$,
>
> $e_h(t_i) C$, for $i = n-1$,
>
> $e_h(t_i) I$, for $i = n$

This principle states that the last three intervals of a group's existence follow the opposite sequence from the integration phase. With impending separation, first comes affection, then control, and finally inclusion. This is the period of "decathecting" the group, or withdrawing investment. This postulate states that investment is withdrawn in the opposite order from that in which it was placed in the group (Chapter 9). If the two parts of Postulate 4 are put together, the sequence of interaction for any interpersonal relation of group is

$$
\begin{array}{ccccccccc}
\text{I} & \text{C} & \text{A} & \text{I} & \text{C} & \text{A} & \dots & \text{A} & \text{C} & \text{I} \\
t_1 & t_2 & t_3 & t_4 & t_5 & t_6 & & t_n\text{--}2 & t_n\text{--}1 & t_n
\end{array}
$$

Theorem 4–1. **(1)** **If a group is high on inclusion compatibility** (K^I)**, but low on** K^C **and** K^A**, group members will be most compatible during the initial stages of their relation.**
(2) **If a group is high on** $\mathbf{K}^C$**, but low on** $\mathbf{K}^I$ **and** $\mathbf{K}^A$**, group members will be most compatible during the middle stages of their relation.**
(3) **If a group is high on** K^A**, but low on** K^I **and** K^C**, group members will be most compatible during the last stages of their relation prior to the separation sequence.**

SUMMARY OF THEORY

There are three interpersonal need areas, inclusion, control, and affection, sufficient for the prediction of interpersonal behavior. Orientations which an individual acquires toward behavior in these areas are relatively invariant over time. Compatibility of two or more persons depends on (a) their ability to satisfy reciprocally each other's interpersonal needs, (b) their complementarity with respect to originating and receiving behavior in each need area, (c) their similarity with respect to the amount of interchange they desire with other people in each need area. "Roles" may be defined in terms of interpersonal requirements in such a way that a measurement can be made of the compatibility of an individual and a role. Compatibility varies with the type of interaction being experienced. If, for example, individuals are engaged in inclusion behavior, or involved in a primary inclusion relation, then compatibility in the inclusion area (K^I) is the most important determinant of their compatibility in the situation itself. Areas and degrees of compatibility are therefore distinguishable which are roughly comparable to personal relations that flourish under one set of circumstances but cannot withstand the stress of a different type of relation.

Every interpersonal relation follows the same general developmental sequence. It starts with inclusion behavior, is followed by control behavior and, finally, affection behavior. This cycle may recur. When the relation approaches termination it reverses direction, and investment from the relation is withdrawn in the order affection, control, and inclusion.

From these postulates it is theoretically possible to predict the course of a relation, if we know the interpersonal orientations of the individual members of the relation and the interpersonal description of the circumstances under which they will interact.

Appendix A
The Rule of Bayes

In the introduction, the rule of Bayes was discussed, and its relations to the plan of organization of the book. Because the idea is felt to be so important, a few more details will be presented here, with special attention given to the application of the rule to behavioral science. Bakan (7) and Meehl (63) have also written in this area.

Before Bayes' rule is discussed in detail, mention should be made that philosophers are by no means in agreement about its value. Historically, it is one of the most controversial concepts in logic. The view presented follows Reichenbach and others who believe the rule has great empirical importance. For a good discussion of a different view, see Carnap (22).

The fundamental idea of confirmation of hypothesis and theory, and the relation of theory to evidence, is embodied in the famous rule of Bayes. In the following discussion we shall follow the presentation of Bayes given, in Reichenbach's *The Theory of Probability* (70). On the importance of the Bayes theorem Reichenbach notes, "... nearly all inquiries into the causes of observed facts are performed in terms of this rule." (p. 94) The Bayes theorem is an expression for the so-called inverse probability; the probability that a certain hypothesis (*B*) is true given a certain outcome (*C*). To put it more formally:

Let *A* be a class of propositions (hypotheses) which are similar to one another in important respects. Let *B* be the class of true propositions. Let *C* be the class of propositions having a particular sort of empirical data relevant to their confirmation. Also let $P(A,B)$ mean the probability that a member of the class *A* is also a member of the class *B*. Then, Bayes rule states

$$P(A.C,B) = \frac{P(A,B) \cdot P(A.B,C)}{P(A,B) \cdot P(A.B,C) + P(A,\bar{B}) \cdot P(A.\bar{B},C)}$$

The term "antecedent probability" used by Reichenbach refers to $P(A,\bar{B})$ and $P(A,B)$. The terms $P(A.B,C)$ and $P(A.\bar{B},C)$ will be called "evidential probabilities," meaning that they refer to the probability that a particular sort of evidence would be forthcoming if a proposition of the class A is true or false, respectively.

The importance of this theorem for empirical science can hardly be overestimated. Reichenbach's discussion makes this point clear (70).

"The method of *indirect evidence,* as this form of inquiry is called, consists of inferences that on closer analysis can be shown to follow the structure of the rule of Bayes. The physician's inferences, leading from the observed symptoms to the diagnosis of a specified disease, are this type; so are the inferences of the historian determining the historical events that must be assumed for the explanation of recorded observation; and, likewise, the inferences of the detective concluding criminal actions from inconspicuous observable data. In many instances the use of probability relations is not manifest because the probabilities occurring have either very high or very low values. Thus, when a corpse is found, it is virtually certain that a murder has been committed; and a fingerprint on the handle of a pistol may be considered as strict evidence for the assumption that a certain person has fired the pistol. That even in such cases the inference has the structure of Bayes' rule is often seen from the fact that appraisals of the antecedent probabilities are made. Thus an inquiry by the detective into the motives of a crime is an attempt to estimate the antecedent probabilities of the case, namely, the probability of a certain person committing a crime of this kind, irrespective of the observed incriminating data. Similarly, the general inductive inference from observational data to the validity of a given scientific theory must be regarded as an inference in terms of Bayes' rule." (p. 94)

To be more specific about the meaning of the Bayes theorem and its applications, each term in the Bayes expression will be discussed.

The antecedent probability is the probability that a certain type of hypothesis is true, regardless of the specific data of confirmation referred to by "C." For example, the probability that a hypothesis of the type under consideration (A), is true (B), regardless of, or prior to, any specific tests of this hypothesis is the antecedent probability of the hypothesis. It is very important to establish at least that the antecedent probability is not zero—that is, could not possibly be true in light of what is already known—since a zero value would render the probability of the theorems zero.

An examination of the formula reveals that the inverse probability, the probability that a given hypothesis having given supporting data is true varies directly with the antecedent probability of that hypothesis. That is, if the hypothesis were antecedently implausible, then a great deal of data is required to establish a high probability for that hypothesis. In particular, the data must be of such a sort that $P(A.\bar{B},C)$ is low; that is, the probability that the same data would be found if some other hypothesis were true must be small.

That science actually operates in this fashion is well illustrated by the general scientific reaction to the experiments on extrasensory perception (ESP). In this research the antecedent probability of the hypothesis that the phenomena reported are caused by extrasensory mechanisms is extremely low, since many of our best established physical laws are called into question if the ESP hypothesis is true (that is, no action at a distance). Consequently, abnormal scrutiny is made of the evidence which is purported to support the ESP hypothesis. If the proposition is true that ESP is an acceptable explanation of the reported phenomenon, then, since from what is now known of the universe prior to ESP experiments the probability of the ESP hypothesis is very low, we demand a high level of certainty from the experiments claiming to support the hypothesis. Using Bayes' terminology, since the antecedent probability is low, then any outcome purporting to support the hypothesis (evidence) must be established repeatedly and with great certainty.

Similarly, if the antecedent probability is high (that is, the hypothesis is clearly consistent with past knowledge), a lower level of certainty is required to establish the probability that the hypothesis accounts for new data. If the confirming evidence is slightly below acceptable standards, there is usually more willingness to accept the phenomenon and try to explain the poor result by pursuing such possibilities as an unreliable measuring instrument, experimental conditions that are awry, and unforeseen factors that are uncontrolled. For example, a classic experiment in the psychology of learning was performed by Blodgett in 1929 (17), in which he demonstrated that a rat learns his surroundings even when unmotivated and can use this learning later to achieve a reward (latent learning). Many years later the data were reanalyzed by Meehl and MacCorquodale (64) and found to be considerably below the standards usually used to accept or reject hypotheses. The thesis of latent learning had such high antecedent probability (that is, seemed so plausible in terms of past experience) that the confirmatory evidence was not required to be convincing. Comparison with the stringent requirement applied to the ESP data illustrates the awareness of the importance of antecedent probability on the behavior of scientists.

Neglect of the implication of the antecedent probability aspect of Bayes' theorem may in part account for the great frequency of negative results in the social sciences. Perhaps if the antecedent probabilities of hypotheses-to-be-tested were systematically investigated by such techniques as reference to past experience and investigations, reanalysis of relevant data, and systematic introspection, then hypotheses finally chosen to be tested would have a better chance of being confirmed. A common objection to antecedent probability is that it is not measurable. This objection seems invalid for behavioral data, since several phenomena under investigation in the behavioral sciences are measured by the same procedure that can be used for measuring antecedent probability, namely: present a scientific hypothesis to a group of judges competent in the content area of the hypothesis, and ask them to answer the question, "How likely is this hypothesis to be confirmed when tested?" Any number of categories may be used and any of several familiar scaling techniques utilized. Amount of agreement among judges would indicate the degree to which the proposed hypothesis is supported by the data now available, hence its antecedent probability. It appears, therefore, that the concept of antecedent probability is as measurable as many respectable scientific concepts in the behavioral sciences.

In summary, science requires, both in theory and practice, higher or lower confirming evidence for a proposition, depending on whether the hypothesis is congenial or contradictory to already existing data. No inference should be made from the concept of antecedent probability regarding the truth or falsity of such hypotheses. That is a separate matter.

The evidential probability is the probability that if the hypothesis is true, then the particular outcome under consideration will follow.

Experiments that test hypotheses are aimed at producing bodies of data which yield decisively high or low values for $P(A.B,C)$ or $P(A.\bar{B},C)$. A hypothesis is offered and a deduction made from it. Then an experiment is performed to test the deduction. To follow the ESP example: the hypothesis may be stated that if a subject has powers of ESP (the event B), then he will correctly guess the symbols on unseen cards more than chance would allow (the event C). An experiment is then performed to determine the frequency of the predicted outcome. This is a standard type of scientific investigation and presents no special problems.

The *antecedent and evidential probabilities* for *alternate* hypotheses (those other than the one under test) have the same meaning as the corresponding probabilities for the hypothesis under test. They are more difficult to discuss in detail. For explanations presented in this book, only informal references are made to other theoretical formulations when the empirical data is discussed. There are, in fact, relatively few quasi-systematic theories existent that have been offered to account for the data under consideration in this book. For any particular postulate or theorem there exist alternate formulations. However, there appear to be few theories that attempt to encompasse *systematically* childhood experiences, mental disorders, group behavior, group development, and interpersonal compatibility. On the other hand, there are theories which cover this scope, such as psychoanalysis, but are not in general oriented toward a systematic description of phenomena, followed by experimentation. The argument for psychoanalytic conceptions lies mainly in the realm of plausibility arguments based in large part on clinical experience. However, it is important to note that the formulation presented here could to some extent be considered a partial test of psychoanalytic theory. It is partial in the sense that although the main outlines of psychoanalysis have been accepted here and several of the principle conceptions are tested (for example, the importance of infantile experience for adult behavior [Chapter 5]), the emphasis in the present theory is on interpersonal relations rather than erogenous zones. The primary extension in the present theory that goes beyond psychoanalytic theory is the formulation of group compatibility and the course of development of interpersonal relations.

The term on the left in the Bayes expression, the *inverse probability*, expresses the probability that, given the experimental results and the antecedent probabilities, the theory presented herein is true. This is a judgment that the reader and future investigators of any theory must make. Obviously, what is presented in this book barely scratches the surface of interpersonal behavior. An enormous amount of work remains to be done, and alterations of the theoretical framework are not only to be expected but hoped for. The present theory represents one attempt to summarize and describe the data, and suggests directions for future investigations.

Appendix B

Experimental Materials

POP
(See Chapter 5, p. 90 ff.)

On each of the following pages you will find a pair of statements about behavior aspects of home life of children. First, you are to read each single statement carefully to see how it fits you. In some cases the statement may not describe exactly how you feel and act; in these cases, estimate which answer **comes closest** to describing your characteristic behavior. Then, at the bottom of the sheet, circle the answer which fits you best.

Please be as frank and as forthright as you possibly can. Do not hesitate to use any of the categories if you honestly feel they are most appropriate. Think each question over carefully. There is no time limit. Put down your considered judgment as to **how your home actually was.**

1	2
In my home my parents actually spent relatively little time interacting with me. I didn't have the feeling very often that they were very much interested in what I was interested in. They didn't spend much time just playing with me instead of doing what they wanted to do. As a result, I really didn't get to know my parents very well. That is, I'd never see them in very many situations so that I'd get to know how they act and feel in a large variety of circumstances.	In my home my parents centered their attention around me. As soon as they were home they would play with me and talk to me and take a great interest in whatever I was doing. We'd interact under all sorts of conditions so that I'd see my parents laugh and cry and get angry, be delighted, and feel fearful. As a result I got to know them very well so that I feel I understand them thoroughly and everything I do is of great interest to them.

Circle the Answer That Best Describes
the Way You **Really** Act and Feel

MY HOME WAS MUCH MORE LIKE 1 THAN IT WAS LIKE 2	MY HOME WAS SOMEWHAT MORE LIKE 1 THAN IT WAS LIKE 2	MY HOME WAS SLIGHTLY MORE LIKE 1 THAN IT WAS LIKE 2	MY HOME WAS SLIGHTLY MORE LIKE 2 THAN IT WAS LIKE 1	MY HOME WAS SOMEWHAT MORE LIKE 2 THAN IT WAS LIKE 1	MY HOME WAS MUCH MORE LIKE 2 THAN IT WAS LIKE 1

3

4

My home was one in which there was strict discipline. My parents decided what was best for the children and enforced their decision. If we didn't comply we were punished for it. There was very little effort made to teach me how to do things on my own or to make me independent.

There was no guidance in my home. I was always given complete independence to do whatever I wanted. Even at a very young age I was on my own and had to do things for myself. There was hardly ever anyone around to show me how to do things or to tell me what was right and what was wrong.

Circle the Answer That Best Describes the Way You **Really** Act and Feel

| MY HOME WAS MUCH MORE LIKE 3 THAN IT WAS LIKE 4 | MY HOME WAS SOMEWHAT MORE LIKE 3 THAN IT WAS LIKE 4 | MY HOME WAS SLIGHTLY MORE LIKE 3 THAN IT WAS LIKE 4 | MY HOME WAS SLIGHTLY MORE LIKE 4 THAN IT WAS LIKE 3 | MY HOME WAS SOMEWHAT MORE LIKE 4 THAN IT WAS LIKE 3 | MY HOME WAS MUCH MORE LIKE 4 THAN IT WAS LIKE 3 |

5

6

My home was very reserved and unemotional. My parents rarely expressed affection to me. They really did not believe in displaying emotions. It was more a matter-of-fact businesslike atmosphere. Expressions of affection either simply never arose or else were actively discouraged.

There was a great display of love and affection in my home. In their own ways both my parents expressed their love for me very openly and without reservation, so that I always had the feeling I was completely loved for myself alone. There was a great emphasis on expressing affection.

Circle the Answer That Best Describes the Way You **Really** Act and Feel

| MY HOME WAS MUCH MORE LIKE 5 THAN IT WAS LIKE 6 | MY HOME WAS SOMEWHAT MORE LIKE 5 THAN IT WAS LIKE 6 | MY HOME WAS SLIGHTLY MORE LIKE 5 THAN IT WAS LIKE 6 | MY HOME WAS SLIGHTLY MORE LIKE 6 THAN IT WAS LIKE 5 | MY HOME WAS SOMEWHAT MORE LIKE 6 THAN IT WAS LIKE 5 | MY HOME WAS LIKE 6 THAN IT WAS LIKE 5 |

OBJECTIVE PROBLEMS

(See Chapter 7, p. 130 ff., and Chapter 8, p. 160 ff.)

Game

This is called "the game." For the purpose of this game four of you will be the players and the fifth will be the coordinator. Your orders are to prevent all opponent's pieces from landing on your base.

Your set of four pieces—each with a different name and each with different possible moves—are the white pieces. They are called Par, Ban, Sky, and Cor. The opponent, played by the experimenter, has four pieces equivalent to yours—Pl, B1, S1, and C1—which can make equivalent moves on the board.

Your team will play against the experimenter with your coordinator moving the pieces on the board. Your object is to capture the opponent's pieces before he can contact the base, and to avoid having any of your pieces taken.

The base is the large square in the center of the board; your pieces are the white ones on the base while the opponent's pieces are the black ones on the edge of the board. The four shapes used to represent the different pieces also represent the direction in which you can move each piece.

The pieces are moved as follows:
The square-shaped Par may be moved one or two squares in a straight direction—up or down, to the right or to the left.

The six-sided Ban may be moved one or two squares in a diagonal direction.

The L-shaped Sky may be moved three squares, two in a straight direction and one in a direction perpendicular to the second square. The move, like the piece, is L-shaped, but the L can be upside down or backward.

The triangular Cor may be moved one square in any direction.

The rules governing the moves are these:
The opponent moves first; then you and the opponent take turns in making moves. We will designate all moves by naming the piece and then the square to which it is to be moved; in other words, Par to F–9 or S1 to A–2. Only one person—the coordinator—moves the pieces on the board, but the group as a whole decides what move to make.

All pieces, except the Cor, may jump other pieces; obviously Cor, which can move only one square, cannot jump another piece.

You capture a piece by landing on a square occupied by another piece. It is then removed from the board.

Your group can protect itself in this way: If any of your pieces could occupy in one move the square now occupied by any other of your pieces, the second one is "protected" by the first and cannot therefore be captured by the opponent. This same protection rule does not hold for the opponent.

If the opponent's piece lands on your base he makes a "contact" and is removed from the board.

The game ends when all pieces on one side are captured or, in the case of the opponent's pieces, have contacted the base.

Points will be awarded in this way:
When you take an enemy piece you get ten points.
When an enemy piece takes one of your pieces you lose twenty points.
When the opponent lands on the base, he gets thirty points.
For any reports which are late you lose ten points.

First you should decide who is coordinator and choose someone to keep score on this sheet. The two sides will take turns making a move; you should all decide as a group which move you want to make. The coordinator is the one who moves the pieces on the board and has the final decision as to which piece shall be moved and where. You will have thirty seconds to make each move in this game. Are there any questions?

(The board is 11 x 11 squares with the "base" in the center square.)

GAME CONTEST

We are now going to have a contest. The results of these contests will count heavily in the final determination of the winning team. We will have two contests this period. Each contest will consist of two games, one game in which this side will be the offending team and one in which that side will be. The total points for the two games will be the result of the contest.

Let me again stress the importance of the coordinator. He will sit in this center seat and have the final decision on all moves to be made.

Concept

In this task we are going to ask you to arrive at a description for a set of figures which we will choose from the figures at this chart: A number of borders, a number of objects inside the borders, the kind of objects inside the borders, and the color of the object or objects.

For each of these characteristics there are three possible values. There are one, or two, or three borders. There are one, or two, or three objects inside the borders; the objects may be one of three kinds: squares, circles, or crosses; and they may be either black, or red, or green.

By specifying values for some of the characteristics, and not specifying the values of the others, we can select a set of figures from the ones on the chart.

For this problem we will use two types of sets. "Regular" and "either-or." In ordinary sets we will choose either one value of the characteristic, e.g., "cross," or the value of each of two characteristics, e.g., "two and square" or "two squares," or one value of each of three characteristics, e.g., "red and three and two borders" or "three red objects with two borders." For example, if I say "positive" for any figure that falls within the set and "negative" for any one falling outside the set, I can illustrate those sets as follows: For the set "cross," if I take the third column and read down, I would call the figure "positive," "negative," etc.

In "either-or" sets we will have two regular set descriptions separated by an "or." In no case will we use two values of the same characteristic, e.g., "black or green." For this task we shall use the following procedure.

We will choose a description of a set of figures, and tell you one of the figures which is a member of the set. A figure will always be specified by means of its row and column. You can then ask about any figure on the chart, and we will tell whether it is a member of the set whose description we have in mind, "positive," or not a member of this set, "negative." Asking for information in this way will be called a "request." You will make all requests simply by specifying the figure you wish information about. After any number of requests you can guess at a description for the set, and we will tell you whether your guess is right or wrong.

The aim of the group is to arrive at the correct description for the set, with the fewest number of requests, in the shortest time, and with the fewest wrong guesses.

The group will be scored as follows:
From an initial score of 500, 5 points will be subtracted for each request, 5 points for each thirty seconds, and 20 points for one wrong guess. (Write points on board.) The time is counted from the time I give you the first positive card until you have correctly solved the problem. If your guess is wrong you must keep going until you get it right.

You are to appoint **two** coordinators for this task, since it is quite complex. They have equal authority and they can make whatever requests or guesses they wish. As soon as either coordinator speaks into this microphone, this will be the group's act. Again you may replace either coordinator at any time. There is one more stipulation—you are not allowed to write anything. Any questions? All right, I'll give you exactly three minutes to appoint coordinators and get organized and then I'll tell you the first positive card.

Toy

For this task we would like you to build a structure like the diagram on the board with the materials in this room. You are to build the figure as quickly as you possibly can, at the same time making it a neat and firm construction, using a minimum number of pipe cleaners.

On that table you will find paper squares with dowels in the seams and over here are paper triangles, also with dowels. On that table are some pipe cleaners which you will use to join the paper pieces, either through the holes in the paper or the holes in the dowels.

In order to do this task you must first designate the group member for each of three jobs.

One of you will be **recorder**. He will be responsible for keeping a complete written record of what the group does, the time it begins working, the method of construction and anything also that he thinks is important. He will begin that **record on this sheet.**

One of you will be the **conserver.** He will be responsible for conserving pipe cleaners and in preventing any torn, bent or broken materials. He should see to it that the structure gets built with the fewest number of pipe cleaners, dowels, and paper pieces possible, and that no materials are damaged.

One of you is the **coordinator.** He has complete charge of the whole construction. He must see to it that the figure gets constructed in the fastest possible time, and that it is as neat and sturdy as possible. He will also have the final say on the description written by the recorder.

When the coordinator is satisfied with the structure and the description of it he will flip this switch which operates a light in my room. I will then return and rate your figure. It will be rated on the basis of speed, neatness and firmness of construction, also of fewest materials and lack of damaged materials.

After that I will give you the signal to disassemble the structure. You are to return all the materials to the exact place they were at the beginning of the period.

To summarize the procedure:

First I will leave the room and give you three minutes to appoint men to these positions and to get organized.

Then I will return and give you the signal to begin building. When, in the opinion of the coordinator, the structure is completed and ready for inspection and the description is satisfactory he will flip this switch. This signal indicates the completion of the task.

I will then return and inspect the structure and rate it. When I finish I will give you the signal to disassemble. Your disassembly will be rated on the basis of (1) time required to complete the disassembly, (2) neatness and completeness.

Disassembly includes returning everything to the place in which it was found, and returning it in the same condition it was originally.

VALUATIVE DISCUSSIONS

(See Chapter 7, p. 130 ff.)

General Instructions

Today I'm going to read you a situation which may be of some interest to you and about which you may have to decide at some time. I want you to decide where you stand on the problem and your reasons for it briefly on this paper. When you finish writing, I'll leave the room, and as a group you will discuss the problem and come to some group decision. You should then choose one of the group to report your decision to me. You may have about twenty minutes to talk about it. When you have come to a group decision, have the man who is going to speak for the group turn over his number. I will take that as a signal to return. Of course there is no right or wrong answer to the problem; we are more interested in the reasons for your decision rather than in the specific conclusion you make. Are there any questions?

Name

First meeting:

Right now we would like you to spend some time choosing a name for your group. You can discuss this and when you have decided on a name, one of you can write it on the board beside your group number.

Sixth meeting:

As you will recall, we asked you to give yourselves a name at the first meeting and told you you would have a chance to change it later. We're now giving you that opportunity. The name you chose was ——————————. You can have fifteen or twenty minutes to discuss the problem and decide whether you wish to keep this name or change it.

Prison

In the recent Boston prison riots four prisoners captured some guards and held them as hostages as a protest against prison conditions. In your opinion what is the one main lesson to be learned from this incident?

Traffic

Mr. Johnson receives a traffic ticket for parking for ten minutes in a no-parking zone in downtown Boston. For some reason he fails to mail in a check for the $2.00 fine until one day after the 21 days allowed. The clerk of the court, following the regulations, returns the check and informs the man that he will shortly receive a summons to appear in court.

Mr. Johnson then writes a letter to the judge stating that it would work a great hardship on him to miss an entire half-day's work, since he would lose pay; also, his employer would be very displeased because this is an extremely busy season and he needs all his employees. Since his wife has just had a child, it is important that he not lose money or jeopardize his job. For those reasons and because the crime was minor and his fine was only a day late, Mr. Johnson requests that the judge accept his check and not require a court appearance.

What would you do if you were the judge? Why?

Answer categories:

———— I definitely would require him to appear in court.
———— I probably would require him to appear in court.
———— I am not sure, but I guess I would require him to appear in court.
———— I am not sure, but I guess I would *not* require him to appear in court.
———— I probably would *not* require him to appear in court.
———— I definitely would *not* require him to appear in court.

Cheat

Your friend, whom you have known for over three years, whom you have double-dated with, and of whom you are quite proud, has a poor math aptitude and is having a difficult time in mastering the math in a course in which you and he are both enrolled. Before the final, he has been bogged down in a time-consuming social science paper, taking all of his spare time.

Before the final, he has asked you to slip him your first blue book after you begin your second so that he can utilize this last chance to pass the course. He needs a passing grade in order to be admitted to Physics 1 in his senior year so that he can complete his pre-medical requirements in time for graduation. At this time, you haven't committed yourself.

The test is in the process of being given, you have just finished your first blue book, the proctor has left the room, and your buddy, sitting beside you, looks at you expectantly. What would you do? Why?

Answer categories:

—————— I would pass him the blue book.
—————— I would not pass him the blue book.

Child

There are many different opinions about how children should be raised. Some parents think that children should be allowed a wide range of freedom to express themselves so that they will develop their natural creativity and an expressive personality. Therefore these parents are permissive and use a negligible amount of discipline or control over their child's behavior.

Some parents, on the other hand, feel that in order for their child to grow up to be a well-integrated, successful member of the larger society, he must learn as a child to accept certain limitations upon his behavior which will be expected as an adult. Therefore these parents feel the necessity of using a considerable amount of discipline to control their child's behavior.

Which principle of child-rearing do you think on the whole is better? Why?

Answer categories:

—————— Permissive
—————— More permissive
—————— More disciplinary
—————— Disciplinary

Groups

There are two main theories as to how groups can improve.

One theory says that groups don't do well because there's not enough attention paid to the individuals in the group. If you want the group improved, you should resolve the personal problems that arise. If any member is not participating, he should be brought into the group by the other members so that he will feel more like contributing. If a member is too bossy or dominating and the other members don't get a chance to participate, somebody should talk to him and try to work out this problem. If people seem to be competing for leadership and this interferes with the group productivity, the problem should be pointed out and something done about it. If some members feel the group is unfriendly—that they hardly even bother to get to know each other—they may not feel like contributing, and they should be talked to by other members.

The other theory says that a group in order to improve should not get involved in personalities in this way. If they're not doing well they should concentrate more on getting the job done. If you get involved with personalities the group will get even worse. The thing to do is to forget about those personal matters and try hard to get your job done. The best groups are those that realize they had a job to do and go about it in a business-like way.

Which theory do you prefer? Why?

Answer Categories:

——————— First theory

——————— Second theory

BEHAVIOR RATINGS

(See Chapter 7, p. 134.)

Below is the description sheet and rating form used by all observers for every meeting. Subjects were given an almost identical form to fill out for their own groups at the fifth and tenth meetings.

I

(First Rating Sheet)

In the following questions we are going to describe various functions that people perform in groups. For most functions we will ask you whether, in your opinion, anyone in the group including yourself clearly **tried to perform** that function, regardless of whether or not he succeeded. We will then ask you if, in your opinion, anyone including yourself clearly **did perform** the function in the group, regardless of whether he tried or not. Again please answer as honestly and accurately as you can. (For each function there is a place on the answer sheet marked "ATTEMPTS" and "SUCCEEDS" where you are to place your answer.)

IN MANY GROUPS THERE IS SOMEONE WHO SEEKS MAINLY TO **GUIDE THE DISCUSSIONS** (IN DISCUSSION TASKS) OR SUPERVISE THE **TASK STRATEGY** (IN PROBLEM TASKS). HE FREQUENTLY DOES THINGS TO KEEP THE GROUP ON THE TRACK, TIES TOGETHER THE CONTRIBUTIONS OF OTHER MEMBERS, SUGGESTS PROCEDURES FOR THE GROUP TO FOLLOW, ACTS AS MODERATOR AND PROVIDES COMPROMISE SOLUTIONS.

6, 7. In your opinion was there any member (or possibly two members) who **tried to perform** this function, including yourself? (If so, put the number, or numbers of the member, next to the word "Attempts," 6 and 7 on the answer sheet.)

8, 9. In your opinion, was there any one member (or possibly two members) who **did perform** this function in the group, including yourself? (If so, put the number or numbers of the members next to the word "Succeeds," 8 and 9 on the answer sheet.)

IN SOME GROUPS SOME MEMBERS **OBSTRUCT** OR DIVERT THE DISCUSSION OR THE TASK SOLUTION BY FOOLING AROUND OR JUST GENERALLY NOT SERIOUSLY PARTICIPATING.

10, 11. In your opinion is there any person or persons in your group who did this, including yourself?

SOME MEMBERS OBSTRUCT THE DISCUSSION OR TASK SOLUTION SIMPLY BECAUSE THEY ARE **INCOMPETENT** IN A CERTAIN TASK AND DON'T REALLY MEAN TO OBSTRUCT.

12. In your opinion is there any member or members who did this in your group, including yourself?

SOME MEMBERS OBSTRUCT THE DISCUSSION OR TASK SOLUTION BECAUSE QUITE OFTEN THEY TRY SO HARD TO ACCOMPLISH THEIR OWN **PERSONAL GOALS** THAT THEY LOSE SIGHT OF THE GROUP GOALS.

13. In your opinion is there any member who did this, including yourself?

14–18. Now rank all the members of the group from the one who most **attempted** to help the discussion and task solutions to move effectively, to the one who least attempted to help.

19–23. Now rank all the members in this group from the one who **actually** helped most to make the discussion and task solutions move effectively, to the one who helped least.

IN MANY GROUPS THERE IS SOMEONE WHO SEEMS MAINLY TO BE THE ONLY ONE WHO **PROMOTES** AND MAINTAINS GOOD **PERSONAL FEELINGS** AMONG THE GROUP MEMBERS. HE WILL FREQUENTLY DO THINGS TO MAKE THE MEMBERS FEEL COMFORTABLE AND AT EASE TOGETHER, MAKE THEM FEEL FREE TO EXPRESS THEMSELVES, ACT VERY SUPPORTIVE TO MEMBERS WHO NEED ASSURANCE, AND CONCILIATE AND MEDIATE IN SITUATIONS WHERE PEOPLE GET ANGRY.

24, 25. In your opinion was there any member (or possibly two members) who **tried to perform** this function, including yourself?

26, 27. In your opinion, was there any member (or possibly two members) who **did perform** this function in the group, including yourself?

IT OFTEN HAPPENS IN GROUPS THAT THERE ARE SOME MEMBERS WHO SEEM TO CAUSE A LOT OF HOSTILITY IN THE GROUP BY BEING **ANTAGONISTIC OR ARGUMENTATIVE,** OR JUST GENERALLY SEEKING TO CAUSE TROUBLE BETWEEN MEMBERS.

28. In your opinion was there any member who did this in your group, including yourself?

IT OFTEN HAPPENS THAT SOME MEMBERS AROUSE HOSTILITY FROM THE OTHERS BECAUSE THEY **WITHDRAW** FROM THE GROUP AND HARDLY PARTICIPATE AT ALL. THEY GIVE THE IMPRESSION THAT THEY ARE **DISDAINFUL** OF THE GROUP—IT IS BENEATH THEM.

29. In your opinion was there any member who did this in your group, including yourself?

30–34. Now rank all the members of this group, including yourself, from the one who most **attempted** to enhance personal feelings among group members to the one who least attempted to do this.

35–39. Now rank all the members of this group, including yourself, from the one who **actually** did most enhance personal feelings among group members to the one who least did this.

IN MANY GROUPS THERE IS SOMEONE WHO, REGARDLESS OF HOW GOOD HIS IDEAS ARE, SEEMS TO HAVE A TREMENDOUS **INFLUENCE** ON THE FINAL GROUP DECISION. HE IS THE MAN WHOSE IDEAS AND OPINIONS SEEM TO BE OVERWHELMINGLY ACCEPTED BY THE GROUP AS ITS FINAL DECISION.

40, 41. In your opinion was there any member (or possibly two members) who **tried to perform** this function, including yourself?

42, 43. In your opinion, is there any member (or possibly two members) who **did perform** this function in the group, including yourself?

IT OFTEN HAPPENS THAT THERE ARE GROUP MEMBERS WHO, REGARDLESS OF HOW GOOD THEIR CONTRIBUTION, SEEM TO HAVE **HARDLY ANY EFFECT** ON THE FINAL GROUP DECISION.

44, 45. In your opinion is there any member or members for whom this was true, including yourself?

46–50. Now, rank all the members of this group, including yourself, from the one who most **attempted** to influence the final group decision, to the one who least attempted to influence the final group decision.

51–55. Now, rank all the members of this group, including yourself, from the one whose ideas and opinions **actually** had the most influence on the group decision to the one who had the least influence.

IN MANY GROUPS THERE IS SOME MEMBER WHOSE **MOOD** SEEMS **CONTAGIOUS** IN THE GROUP; WHETHER JOKING AND LIGHTHEARTED, VERY SERIOUS AND INTENT, OR PERHAPS SARCASTIC AND RIDICULING, THE REST OF THE GROUP SEEMS TO GO ALONG WITH HIS MOOD.

56, 57. In your opinion is there any member (or possibly two) who **tried** to influence the group with his moods in this way, including yourself?

58, 59. In your opinion was there any one member (or possibly two) who **created** the atmosphere very frequently for the group, including yourself?

IT OFTEN HAPPENS IN MANY GROUPS THAT SOME MEMBER FOR SOME REASON NEVER CAN SEEM TO GET ANYONE TO GO ALONG WITH HIS MOOD, PEOPLE JUST **DON'T** SEEM TO **RESPOND TO HIM** THE WAY HE SEEMS TO WANT THEM TO.

60, 61. In your opinion is there any member or members for whom this is true, including yourself?

62–66. Now, rank all the members of this group, including yourself, from the one who most **attempted** to influence the feelings and atmosphere of the group to the member who least attempted to do this.

67–71. Now, rank all the members of this group, including yourself, from the one whose feelings **actually** did most often influence the atmosphere of the group, to the member whose feelings least often do this.

IN MANY GROUPS THERE IS SOMEONE WHO, REGARDLESS OF HOW EFFECTIVE HIS OPINIONS ARE IN THE GROUP, SEEMS TO HAVE EXCEPTIONALLY **GOOD IDEAS.** HE FREQUENTLY SHOWS A VERY GOOD GRASP OF THE PROBLEM, HAS KEEN INSIGHT, AND A VERY CLEAR REASONING ABILITY.

72, 73. In your opinion, was there any member (or possibly two members) who showed this **exceptional** ability, including yourself?

IT OFTEN HAPPENS IN GROUPS THAT SOME MEMBERS, FOR WHATEVER REASON, JUST DON'T SEEM TO GRASP THE BASIC PRINCIPLES OF THE PROBLEMS THE GROUP IS TRYING TO SOLVE AND, AS A RESULT THEIR **IDEAS ARE NOT TOO SHARP.**

74. In your opinion was there any member like this in your group, including yourself?

75–79. Now, rank all the members of this group from the one who, in your opinion, had the best ideas, regardless of how the group felt about them, to the one with the least good ideas.

II

(Second Rating Sheet)

IN MANY GROUPS THERE IS SOMEONE WHO TRIES TO GIVE THE IMPRESSION THAT HE IS A VERY IMPORTANT PERSON AND WHAT HE HAS TO SAY SHOULD BE LISTENED TO. HE DOESN'T NECESSARILY WANT TO BE LIKED OR EVEN NECESSARILY WANT TO BE LEADER. HE WANTS TO BE LOOKED UPON AS A **HIGH STATUS** MEMBER OF THE GROUP.

6, 7, 8. In your opinion is there any member, or members, of this group, including yourself, who are obviously **striving** very hard to become a high status member.

9, 10. In your opinion is there any member (or possibly two members), of this group who actually **are** high status members, including yourself?

IT OFTEN HAPPENS THAT IN MANY GROUPS SOME MEMBERS TRY TO **AVOID** BEING **PROMINENT** IN THE GROUP.

11, 12. In your opinion is there any member (or possibly two) who does this in your group, including yourself?

13–17. Now, rank all the members of this group from the one, who is most **striving** for high status to the one who is striving least.

18–22. Now, rank all the members of this group from the member who **actually** has the most status to the one who actually has the least.

IN MANY GROUPS THERE IS SOMEONE WHO SEEMS TO BE **TRYING** EXCESSIVELY HARD **TO BE LIKED** BY THE MEMBERS OF THE GROUP.

23, 24. In your opinion is there any one member (or possibly two) who is obviously striving **very strongly** to be well-liked by the group?

IT OFTEN HAPPENS THAT SOME GROUP MEMBERS GIVE THE IMPRESSION THAT THEY **DON'T CARE** AT ALL WHETHER PEOPLE **LIKE** THEM OR NOT.

> 25, 26. Was there anyone in this group, including yourself, who gave you that impression?

> 27–31. Now, rank all the members of this group, including yourself, from the one who seems most to be **striving** to be liked to the one who seems to be striving least.

IN MANY GROUPS DIFFERENCES IN THE AMOUNT OF **PARTICIPATION** ARE GREAT. SOME MEMBERS FREQUENTLY PARTICIPATES MUCH MORE THAN THE OTHERS.

> 34, 33. Is there any member (or possibly two members) who, in your opinion participates **far more** than others?

IT OFTEN HAPPENS THAT SOME MEMBER OF THE GROUP SEEMS TO **WITHDRAW** FROM MOST OF THE ACTIVITIES OF THE GROUP AND HARDLY PARTICIPATES AT ALL.

> 34, 35. Is there any member (or possibly two members) who does this?

> 36–40. Now, rank all the members of your group, including yourself, from the highest participator to the lowest.

IN SOME GROUPS THERE IS ONE MEMBER WHO DISRUPTS THE GROUP'S FUNCTIONING BY BEING **BOSSY**, DOMINATING, AND AGGRESSIVE.

41. In your opinion is there any member of your group who does this?

42. If there is a member of your group like this, how did the group handle him:
    (1) He was toned down and integrated into the group.
    (2) He was toned down, but he is not really a member of the group.
    (3) He was not handled by the group at all.

IN SOME GROUPS THERE IS ONE MEMBER WHO IMPAIRS THE GROUP'S PERFORMANCE BY **NOT ASSUMING** HIS SHARE OF THE **RESPONSIBILITY** AND NOT INTEGRATING HIMSELF INTO THE GROUP.

43. In your opinion is there any member of your group who does this?

44. If there is a member of your group like this, how did the group handle him? (1) He was integrated into the group. (2) He was not integrated into the group.

Rating Form

1———— Rater
2———— Group
3————
4———— Meeting
5———— Rating (1, 2)

Guides discussion or task strategy
6———— Attempts
7———— Attempts
8———— Succeeds
9———— Succeeds

Obstructs discussion or task accomplishment
10———— Attempts (not task orient.)
11———— Attempts (not task orient.)
12———— Succeeds (incompetence)
13———— Succeeds (self-orient. behavior)

Rank: Guides
14———— Attempts
15————
16————
17————
18————
19———— Succeeds
20————
21————
22————
23————

Promotes personal good feelings
24———— Attempts
25———— Attempts

Rank: Influences
46———— Attempts
47————
48————
49————
50————
51———— Succeeds
52————
53————
54————
55————

Has contagious moods
56———— Attempts
57———— Attempts
58———— Succeeds
59———— Succeeds
60———— Gets no response
61———— Gets no response

Rank: Contagion
62———— Attempts
63————
64————
65————
66————
67———— Succeeds
68————
69————
70————
71————

Has good ideas
72———— Good ideas
73———— Good ideas
74———— Poor ideas

26———— Succeeds
27———— Succeeds
28———— Acts antagonistic
29———— Acts disdainful

Rank: Feelings

30———— Attempts
31————
32————
33————
34————
35———— Succeeds
36————
37————
38————
39————

Influences decisions

40———— Attempts
41———— Attempts
42———— Succeeds
43———— Succeeds
44———— No influence
45———— No influence

Rank: Ideas

75————
76————
77————
78————
79————
80———— FIRO group type

How do you feel?————

————————

————————

————————

————————

Second Rating Form

1———— Rater
2———— Group
3————
4———— Meeting
5———— Rating (1, 2)

Has status and prominence

6———— Attempts
7———— Attempts
8———— Attempts
9———— Succeeds
10———— Succeeds
11———— Tries to avoid prominence
12———— Tries to avoid prominence

Rank: Status

13———— Attempts
14————
15————
16————
17————
18———— Succeeds
19————

Rank: Being liked

27———— Attempts
28————
29————
30————
31————

Participation

32———— High participation
33———— High participation
34———— Low participation
35———— Low participation

Rank: Participation

36————
37————
38————
39————
40————
41———— Aggressive problem member
42———— How handled?
1. integrated. 2. expelled.
3. not

20————
21————
22————

Liked by others
23———— Attempts
24———— Attempts
25———— Definitely not trying
26———— Definitely not trying

43———— Non-integrated   problem
        member
44———— How handled?
        1. integrated. 2. not
45———— Coercion user
46———— Very dominant
47———— Dominant
48———— Influenced by coercion
49———— Influenced by coercion

ASIA

(Chapter 7, p. 148 ff.)

NAME ———————— ————————

GROUP ————————————————

Directions: Rank the two most likely reasons 1 and 2
            and the two least likely reasons 5 and 6.

PLEASE ANSWER AS CAREFULLY, BUT AS QUICKLY AS POSSIBLE.

A usually does everything together with other people. When he
is doing something he includes other people, and when others
are doing something he joins them.

However, sometimes he feels that he would enjoy his relationships with people more if he did not always do things with
others.

Why would you guess he does not behave differently?

A is afraid that if he did more things alone ...

———————— People would be more likely to ignore him.

———————— People would allow him to take more responsi-
          bility than he can handle.

———————— Certain individuals would try to become more
          intimate and personal with him than he would
          like.

———————— He wouldn't have as much of a chance to be
          alone when he wants to since people would try to
          get him involved in their activities.

———————— People would be more likely to try to tell him
          what to do.

———————— Certain individuals would be likely to be less
          friendly toward him.

When **C** is with people he is usually rather cool and reserved. He does not get very close to people and doesn't confide to them his feelings and worries.

However, sometimes he feels that he might enjoy his relationships with people more if he were not so cool and reserved.

Why would you guess he does not behave differently?

C is afraid that if he were close and personal ...

—————— Certain individuals would be likely to be less friendly toward him.

—————— Certain individuals would try to become more intimate and personal with him than he would like.

—————— People would be more likely to ignore him.

—————— People would be more likely to try to tell him what to do.

—————— He wouldn't have as much of a chance to be alone when he wants to, since people would try to get him involved in their activities.

—————— People would allow him to take more responsibility than he can handle.

When **D** is with people he is usually quite dominant. He often takes charge of things and decides what is to be done.

However, sometimes he feels that he might enjoy his relationships with people more if he were not so dominant.

Why would you guess he does not behave differently?

D is afraid that if he weren't so dominant ...

—————— People would allow him to take more responsibility than he can handle.

—————— He wouldn't have as much chance to be alone when he wants to, since people would try to get him involved in their activities.

—————— People would be more likely to try to tell him what to do.

—————— Certain individuals would try to become more intimate and personal with him than he would like.

——————— Certain individuals would be likely to be less friendly toward him.

——————— People would be more likely to ignore him.

When **P** is with people he usually becomes very close and personally involved. He confides to them his innermost feelings and his worries about himself.

However, sometimes he feels he would enjoy his relationships with people more if he did not become so close and personally involved.

Why would you guess he does not behave differently?

P is afraid that if he were cool and reserved ...

——————— He wouldn't have as much of a chance to be alone when he wanted to, since people would try to get him involved in their activities.

——————— People would be more likely to ignore him.

——————— People would allow him to take more responsibility than he can handle.

——————— Certain individuals would be likely to be less friendly toward him.

——————— Certain individuals would try to become more intimate and personal with him than he would like.

——————— People would be more likely to try to tell him what to do.

When **S** is with people he rarely takes charge of things even when it might be appropriate. He usually does not take much responsibility for deciding what people should do.

However, sometimes he feels that he would enjoy his relationships with people more if he were not so reluctant to take charge.

Why would you guess he does not behave differently?

S is afraid that if he took charge more often ...

——————— People would be more likely to try to tell him what to do.

———————— Certain individuals would be likely to be less friendly toward him.

———————— He wouldn't have as much of a chance to be alone when he wanted to, since people would try to get him involved in their activities.

———————— People would be more likely to ignore him.

———————— People would allow him to take more responsibility than he can handle.

———————— Certain individuals would try to become more intimate and personal with him than he would like.

W usually does things by himself. He seldom includes other people in his activities and does not often join in theirs.

However, sometimes he feels that he would enjoy his relationships with people more if he didn't always do things by himself.

Why would you guess he does not behave differently?

W is afraid that if he did more things together with other people ...

———————— Certain individuals would try to become more intimate and personal with him than he would like.

———————— People would be more likely to try to tell him what to do.

———————— Certain individuals would be likely to be less friendly toward him.

———————— People would allow him to take more responsibility than he can handle.

———————— People would be more likely to ignore him.

———————— He wouldn't have as much of a chance to be alone when he wanted to, since people would try to get him involved in their activities.

1. Which of these people comes closest to describing you?
   (Put a 1 by your first choice, 2 by your second choice.)

   A   ———————
   C   ———————
   D   ———————
   P   ———————
   S   ———————
   W ———————

2. Which of these people least describes you?
   (Put a 6 by the one which least describes you, and a 5
   by the next.)

   A   ———————
   C   ———————
   D   ———————
   P   ———————
   S   ———————
   W ———————

3. Do you feel that the people described are realistic?
   Why?

ASIA SCORING SHEET

SUBJECT NUMBER————

GROUP————

	IGNORE		RESPONSIBLE		INTIMATE		INVOLVED		TELL		UNFRIENDLY		CHOICE
A	A		B		C		D		E		F		
C	C		F		B		E		D		A		
D	F		A		D		B		C		E		
P	B		C		E		A		F		D		
S	D		E		F		C		A		B		
W	E		D		A		F		B		C		
TOTAL													
DECILE													

Bibliography

1. Abelow, Arnold. "The Tigers: A Study of a Street Corner Gang." Unpublished honors thesis, Harvard University, 1956.
2. Adorno, T. W., Else Frenkel-Brunswik, D. J. Levinson, and R. N. Sanford. *The Authoritarian Personality*. New York: Harper, 1950.
3. Alexander, W. B., R. A. Gonzales, J. F. Herminghaus, G. Marwell, and L. Wheeless. "Personality Variables and Predictability of Interaction Patterns in Small Groups." Unpublished term paper, Massachusetts Institute of Technology, 1957.
4. American Psychological Association, Inc. *Technical Recommendations for Psychological Tests and Diagnostic Techniques*. The Association, 1954.
5. Asch, S. "Effects of Group Pressure upon the Modification and Distortion of Judgment," in *Groups, Leadership and Men*, ed. H. Guetzkow. Pittsburgh: The Carnegie Press, 1951.
6. Back, K. "Influence through Social Communication," *Journal of Abnormal and Social Psychology*, 46, 1951, 9–23.
7. Bakan, D. "Learning and the Principle of Inverse Probability," *Psychological Review*, 60, No. 6, 1953, 360–370.
8. Baldwin, A., J. Kallhorn, and F. Breese. "Patterns of Parent Behavior," *Psychological Monographs*, 58, No. 268, 1945, 1–75.
9. Bales, R. F., and A. Couch. Unpublished work, Harvard University, 1956.
10. Bavelas, A. "Communication Patterns in Task Oriented Groups," *Journal of Accoustical Society of America*, 22, 1950, 725–730.
11. Benne, K., and P. Sheats. "Functional Roles of Group Members," *Journal of Social Issues*, 4, 1948, 41–49.
12. Bennis, W. "Working Paper on Group Development." Staff Memorandum No. 12, Massachusetts Mental Health Center Group Research Project, 1957.
13. ———, and D. Peabody. "The Relationship between Some Personality Dimensions and Group Development." Unpublished paper, 1956.
14. ———, and H. A. Shepard. "A Theory of Group Development," *Human Relations*, 9, 1956, 415–437.

15. Bettleheim, B., and M. Janowitz. *Dynamics of Prejudice*. New York: Harper, 1950.
16. Bion, W. "Experiences in Groups: III, IV," *Human Relations*, 2, 1949, 13–22.
17. Blodgett, H. C. "The Effect of the Introduction of Reward upon the Maze Performance of Rats," *University of California Publications in Psychology*, 4, 1929, 113–134.
18. Blum, G. S. *The Blacky Pictures: A Technique for the Exploration of Personality Dynamics*. New York: The Psychological Corporation, 1950.
19. ———. "Procedure for the Assessment of Conflict and Defense." Unpublished paper, University of Michigan, 1954.
20. Bruner, J. S., J. Goodnow, and G. Austin. *A Study of Thinking*. New York: Wiley, 1956.
21. Bunker, Douglas. "Experimental Studies of Attitude Change." Unpublished term paper, Department of Social Relations, Harvard University, 1957.
22. Carnap, R. *Logical Foundations of Probability*. Chicago: University of Chicago Press, 1950.
23. Carter, L. "Recording and Evaluating the Performance of Individuals as Members of Small Groups," in *Small Groups: Studies in Interaction*, edited by A. P. Hare, E. F. Borgatta, and R. F. Bales. New York: Knopf, 1955.
24. Champney, H. "The Variables of Parent Behavior," *Journal of Abnormal and Social Psychology*, 36, 1941, 525–542.
25. Christie, L. S., R. D. Luce, and J. Macy. *Communications and Learning in Task Oriented Groups*. Cambridge, Mass.: Research Laboratory of Electronics, 1952.
26. Clark, R. A. "Analyzing the Group Structure of Combat Rifle Squads," *American Psychologist*, 8, 1953, 333.
27. Cohen, Bernard P. Unpublished study of personality and group conformity, Harvard University, 1957.
28. Copi, I. M. *Symbolic Logic*. New York: Macmillan, 1954.
29. Corsini, R., and B. Rosenberg. "Mechanisms of Group Psychotherapy: Processes and Dynamics," *Journal of Abnormal and Social Psychology*, 51, 1955, 406–411.
30. Crutchfield, R. S. "Conformity and Character," *American Psychologist*, 10, 1955, 191–198.
31. Dodd, S. *Dimensions of Society*. New York: Macmillan, 1942.
32. Drinkwater, J. *The Outline of Literature*. New York: Putnam, 1923.
33. Edwards, A. L. *Edwards Personal Preference Schedule*. New York: The Psychological Corporation, 1953.
34. Fenichel, O. *The Psychoanalytic Theory of Neuroses*. New York: Norton, 1945.
35. French, T. *Summary of Factor Analytic Studies of Personality*. Princeton, N.J.: Educational Testing Service, 1956.
36. Freud, S. *Group Psychology and the Analysis of the Ego*. London: Hogarth, 1922.
37. ———. "Libidinal Types," in *Collected Papers*. London: Hogarth, 1950, V, 247–251.
38. ———. *An Outline of Psychoanalysis*. New York: Norton, 1949.

39. Fromm, E. *Man for Himself.* New York: Rinehart, 1947.

40. Glueck, S., and Eleanor Glueck. *Unraveling Juvenile Delinquency.* New York: Commonwealth Fund, 1950.

41. Goldfarb, W. "The Effects of Early Institutional Care on Adolescent Personality," *Journal of Experimental Education,* 12, 1943, 106–129.

42. Gross, Eugene F. "An Empirical Study of the Concepts of Cohesiveness and Compatibility." Unpublished honors thesis, Department of Social Relations, Harvard University, 1957.

43. Guilford, J. P. *An Inventory of Factors STDCR.* Beverly Hills, Calif.: Sheridan Supply Company, 1940.

44. Guttman, L. "The Basis for Scalogram Analysis," in S. A. Stouffer *et al., Measurement and Prediction.* Princeton, N.J.: Princeton University Press, 1950, 60–90.

45. ———. "Principal Components of Scalable Attitudes," in *Mathematical Thinking in the Social Sciences,* ed. P. Lazarsfeld. Glencoe, Ill.: Free Press, 1954.

46. Hampton, Catherine. "Prediction of 'Appropriate' Behavior in Small Groups." Unpublished paper, Department of Social Relations, Harvard University, 1955.

47. Hare, A. P. *Social Interaction: An Analysis of Behavior in Small Groups.* Forthcoming.

48. Holzinger, K. J., and H. Harman. *Factor Analysis: A Synthesis of Factorial Methods.* Chicago: University of Chicago Press, 1941.

49. Horney, Karen. *Our Inner Conflicts.* New York: Norton, 1945.

50. Hull, C. L. *Principles of Behavior.* New York: Appleton-Century-Crofts, 1943.

51. Jenkins, D. J., and R. Lippitt. *Interpersonal Perception in Teachers, Students and Parents.* Washington, D.C.: National Education Association, 1951.

52. Jones, Richard. "The Effect of Experimentally Increased Self-Acceptance on Ethnic Attitudes: An Experiment in Education." Unpublished doctoral dissertation, Harvard University, 1956.

53. Kaplan, A. "Definition and Specification of Meaning," *Journal of Philosophy,* XLIII, No. 11, May, 1946, 281–288.

54. LaForge, R., and R. Suczek ."The Interpersonal Dimension of Personality: An Interpersonal Checklist," *Journal of Personality,* 24, No. 1, 1955, 94–112.

55. Lazarsfeld, P., and A. Barton. "Qualitative Measurement in the Social Sciences," in D. Lerner and H. Lasswell, *The Policy Sciences.* Stanford, Calif.: Stanford University Press, 1951.

56. ———, B. Berelson, and Hazel Gaudet. *The People's Choice.* New York: Duell, Sloan, Pearce, 1944.

57. Leary, T. *The Interpersonal Diagnosis of Personality.* New York: Ronald, 1957.

58. ———, M. B. Freedman, A. G. Ossorio, and H. S. Coffey. "Th Interpersonal Dimension of Personality," *Journal of Personality,* 20, 1951, 143–161.

59. Lewin, K., R. Lippitt, and R. K. White. "Patterns of Aggressive Behavior

in Experimentally Created Social Climates," *Journal of Social Psychology,* 10, 1939, 271–279.

60. McElheny, Victor. "Interpersonal Orientations and Political Opinion." Unpublished honors thesis, Department of Social Relations, Harvard University, 1957.

61. McKinsey, J. C. C., A. C. Sugar, and P. Suppes. "Axiomatic Foundations of Classical Particle Mechanics," *Journal of Rational Mechanics and Analysis,* 2, 1953, 253–272.

62. Mann, J. "Group Therapy with Adults," *American Journal of Orthopsychiatry,* 23, No. 2, 1953, 332–337.

63. Meehl, P. "Wanted: A Good Cookbook," *American Psychologist,* 11, No. 6, June 1956, 263.

64. ———, and K. MacCorquodale. "Drive Conditioning as a Factor in Latent Learning," *Journal of Experimental Psychology,* 45, 1953, 20–24.

65. Miller, N. E., and J. Dollard. *Social Learning and Imitation.* New Haven, Conn.: Yale University Press, 1941.

66. Munroe, Ruth. *Schools of Psychoanalytic Thought.* New York: Dryden, 1956.

67. Parsons, T. *The Social System.* Glencoe, Ill.: Free Press, 1951.

68. ———, and E. Shils. *Toward a General Theory of Action.* Cambridge, Mass.: Harvard University Press, 1951.

69. Redl, F. "Group Emotion and Leadership," *Psychiatry,* 5, 1942, 573–596.

70. Reichenbach, H. *The Theory of Probability.* Berkeley: University of California Press, 1949.

71. Rhine, J. B. *New Frontiers of the Mind.* New York: Rinehart, 1937.

72. Rubin, H., and P. Suppes. "Transformations of Systems of Rationalistic Particle Mechanics," *Pacific Journal of Mathematics,* 4, 1954, 563–601.

73. Rudner, Richard. Unpublished paper on small group problem solving, 1953.

74. Sakoda, J. M. "Factor Analysis of OSS Situational Tests," *Journal of Abnormal and Social Psychology,* 47, 1952, 843–852.

75. Sarbin, T. "Role Theory," in *Handbook of Social Psychology,* ed. G. Lindzey. Cambridge, Mass.: Addison-Wesley, 1954, Vol. I.

76. Schachter, S., N. Ellertson, D. McBride, and D. Gregory. "An Experimental Study of Cohesiveness and Productivity," *Human Relations,* 4, 1951, 229–238.

77. Schutz, W. C. "What Makes Groups Productive?" *Human Relations,* 8, 1955, 429–465.

78. Semrad, E. V., and J. Arsenian. "The Use of Group Processes in Teaching Group Dynamics," *American Journal of Psychiatry,* 108, 1951, 358–363.

79. Sewell, W., P. Mussen, and C. Harris. "Relationships among Child Training Practices," *American Sociological Review,* 20, 1955, 137–148.

80. Shapiro, D. "Issues in Semrad Groups: Themes and Variations," Staff Memorandum No. 4, Massachusetts Mental Health Center Group Research Project, 1957.

81. Sister Marie Augusta. "A Study of the Expression of the Three Interpersonal Needs." Unpublished term paper, Department of Social Relations, Harvard University, 1957.

82. Slater, Phillip. *Psychological Factors in Role Specialization.* Unpublished doctoral dissertation, Harvard University, 1955.

83. Small, M. H. "On Some Psychical Relations of Society and Solitude," *Pedagogical Seminary*, 7, 1900, 13–69.

84. Spitz, R. "Anaclitic Depression," in *Psychoanalytic Study of the Child*, ed. Anna Freud. New York: International Universities Press, 1947, II, 313–342.

85. ———. "Hospitalism: An Enquiry into the Genesis of Psychiatric Conditions in Early Childhood," in *Psychoanalytic Study of the Child*, ed. Anna Freud. New York: International Universities Press, 1945, I, 53–74.

86. Stephenson, W. *The Study of Behavior: Q-Technique and Its Methodology*. Chicago: University of Chicago Press, 1953.

87. Stock, Dorothy, and H. Thelen. *Emotional Dynamics and Group Culture*. In press.

88. Sullivan, H. S. *The Interpersonal Theory of Psychiatry*. New York: Norton, 1954.

89. Sutton, Margaret. *Who Will Play with Me?* New York: Wonder Books (Grosset), 1951.

90. Swanson, G. "Some Effects of Member Object-Relationships on Small Groups," *Human Relations*, 4, 1951, 355–380.

91. Thurstone, L. L. *Multiple Factor Analysis*. Chicago: University of Chicago Press, 1947.

92. Varon, Edith. "Recurrent Phenomena in Group Psychotherapy," *International Journal of Group Psychotherapy*, 3, 1953, 49–58.

93. Warner, W. L. *A Black Civilization*. New York: Harper, 1937.

94. Whyte, W. H., Jr. *The Organization Man*. New York: Simon & Schuster, 1956.

95. Winch, R. F. *The Modern Family*. New York: Holt, 1953.

96. Woodger, J. H. *The Technique of Theory Construction*. Chicago: University of Chicago Press, 1939.

Index